IMAGES
of Rail

Iowa's Last Narrow-Gauge Railroad

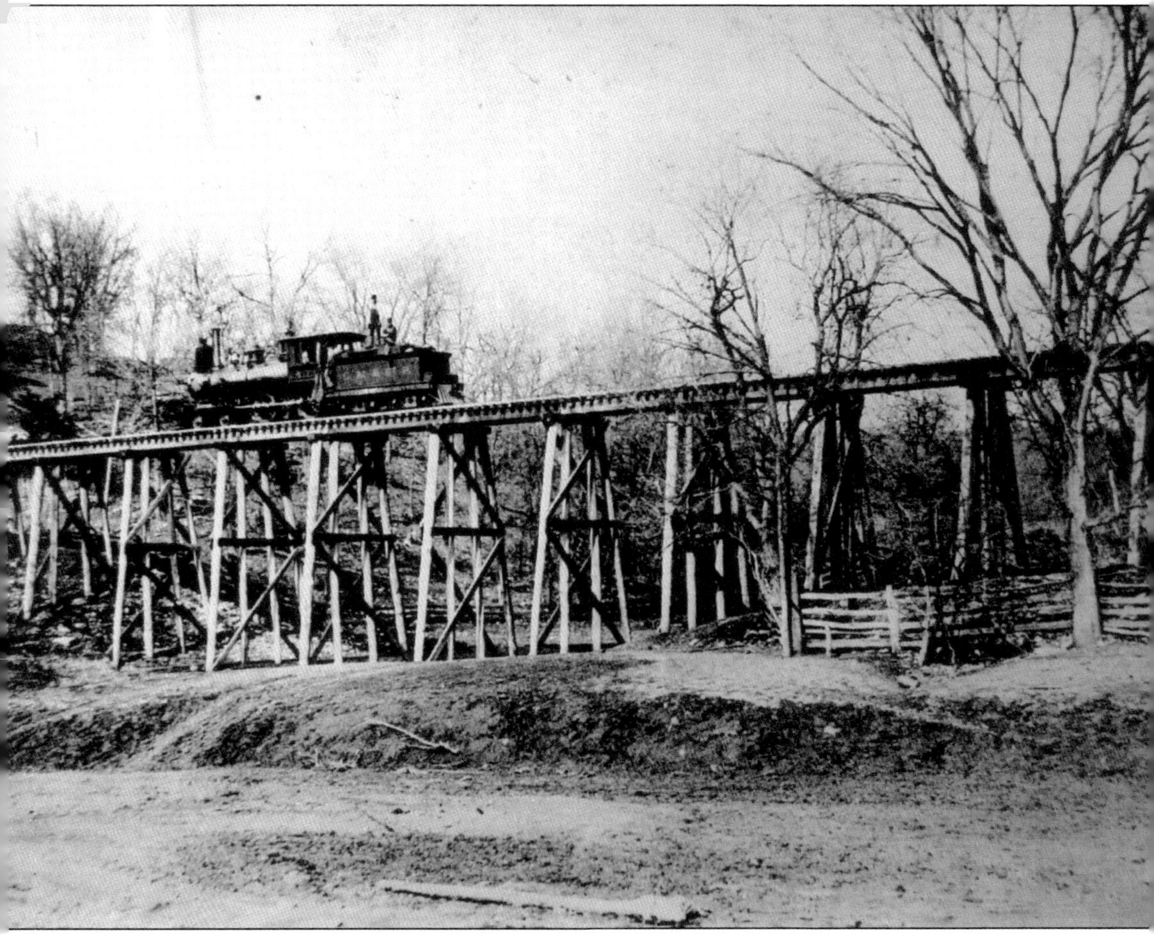

Long trestles, long and short grades, one long grade of 2.8 percent, tight curves, and few straight stretches of track made up the main line of Iowa's last narrow-gauge railroad.

On the cover: Please see page 71. (Streuser.)

IMAGES
of Rail

Iowa's Last Narrow-Gauge Railroad

John Tigges and James Shaffer

ARCADIA
PUBLISHING

ISBN 978-0-7385-4118

Published by Arcadia Publishing
Charleston, South Carolina

Printed in the United States of America

Library of Congress Catalog Card Number: 2006933045

For all general information contact Arcadia Publishing at:
Telephone 843-853-2070
Fax 843-853-0044
E-mail sales@arcadiapublishing.com
For customer service and orders:
Toll-Free 1-888-313-2665

Visit us on the Internet at www.arcadiapublishing.com

To the early citizens of Cascade, Iowa, who fought long and hard to get "their" railroad. And to the citizens of Bellevue, Iowa, the eastern terminus of this narrow-gauge railroad. In all its quaintness, the railroad is still recalled and associated with a time long gone . . . when life was more simple.

Contents

ACKNOWLEDGMENTS

We are grateful to the photographers and aficionados who generously opened their collections of Iowa's last narrow-gauge railroad: John Adney, Thomas Berg, Richard Bogue, John Bradley, Roy Campbell, Robert W. Courtney, Lester Deppe, Jeff Dyer, Arne Hachmann, ? Higbe, Raymond Kemerer, J. Kreuzberger, Albin Lee, Carl Leffert, Rose Moorman, ? Neiers, C. Nemmers, Ralph Otting, Keith Pregler, Theodore Schnepf, Margaret Schroeder, John D. Smith, ? Streuser, W. Talbert, Marie Weber-Cook, D. F. Wood, and Claude Wyrick. The last name of those who provided photographs is given at the end of the caption accompanying the photograph.

The following also lent a helping hand: the Cascade Pioneer, Kalmbach Publishing Company, the late, great Milwaukee Road, the Quad City Times, and the Telegraph Herald. Special thanks go to Bette Shaffer and Kathryn Tigges for their assistance.

INTRODUCTION

In 1848, the citizens of Cascade quickly became concerned about a railroad passing through their community. Dire predictions were that any town without trains would soon wither and disappear.

Following the Civil War, the largest rail boom in history began. The Transcontinental Railroad was completed in 1869. Included with the spreading spiderweb of steel across the country were narrow-gauge railroads of various widths, the most prominent being three feet. The philosophy was that narrow railroads demanded a lesser cost because of lighter rails, less grading, and less expensive locomotives and cars. The general belief was that these "little" railroads would be taken over by the standard railroads and the gauge widened to four feet eight and one-half inches. In most cases, the prediction was right. Today, in the 21st century, Colorado and several other locations still have 19th-century narrow-gauge railroads that are great tourist attractions.

Completed in 1879, the Chicago, Bellevue, Cascade, and Western Railway Company was purchased outright by the Milwaukee Road in 1880. The people of Cascade were joyful. Everything was going according to the narrow-gauge philosophy. Of course, the new owner would widen the rails as soon as possible. Their joy turned to frustration and finally to begging the Milwaukee Road to widen the track.

Outside expert engineers, along with the Milwaukee Road's brainpower and the Iowa Railroad Commission, deemed the topography to be too hilly and that an existing 2.8-percent grade would present expensive problems that, even if overcome, would likely never be profitable. However, Iowa's last narrow-gauge railroad would never be widened. As a result, the little trains continued plying the eastern Iowa hills much to the disgruntlement of businessmen and patrons.

In addition to the complaints, the winter seasons proved to be almost as detrimental to the railroad, with unbelievable snowfalls most years. When standard railroads shut down, the branch line did as well. Sometimes—a lot of times—the narrow gauge was snowed in while the bigger trains remained unaffected. No one blamed the men working for the Milwaukee Road. They catered to the customers, who in turn were more than appreciative. Some firemen, brakemen, and gandy dancers, who kept the rails in gauge, came from the towns and villages along the line. Steam locomotive engineers were generally Milwaukee Road employees.

The advances made in automobiles and eventually paved highways proved to be the line's coup de grâce. Trucks took away the business formerly controlled by the narrow gauge. Before the roads were paved, cars or trucks could drive the 25 miles from Cascade to Dubuque in three or four hours—if no flat tires interrupted the trip. The time was lowered by an hour or two once the road became concrete. The narrow gauge still took over three hours to reach Bellevue, where passengers or freight were still 20 miles or so south of Dubuque.

Of the four steam locomotives on the branch line in the late 1920s, one had a leaky flue and one cylinder of another had cracked and could not be repaired. The Milwaukee had ordered a one-of-a-kind snowplow to keep the branch line open and a dual-gauge crane to assist in transferring freight from standard to narrow gauge and vice versa. By 1932, the Milwaukee Road was ready to abandon the 36 miles of track. Before the company could pull the pin, Minnesota businessman Earl Bradley stepped forward in 1933 and offered to purchase the property.

After an amount had been reached, Bradley made his plans known. He needed a test track to evaluate a new concept in railroading: rubber-tired wheels running on steel rails. Along with that innovation came luck that would prove unbelievably bad. From careless employees to uncommonly bad choices, Bradley had had enough in less then three years. When a government loan was not forthcoming, Bradley contacted short-line railroad expert William G. Bell and his partner, Joseph Schoenthal. Bell would either make the railroad operate at a profit or scrap it. When he had to confront heavy snowfalls without a snowplow and had to hire men to shovel open the branch line, he opted for his alternate plan and scrapped everything.

By 1937, the railroad itself was only a memory. However, many artifacts still exist today, including a life-size duplicate caboose built by a Bellevue contractor, the late James Schroeder, in 1980. Today the car resides at Mount Pleasant on the Midwest Central Railroad. A boxcar was also built by Schroeder for the Cascade Historical Society.

Many things have been written and said about this memorable railroad. Perhaps the most notable is Richard Bogue's statement: "It's 36 by 36 by 36 . . . 36 inches wide and 36 miles long and sometimes it could take 36 hours to get there."

One

Cascade Needs a Railroad

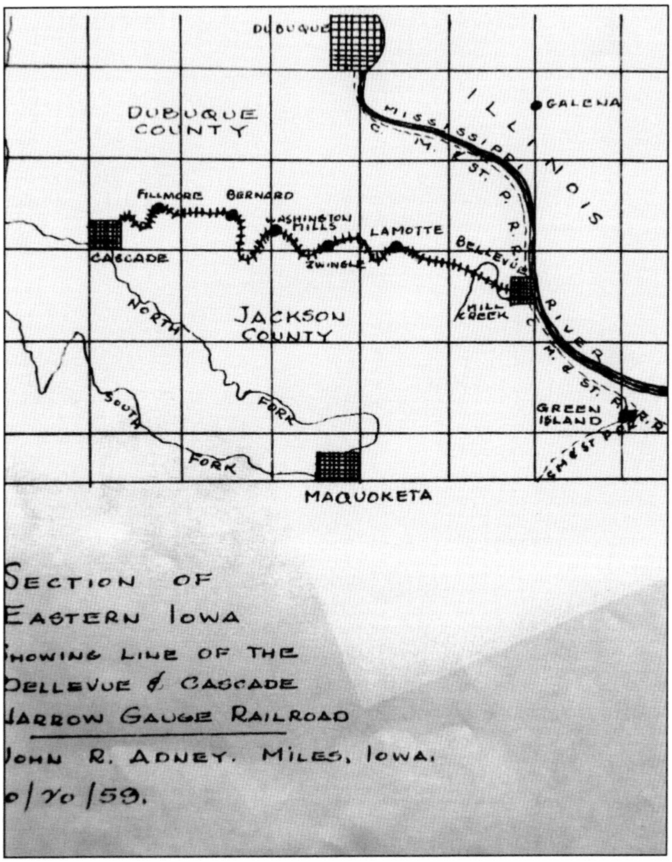

This map was drawn by John Adney in 1959. The former Milwaukee Road employee loved the railroad and took many photographs of the narrow gauge. (Adney.)

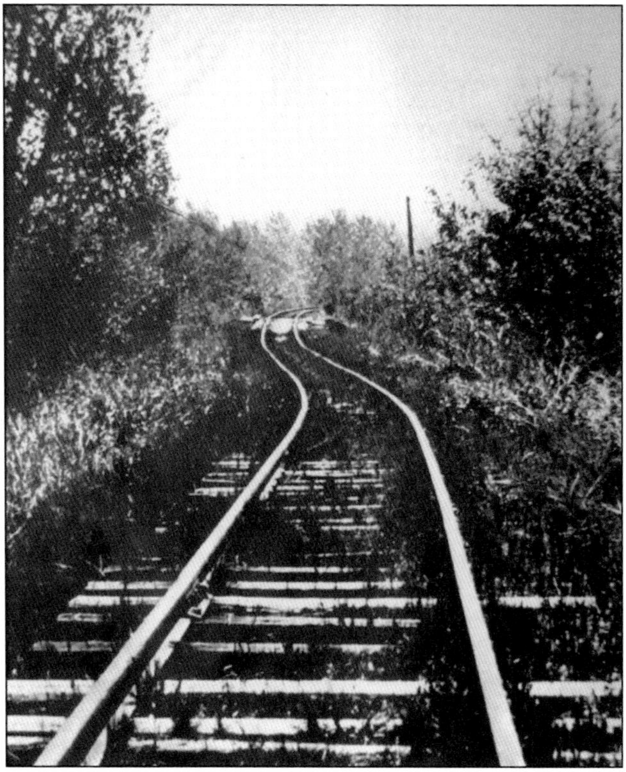

Three-foot-gauge rails were more economical to lay then the four-foot-eight-and-a-half-inch standard gauge. The locomotives were smaller and lighter. A slight rise could be avoided and thus save time and money without excavating, as shown on the left. (Leffert.)

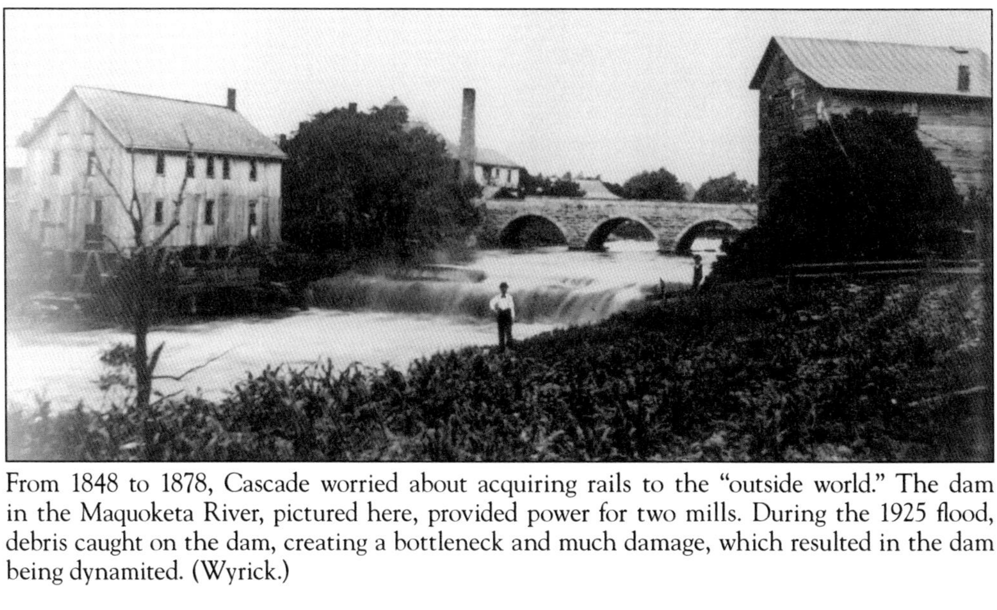

From 1848 to 1878, Cascade worried about acquiring rails to the "outside world." The dam in the Maquoketa River, pictured here, provided power for two mills. During the 1925 flood, debris caught on the dam, creating a bottleneck and much damage, which resulted in the dam being dynamited. (Wyrick.)

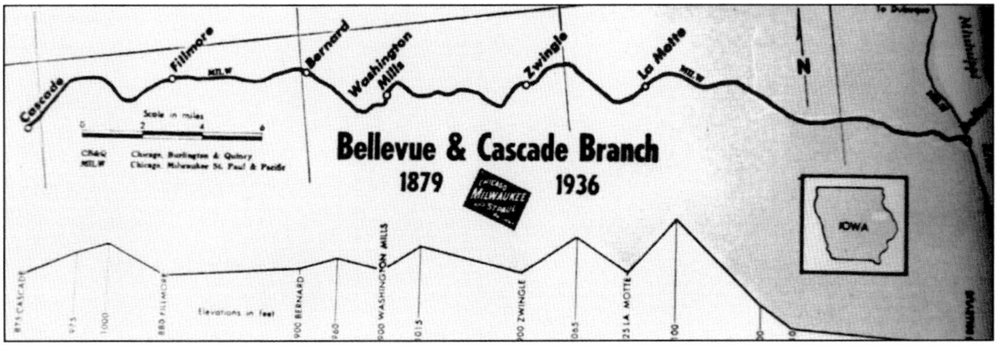

This map shows the terrain the little railroad had to traverse between Bellevue and Cascade. (Kalmbach Publishing Company.)

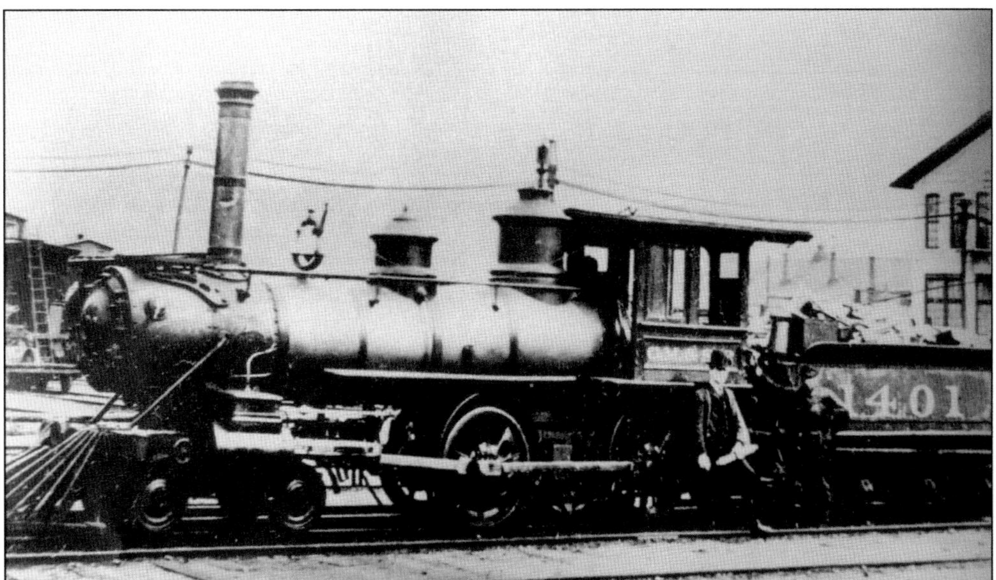

Seen here is the first locomotive used on the Chicago, Bellevue, Cascade, and Western Railway. The straight-stacked Pittsburgh-built engine had 11-by-16-inch cylinders, which proved to be too small for efficient operation. After the Chicago, Milwaukee, and St. Paul acquired the road, the locomotive was given transfer-table power duty in Milwaukee.

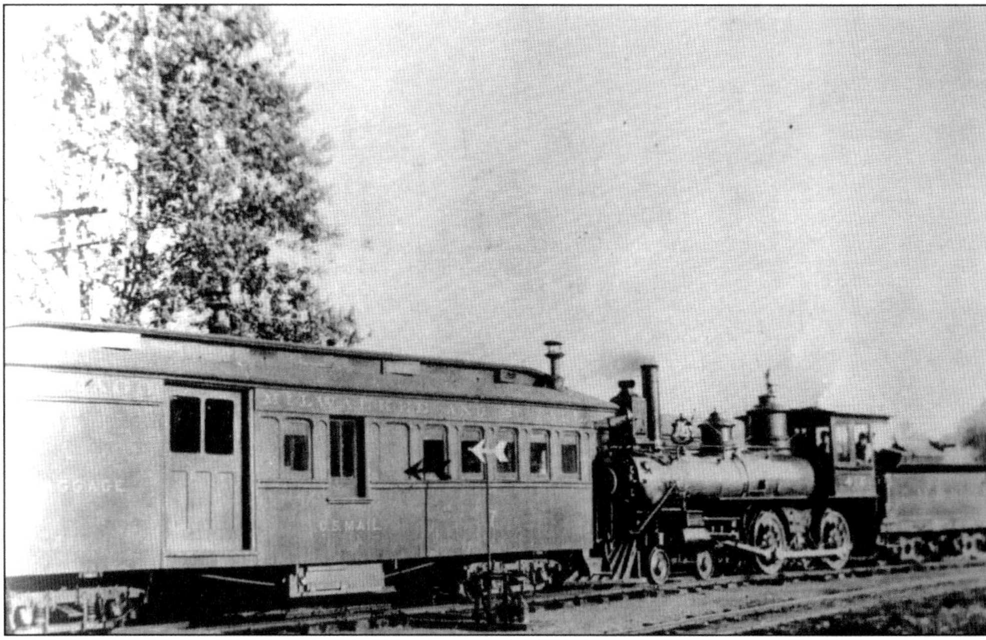

Engine No. 416 gently pushes combine No. 7 to be coupled to the rear of a freight train. Notice the arrow on the switch stand indicating the position of the rails.

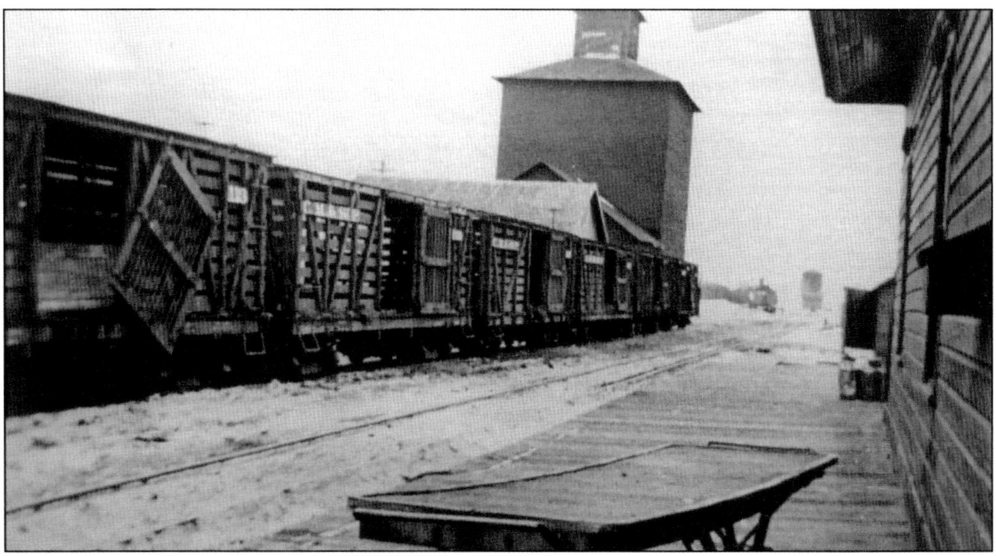

This string of stock cars is possibly shipping farmer G. G. Banghart's livestock to market. Banghart was a proponent for the narrow-gauge railroad (Neiers.)

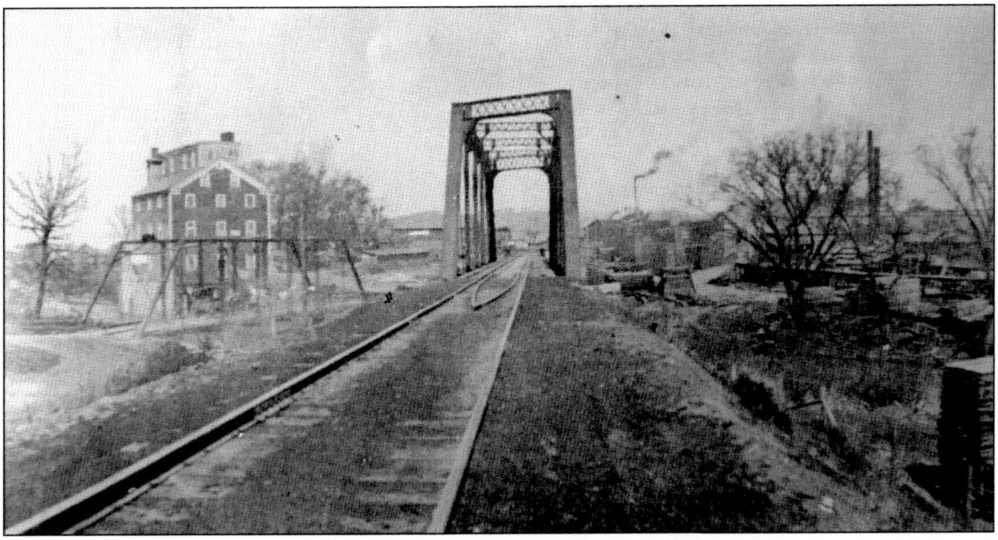

Before the Milwaukee Road entered the picture, the standard-gauge River Road passed through Bellevue. The railroad bridge lies next to the road bridge to the left, and Potter's Mill appears beyond.

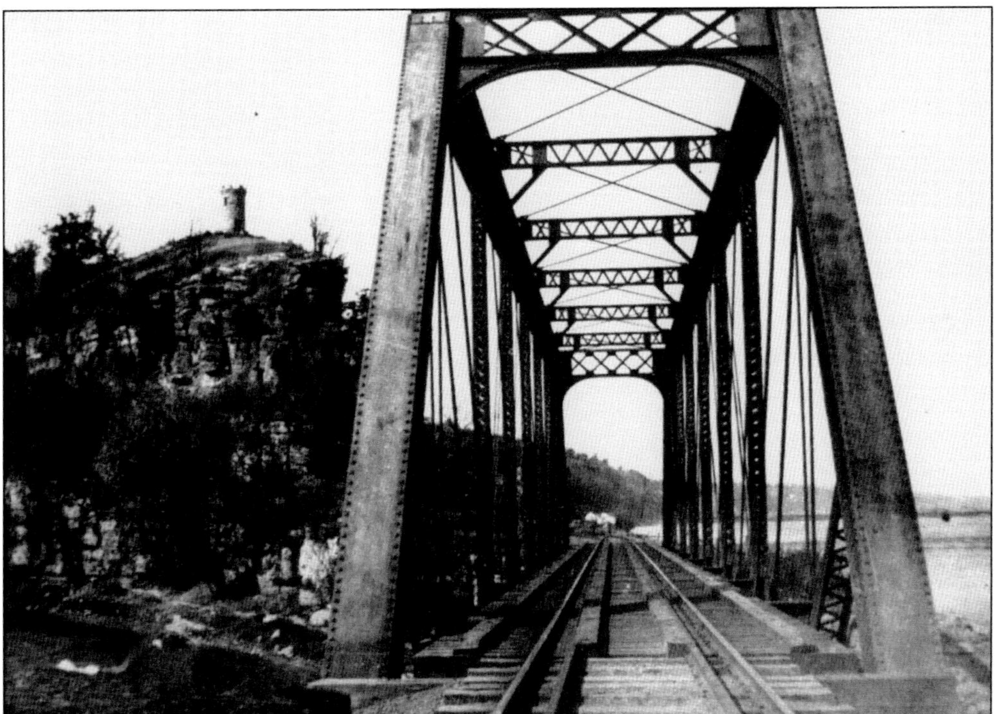

North of Bellevue, the River Road spans Catfish Creek. The tower in the upper left marks the spot where the city of Dubuque's namesake was interred. Civil War artist Alexander Simplot designed the monument.

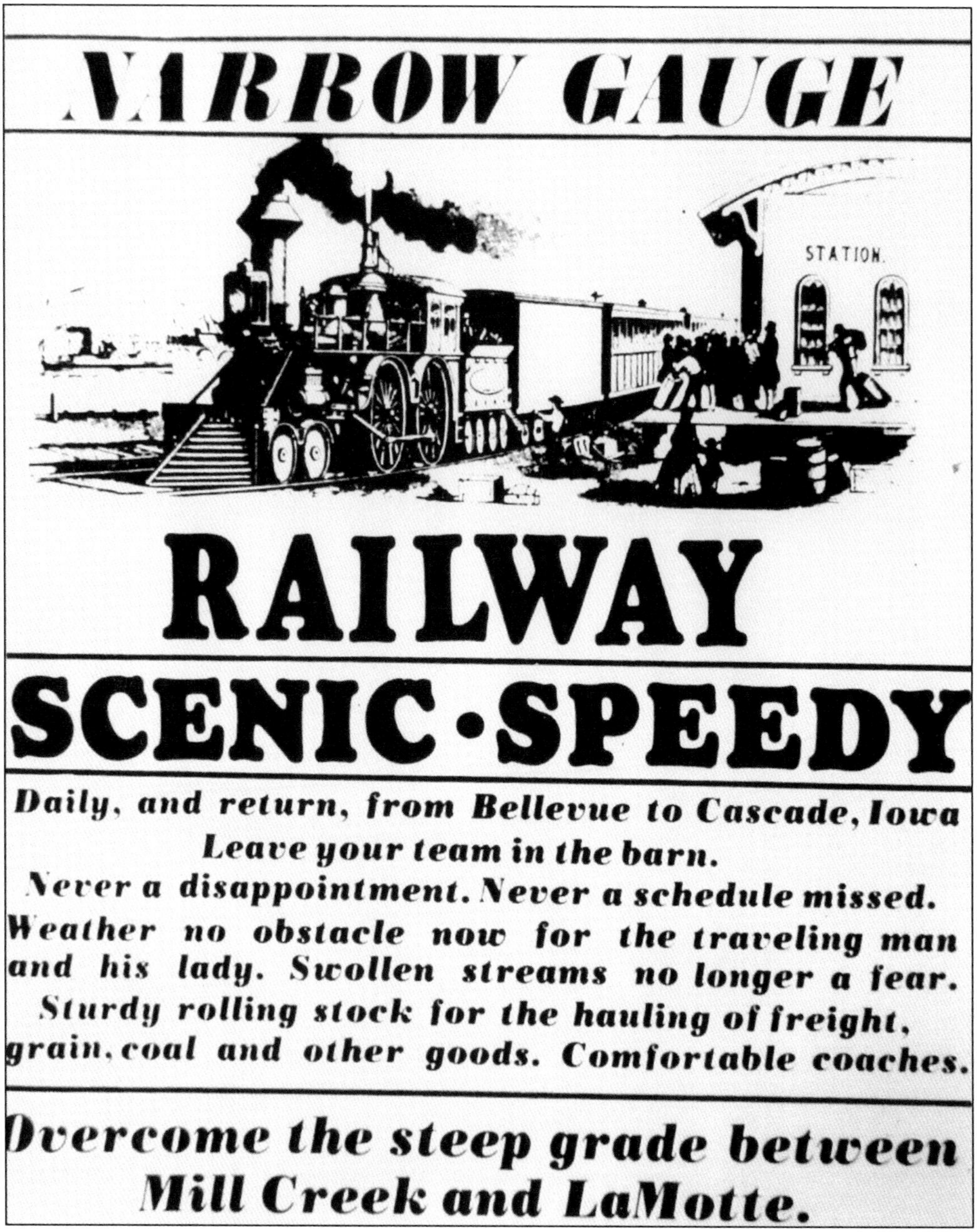

Over the years, Iowa's last narrow-gauge railroad attracted attention far and wide. In 1972, about 36 years after the rails were pulled up, the *Quad City Times* in Davenport created this to accompany a story in its supplement paper, *Focus*. (Quad City Times.)

Two

ENTER THE MILWAUKEE ROAD

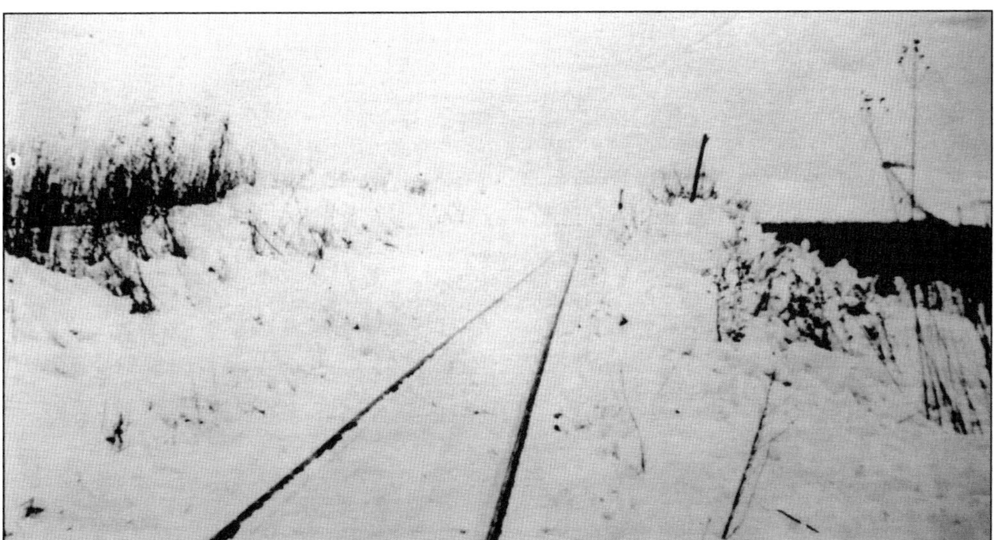

This snowfall did not stop the trains from operating. (Deppe.)

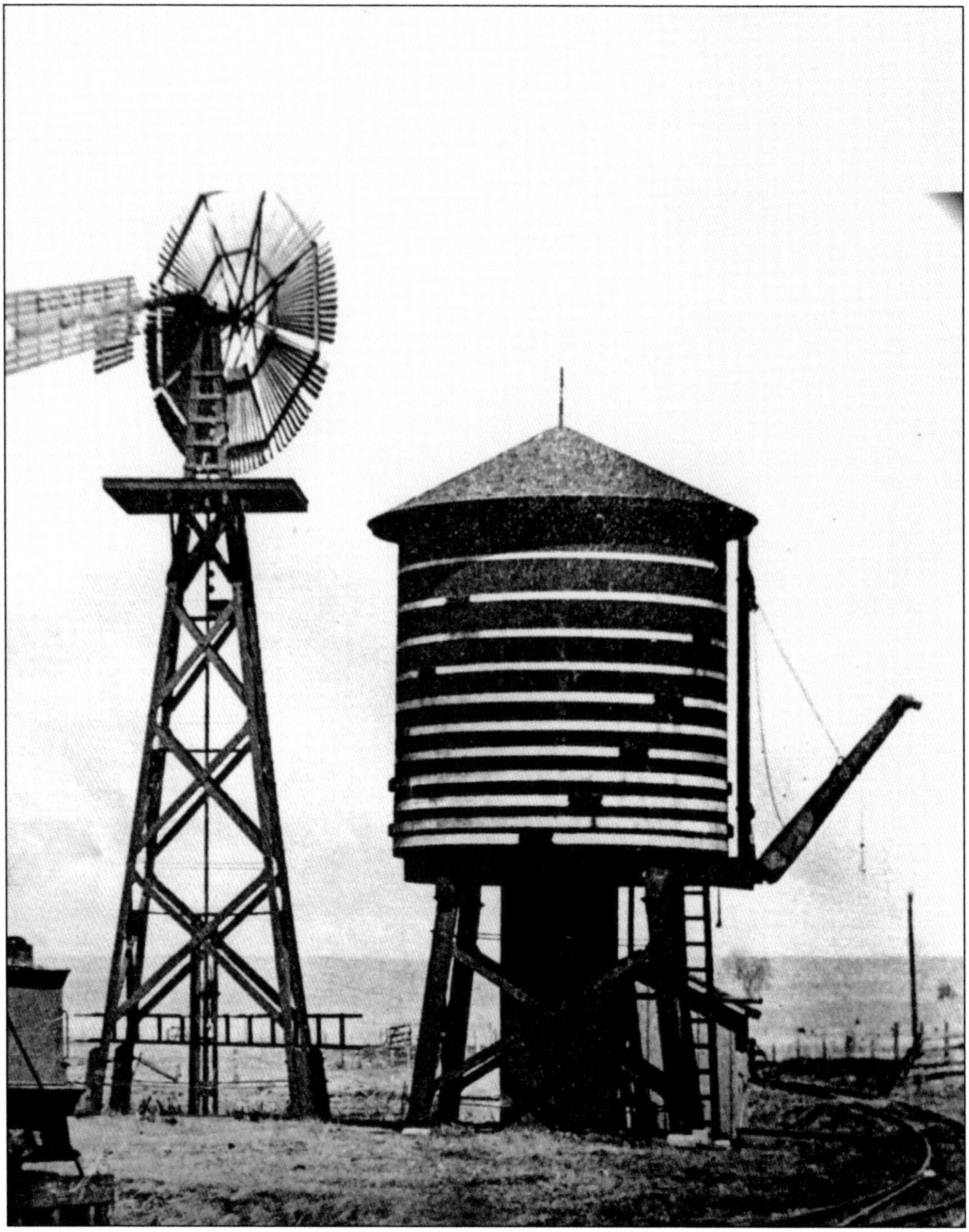

Here the water tank at Cascade and its windmill stand in the rail yards. Before the tanks were built, the locomotives were watered by using a siphon hose. Water from the creeks over which the railroad passed had sufficed. (Wyrick.)

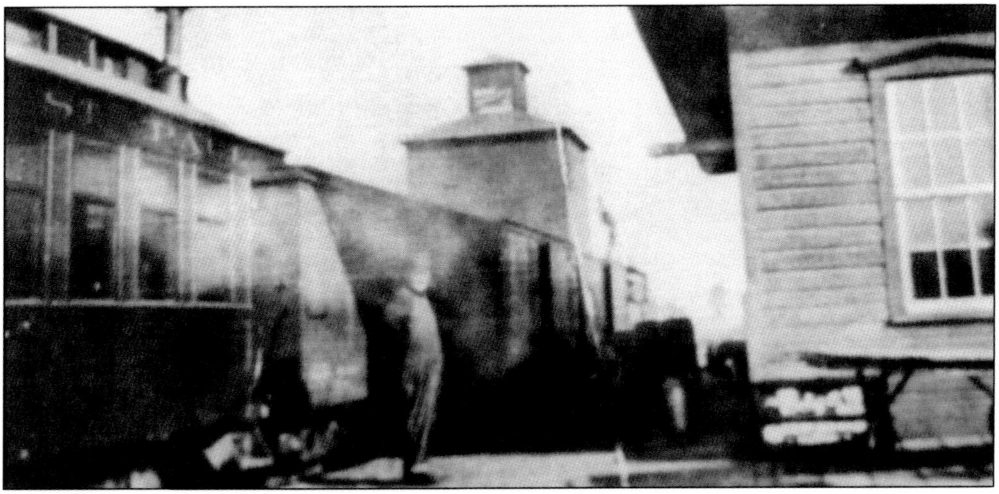

An eastbound, or "down," train readies to leave Cascade for Bellevue.

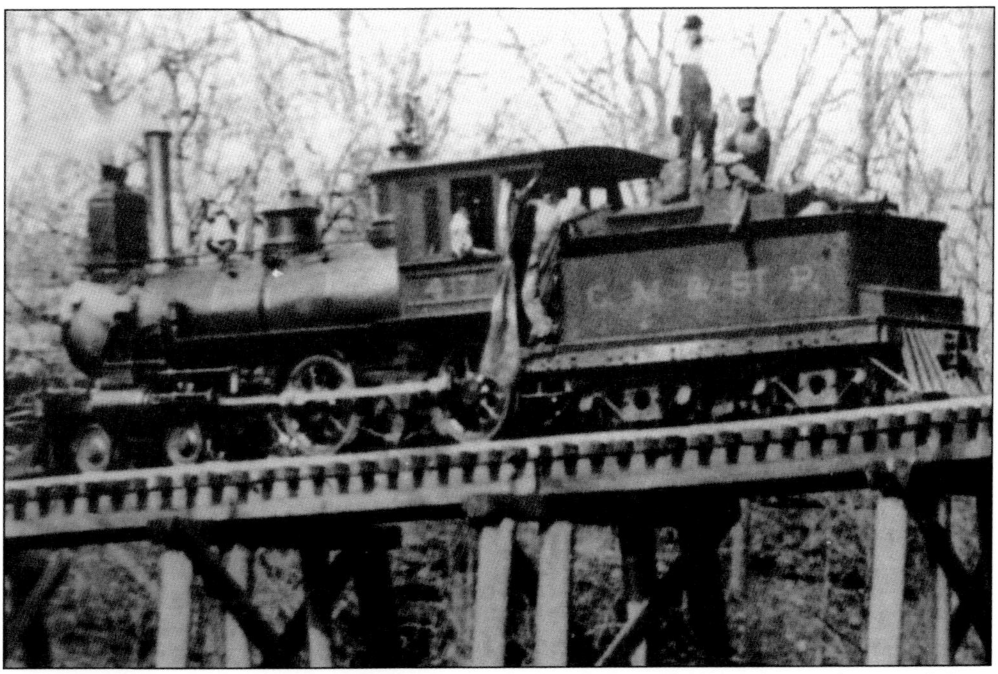

No. 417, while never formally assigned to the Bellevue-Cascade branch, was borrowed from the Preston, Minnesota, line to help in an emergency. Nos. 416 and 419 were probably at the Dubuque shops for maintenance when help was needed.

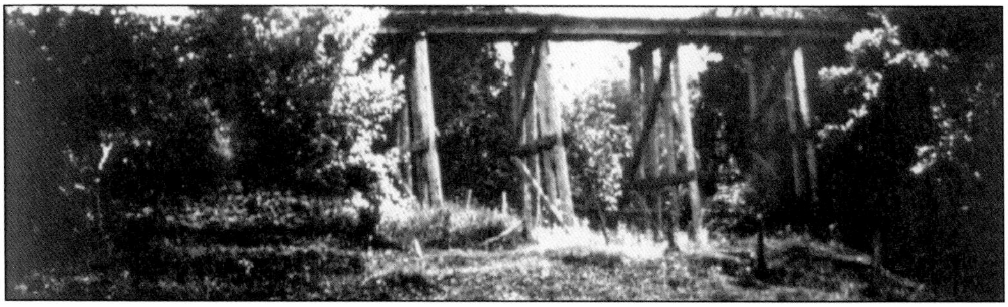

The rugged topography featured deep gullies and ravines, as well as creeks along the branch line's right-of-way. Passengers must have been thrilled with the scenery. (Deppe.)

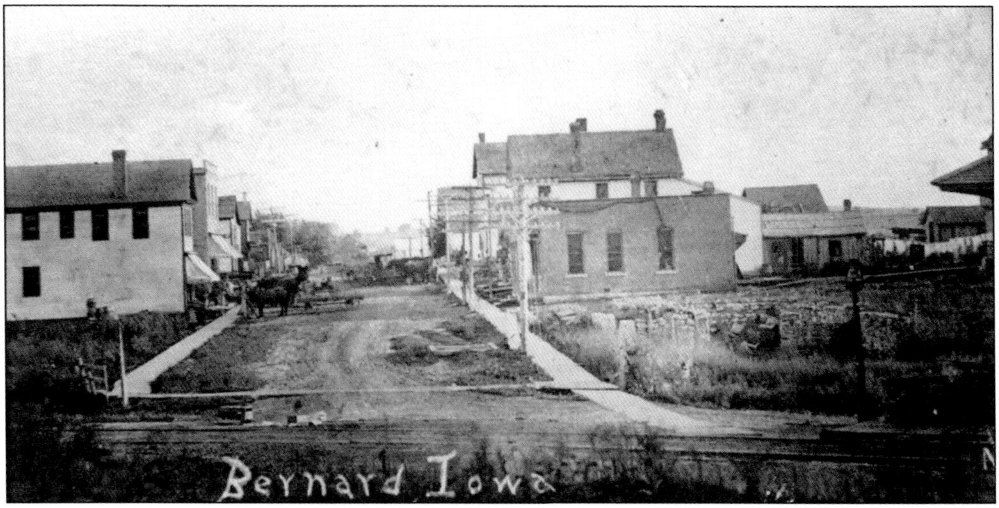

Horse-drawn vehicles line the Bernard business district in the early 1880s. A new grain elevator would soon be operating. Everyone involved with the three-foot-gauge line felt pride. (Higbe.)

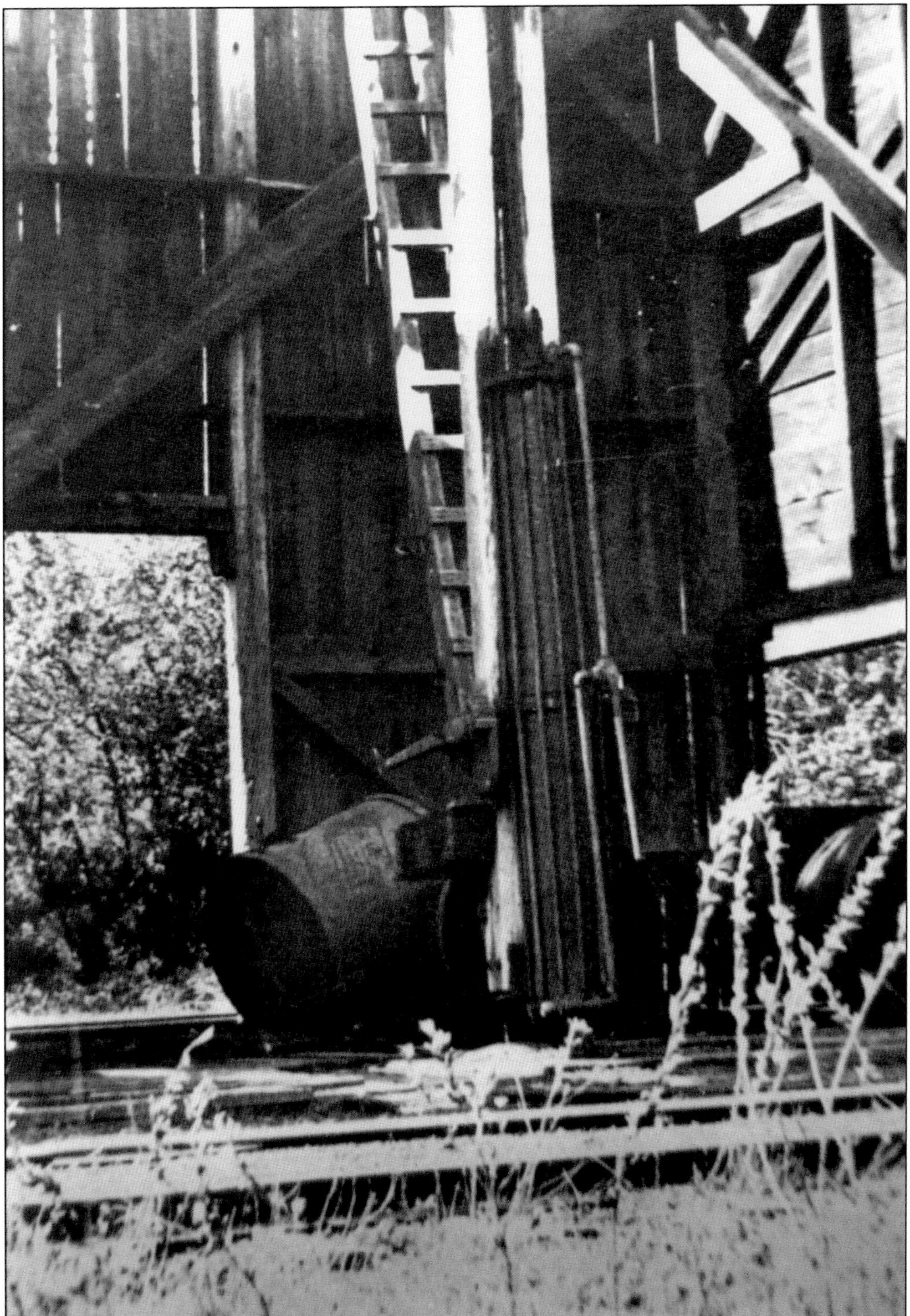

A winch lifted a half ton of coal above the tender and dumped the bucket. That method was just as unorthodox as siphoning water for the locomotives from a creek. In time, the advent of air brakes allowed a modification to a lifting mechanism operated by the engine's air pumps.

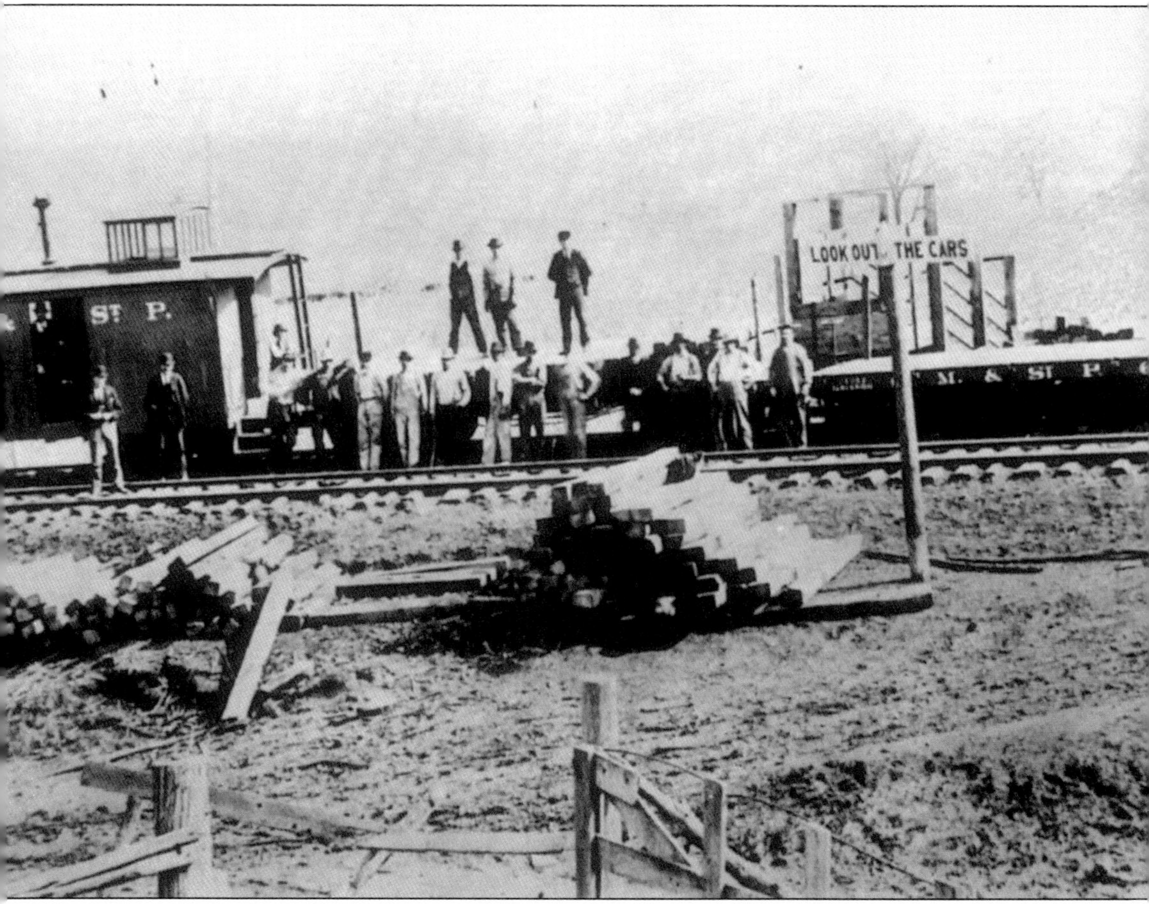

By the late 1880s, the Milwaukee owned the 37 miles of track, and because of the amount of business being generated along the main line, some sidings were lengthened. In this photograph, the section gang poses near Sylva switch.

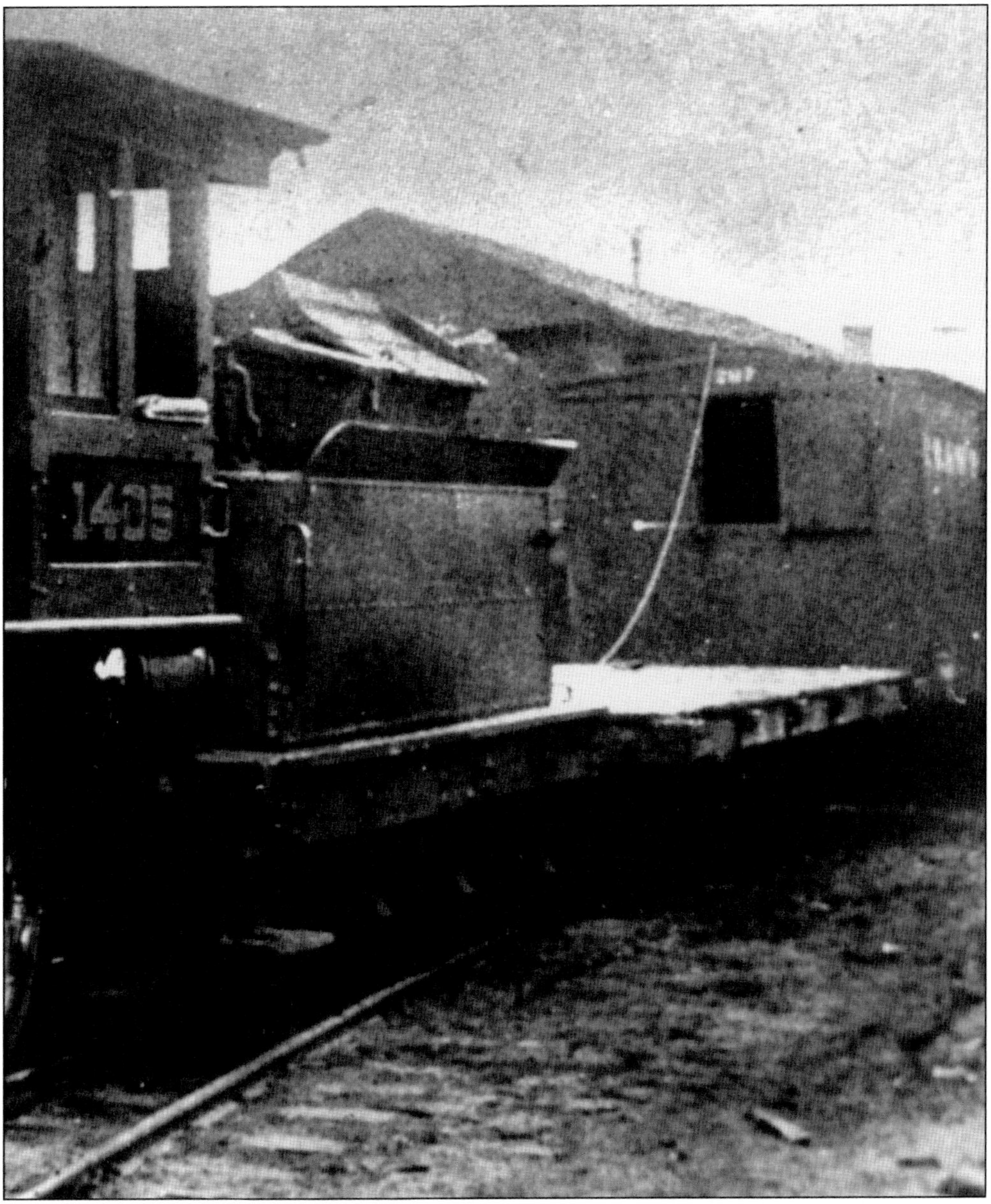

A rope dangles across a flatcar. While the train was running, the crew was able to communicate with the caboose—and vice versa—through a series of rope pulls.

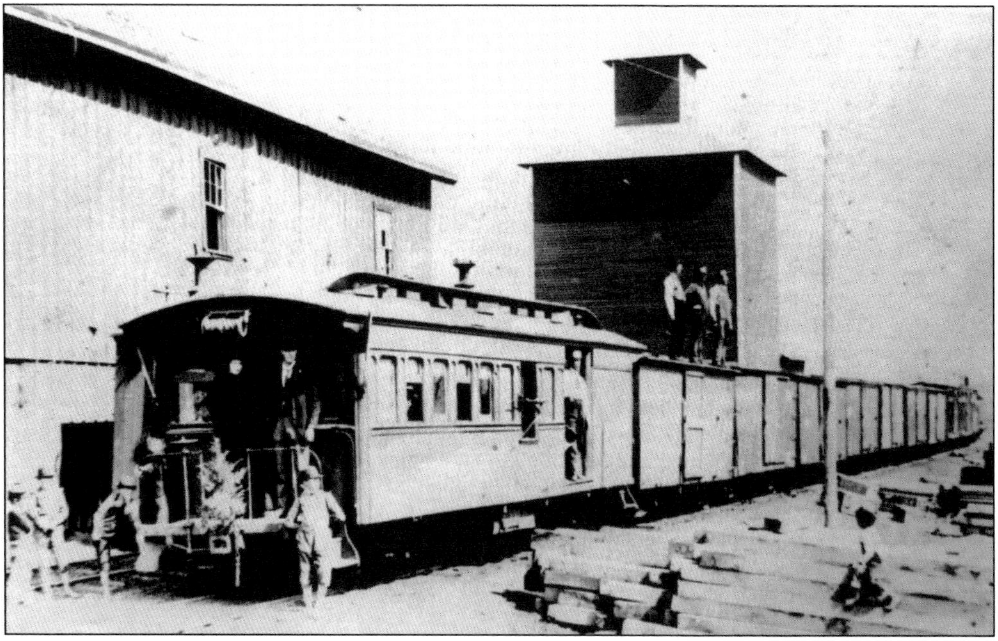

Here the communication rope can be seen on its drum. The rope stretched the full length of combine No. 7, through seven boxcars and two stock cars to the engine. The small Christmas tree on the rear platform was displayed every year during the holidays to create goodwill and garner food gifts for the crews from farmers along the route.

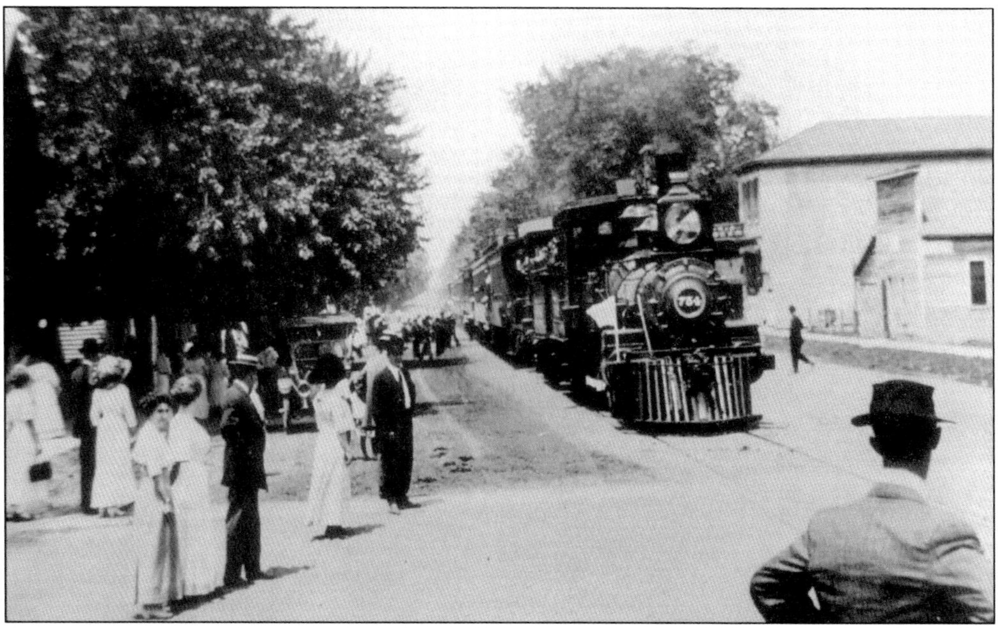

Trains of the Milwaukee standard gauge are pictured in Bellevue, as they were usually scheduled to be there when the small train arrived. Shoppers' specials, which carried the white flags of an extra train, existed from the 1890s well into the 20th century until better roads were laid. No. 754 was built in 1877 by the Schenectedy Locomotive Works. This photograph was taken sometime between 1899 and 1912.

The tiny community of Washington Mills, whose main industry was the mill house shown on the right, is seen in this westward view.

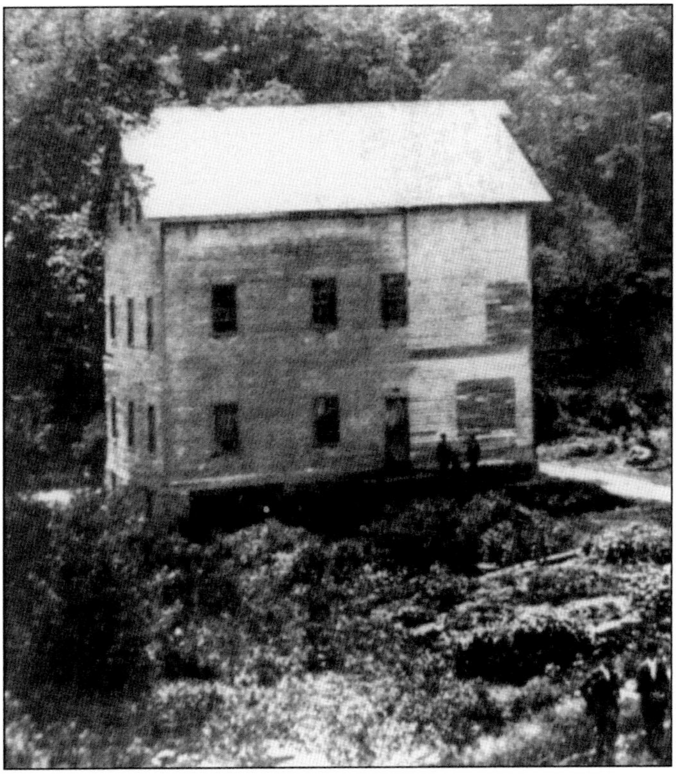

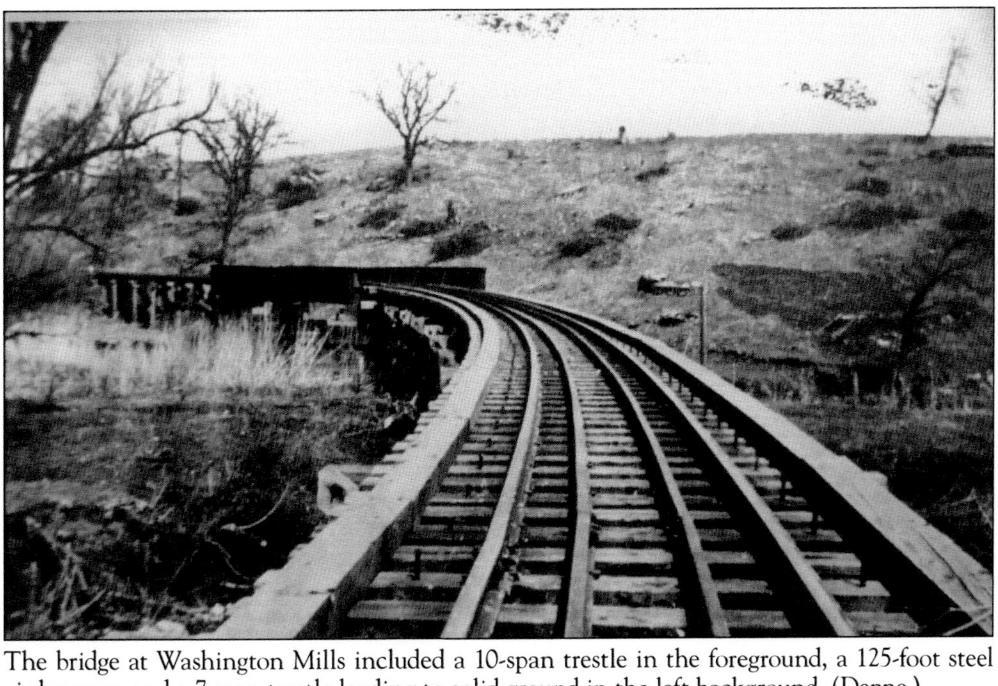

The bridge at Washington Mills included a 10-span trestle in the foreground, a 125-foot steel girder span, and a 7-span trestle leading to solid ground in the left background. (Deppe.)

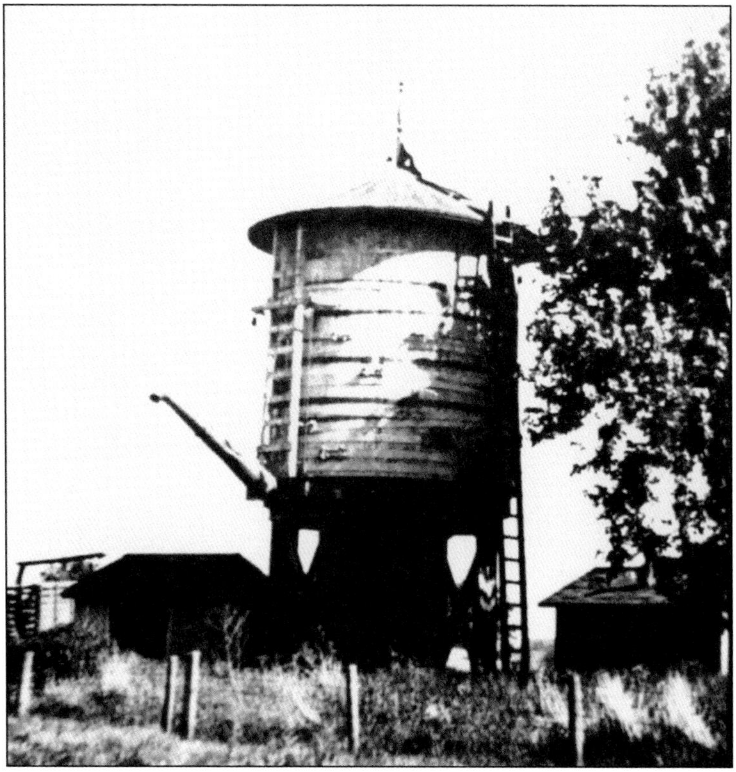

In this view looking northwest, the Cascade water tank is seen in the yards. Some of the stockyards are visible on the left.

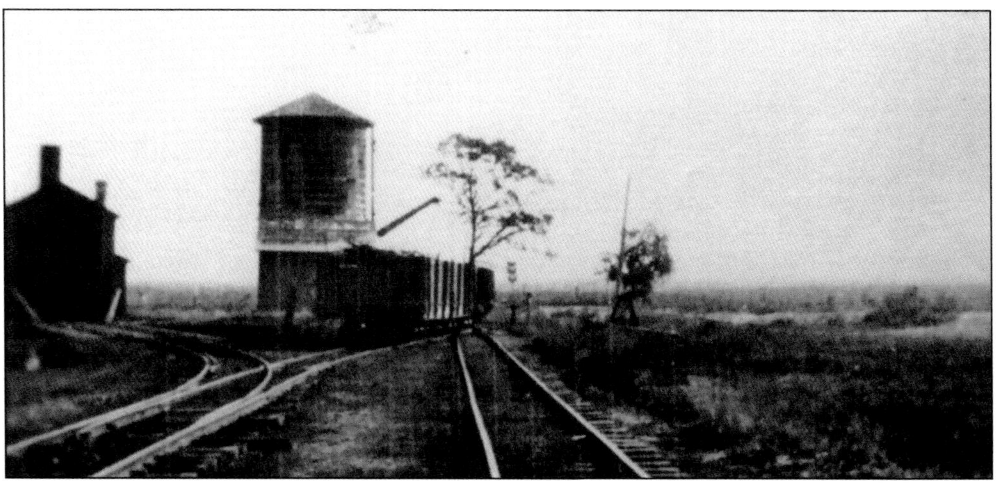

This scene shows the single-stall engine house in Cascade, the water tank, and a cut of gondolas. Just beyond the switch at left, a turntable was armstrong powered.

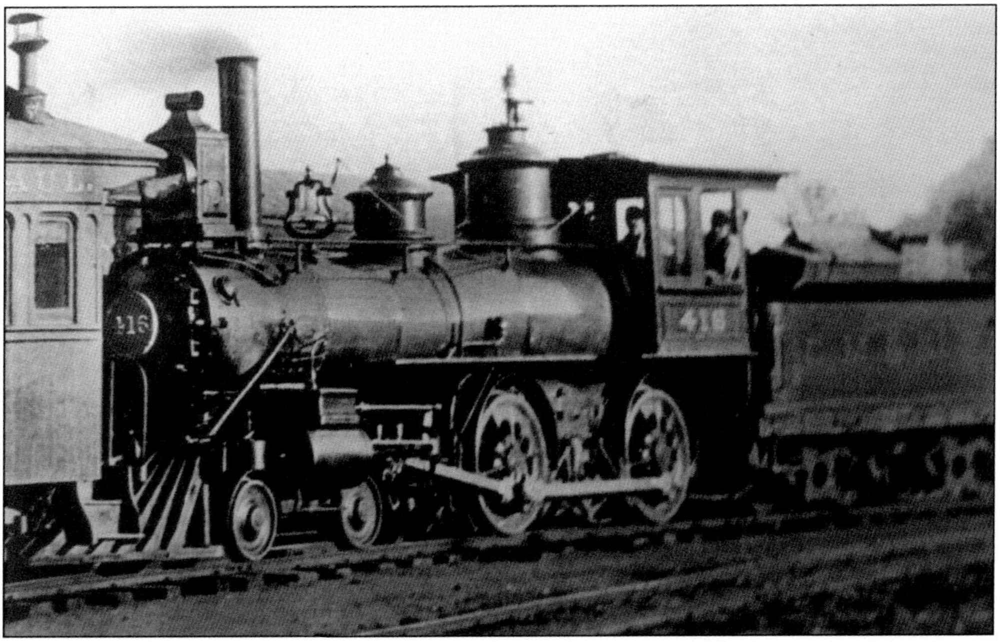

Here No. 416 pushes a car toward its train. The Pittsburgh locomotive served on the narrow gauge for 39 years (Streuser.)

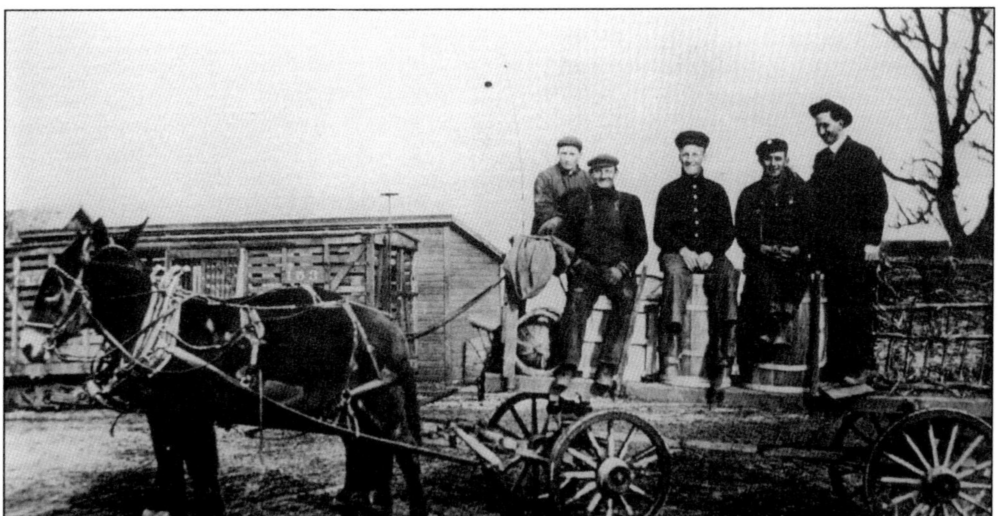
Once freight reached the western terminus, Cascade, the only way to deliver shipped goods was by wagon, drawn by mules or horses. None of these men are identified. Stock car No. 153 is in the background.

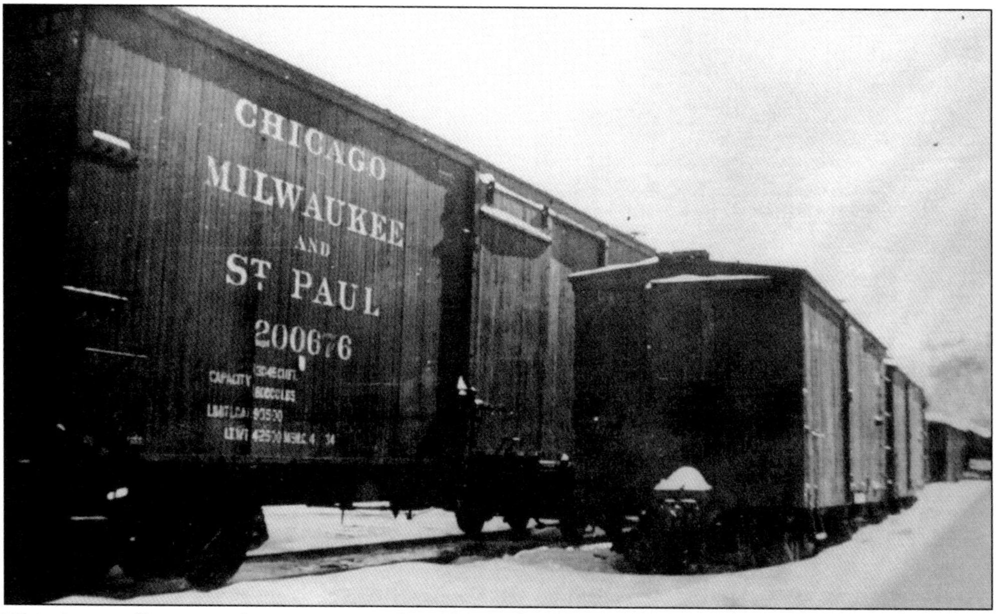

This image illustrates the expense and work involved in transferring goods from small to large cars, and vice versa. (Deppe.)

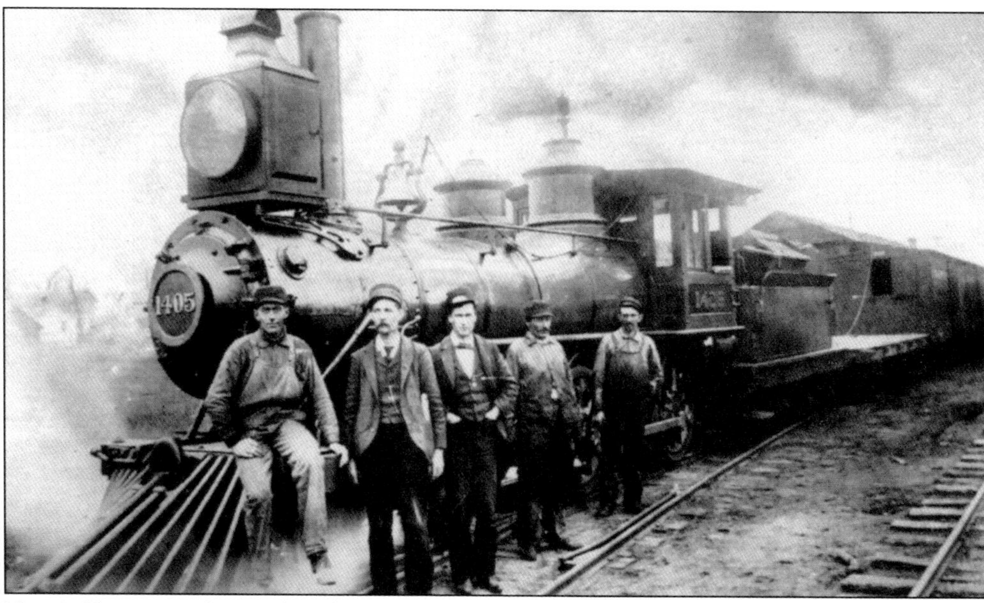

No. 1405, previously numbered 416, waits patiently while a photograph is taken. Pictured here, from left to right, are Phillip Webber (brakeman), John Dunn (conductor), O. E. Winter (Cascade depot agent), Edward Butler (engineer), and John Theilen (fireman). The locomotive's headlight lens was 24 inches across. (Streuser.)

Cascade Branch—(Narrow Gauge). (Table 49)

103	Mls	STATIONS.	126
AM			PM
†8.50	0.	Lv. **Bellevue(k)** Ar	**4.30**
10.05	11.4	" ... La Motte ... Lv	**3.05**
10.30	15.7	" .... Zwingle .... "	**2.35**
11.00	22.0	" Washingt'n Mills "	**1.55**
11.20	25.2	" .... Bernard .... "	**1.35**
11.35	29.7	" .... Fillmore .... "	**1.10**
11.55	35.6	Ar ... Cascade ... Lv	**†12.45**

According to this timetable, train No. 103 took three hours and five minutes to reach Cascade from Bellevue. Eastbound train No. 126 took three hours and 45 minutes. Brakes on each car had to be set by hand to descend the summit grade between LaMotte and Bellevue.

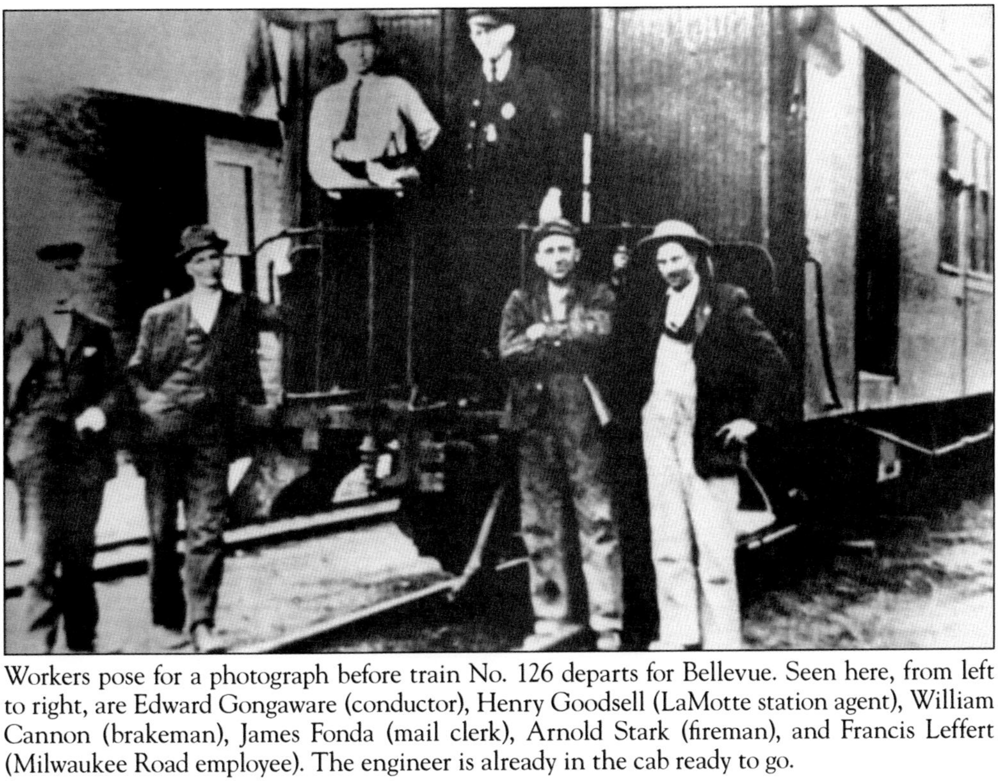

Workers pose for a photograph before train No. 126 departs for Bellevue. Seen here, from left to right, are Edward Gongaware (conductor), Henry Goodsell (LaMotte station agent), William Cannon (brakeman), James Fonda (mail clerk), Arnold Stark (fireman), and Francis Leffert (Milwaukee Road employee). The engineer is already in the cab ready to go.

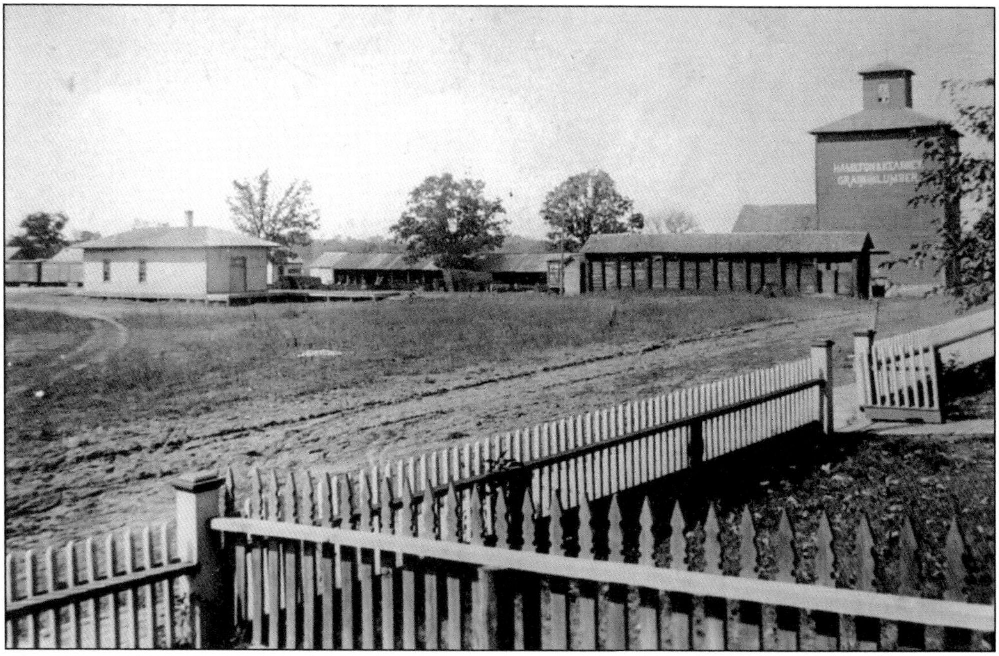

This image shows Locust Street, which runs parallel to the picket fence. The Cascade depot (left) and the lumberyard (center) are dwarfed by the Hamilton and Kearney Grain and Lumber elevator.

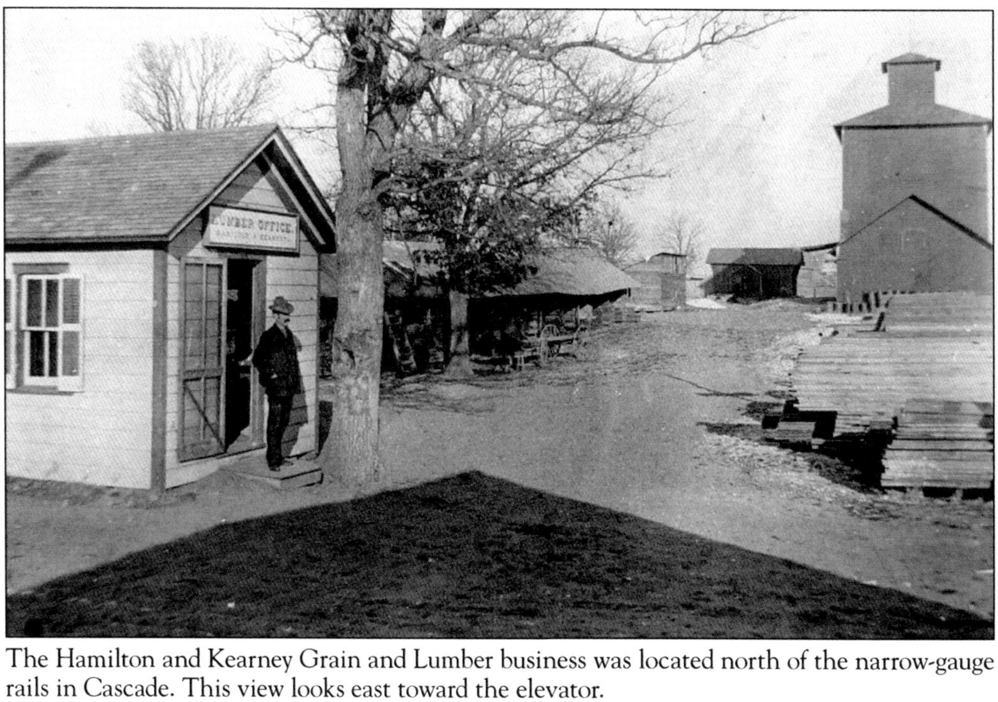

The Hamilton and Kearney Grain and Lumber business was located north of the narrow-gauge rails in Cascade. This view looks east toward the elevator.

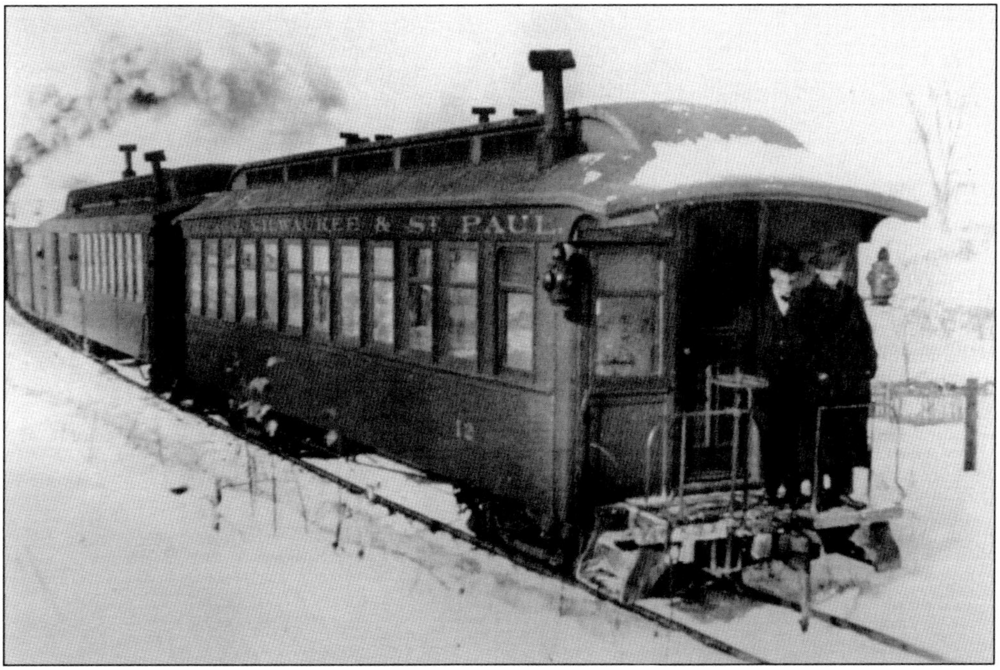

It could be said that the eastern Iowa narrow-gauge railroad did its very best to provide comfort for its passengers. Here two unidentified patrons pose on a cold winter day while train No. 103 leaves the Bellevue yards.

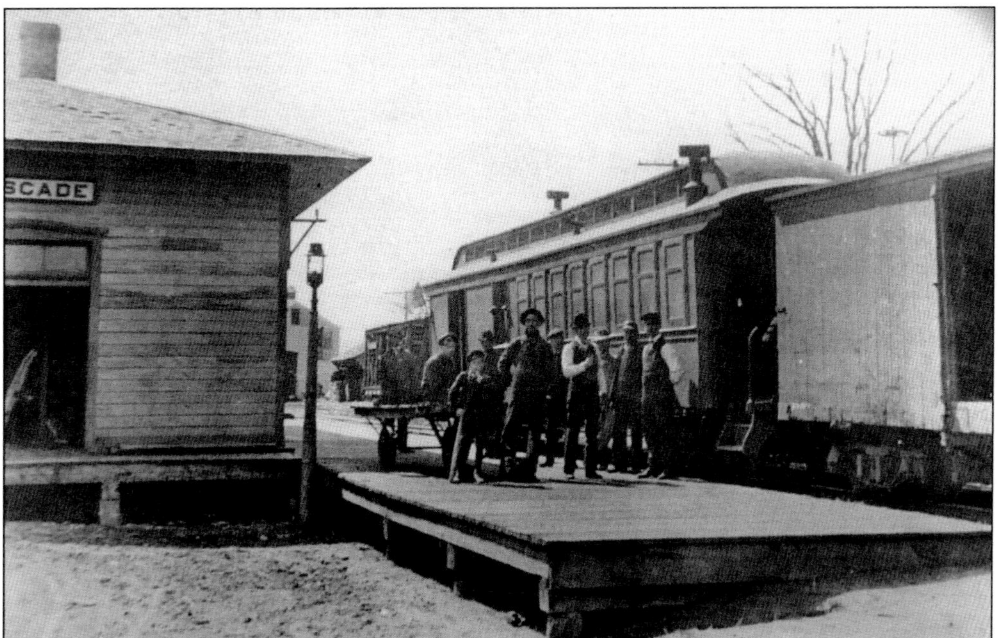

This 1880s image, depicting Cascade's depot, eight unidentified men, and a boy dressed in a suit, was taken next to combine No. 8 before it headed east toward Bellevue.

CHICAGO, MILWAUKEE & ST. PAUL RAILWAY.

Cascade Branch.

GOING WEST.							STATIONS. U. S. Express Co. Dec. 6, 1903.	GOING EAST.				
			No109 Mix'd	No103 Mix'd	Mls			Population	No104 Mix'd	No110 Mix'd		
			P M	A.M.					P.M.	A.M.		
......	......	......	b 6 55	b 9 30	....	lv	.....*Bellevue ....ar	1607	b4 30	b 8 40	......	......
......	......	......	7 35	10 30	11		.......La Motte.......	272	3 15	8 05	......	......
......	......	......	7 50	10 50	16		........Zwingle	241	2 40	7 53	......	......
......	......	......	8 10	11 15	22		...Washington Mills ..	112	2 00	7 37	......	......
......	......	......	8 20	11 30	25		.........Bernard.......	113	1 45	7 27	......	......
......	......	......	8 33	11 45	30		.......Fillmore	115	1 25	7 15	......	......
......	......	......	8 50	12 05	36	ar	......Cascade lv	1266	1 00	7 00	......	......
			P.M.	P.M.					P.M.	A.M.		

The December 6, 1903, timetable shows that two mixed dailies made two round-trips between the terminals. The population of each town is given in the right-hand columns.

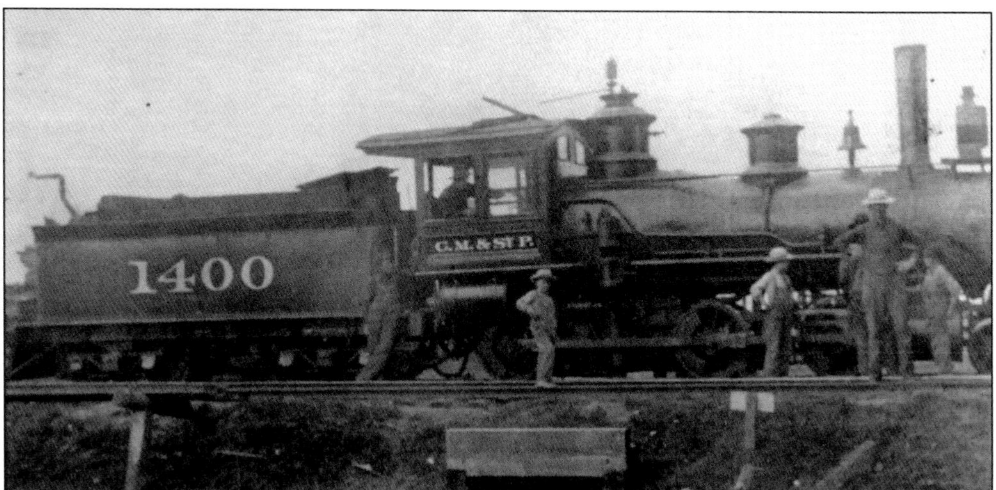

In 1905, a secondhand Brooks Mogul 2-6-0 was acquired. Of its total 46 years service, 30 were spent on the last narrow gauge in Iowa. The crew and boys are unidentified.

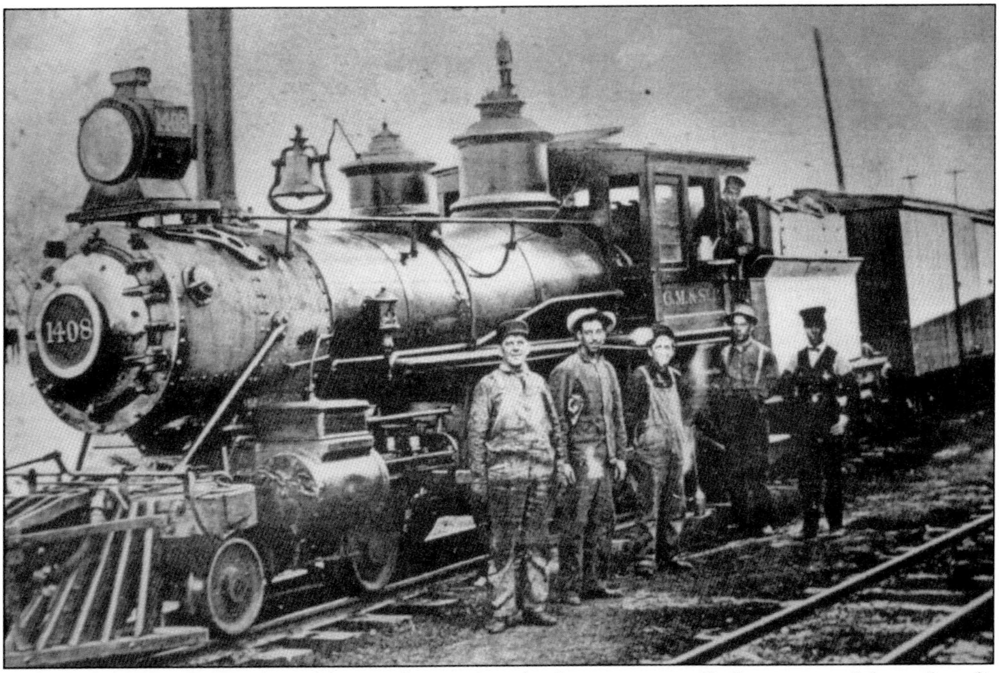

Between 1905 and 1906, knuckle couplers and air brakes were installed on most of the railroad's equipment. From left to right, Edward Horning Sr., three unidentified men, and Edward Gongaware (conductor) stand by No. 1408. The man in the cab is unidentified.

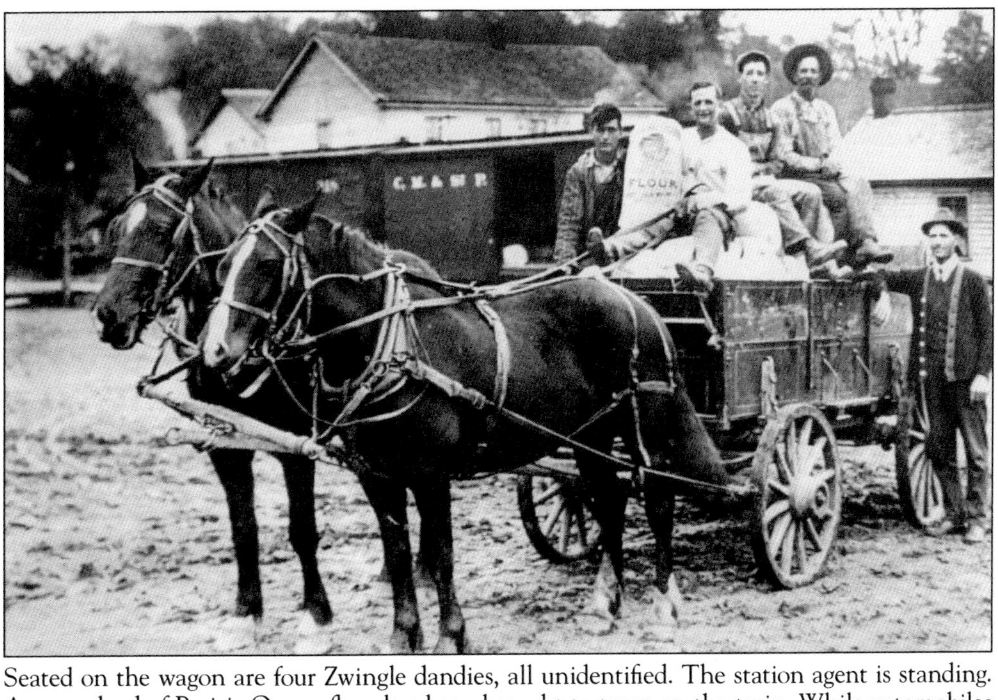

Seated on the wagon are four Zwingle dandies, all unidentified. The station agent is standing. A wagonload of Prairie Queen flour has been brought to town on the train. While automobiles were beginning to show up along the Milwaukee branch line, most people depended on a good team of horses or mules for transportation and work.

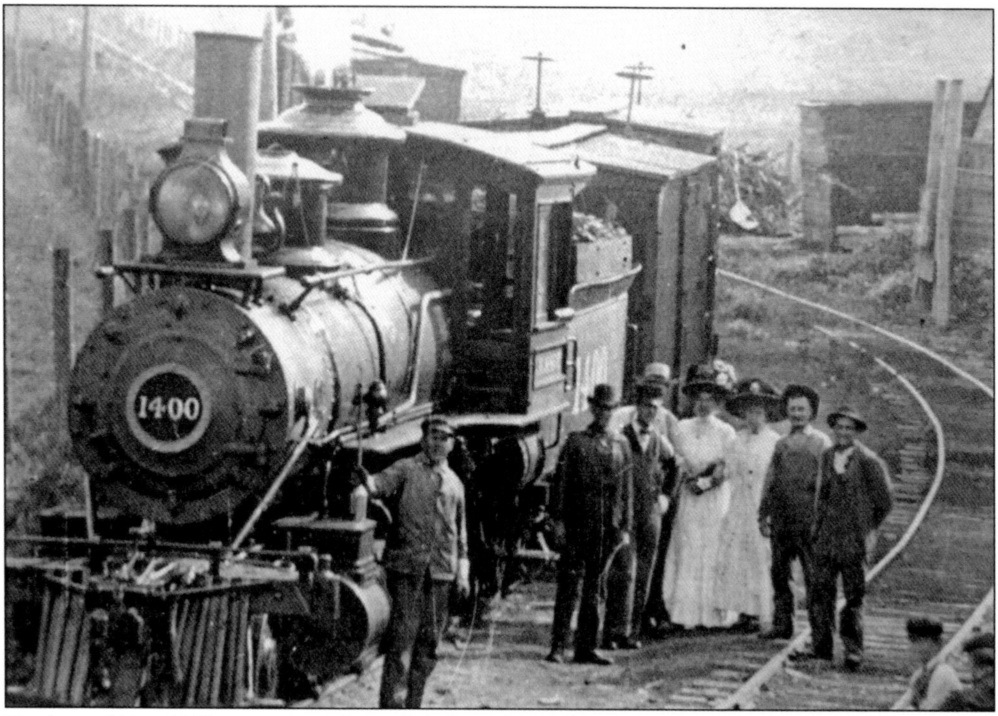

Eastbound No. 1400 prepares to leave LaMotte for Bellevue in 1906. For decades, train arrivals were always exciting in small-town America.

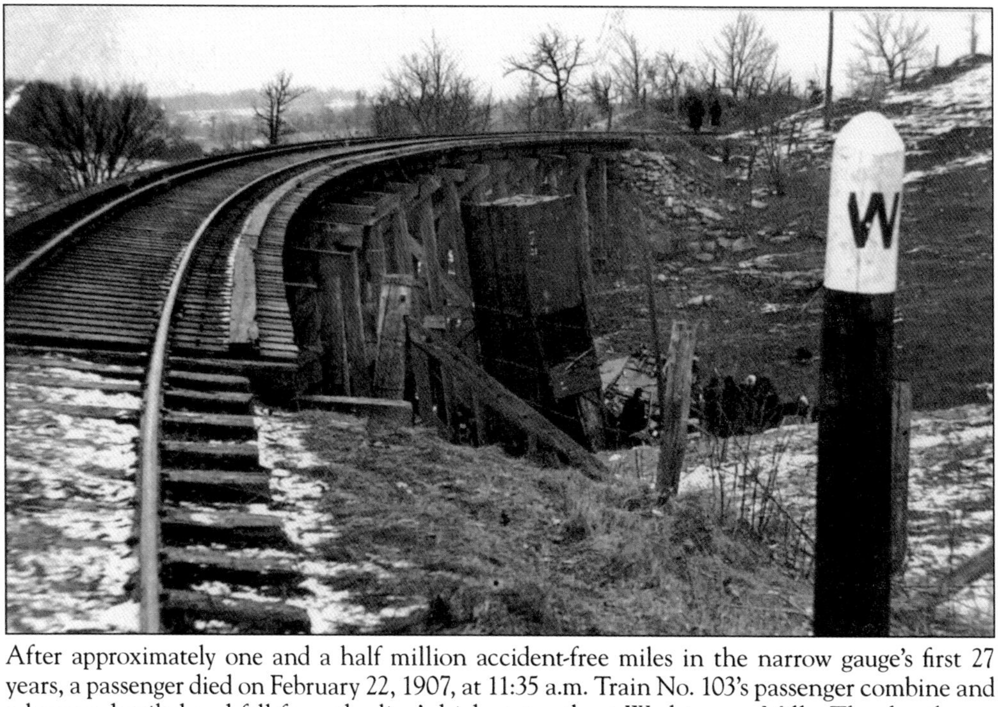

After approximately one and a half million accident-free miles in the narrow gauge's first 27 years, a passenger died on February 22, 1907, at 11:35 a.m. Train No. 103's passenger combine and a boxcar derailed and fell from the line's highest trestle at Washington Mills. The derailment occurred at the middle of the curved trestle after passing through the rock cut. (Wyrick.)

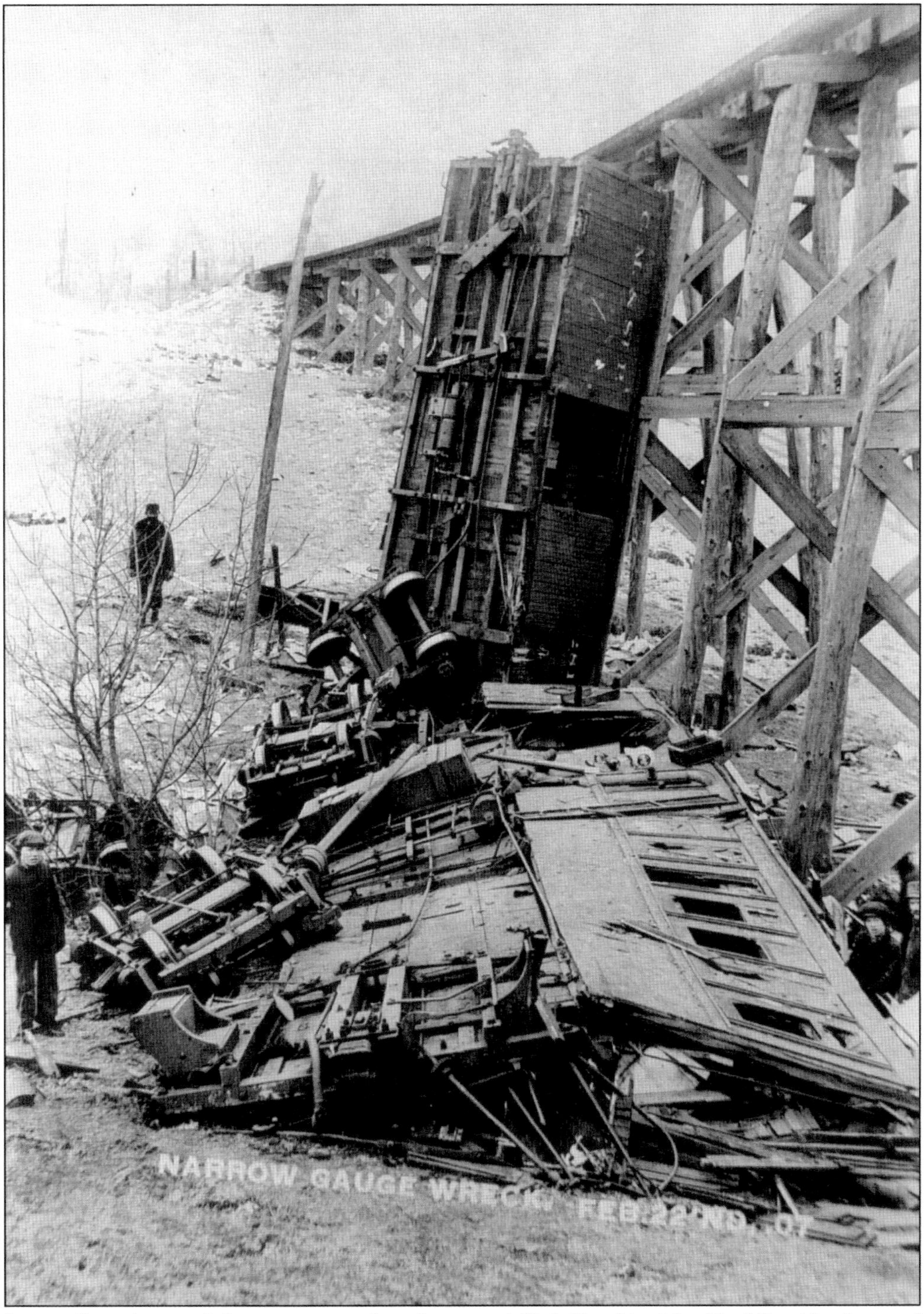

It was a "wonderment" that everyone onboard was not killed. Combine No. 6 had "its sides slammed together, not unlike the covers of a closed book," reported the *Cascade Pioneer-Advertiser.* (Wyrick.)

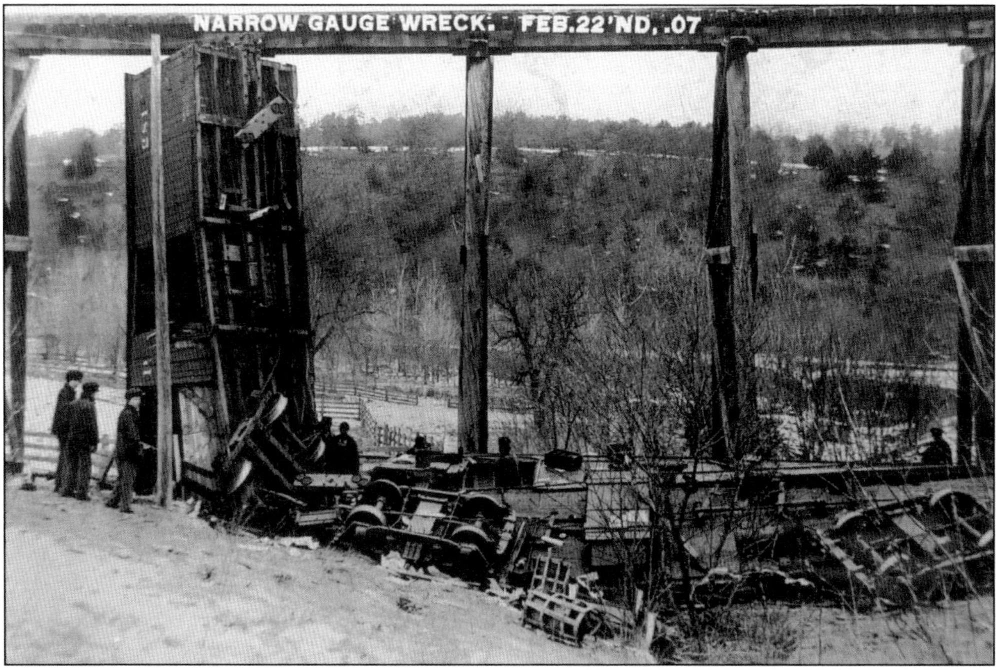

In this photograph of the 1907 accident, the gawkers who have gathered to see the results prove that people have always been interested in others' misfortunes. (Nemmers.)

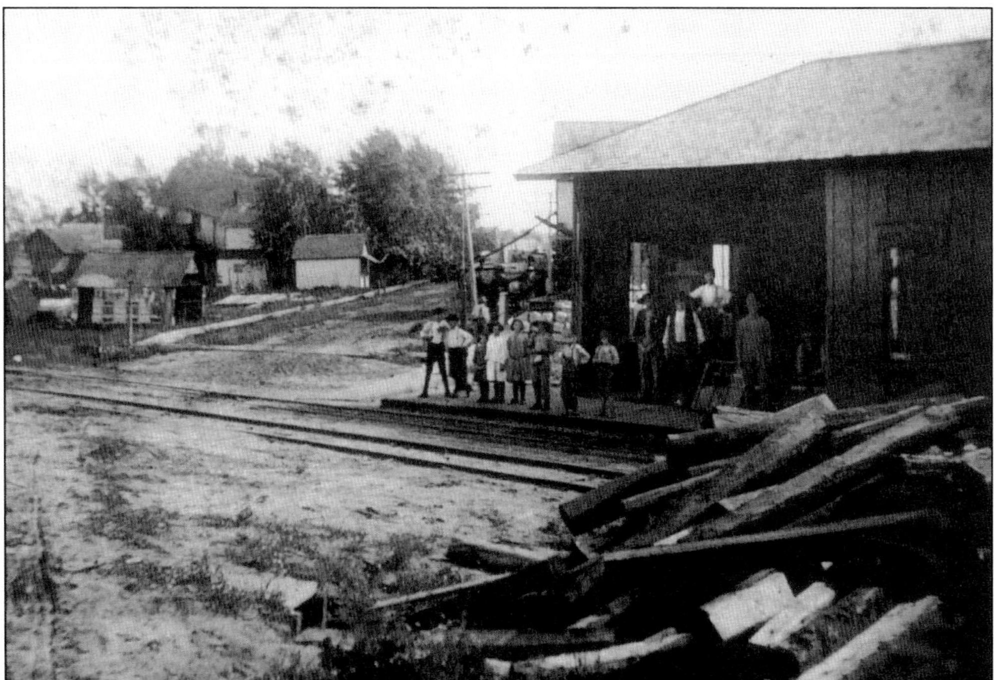

The depot in Bernard was struck by a tornado in 1907. The open portion had an upper wall that hung down two-fifths of the way. That area acted as a waiting room. The storm probably took the facade. In the background are an overturned shed and a house twisted off its foundation.

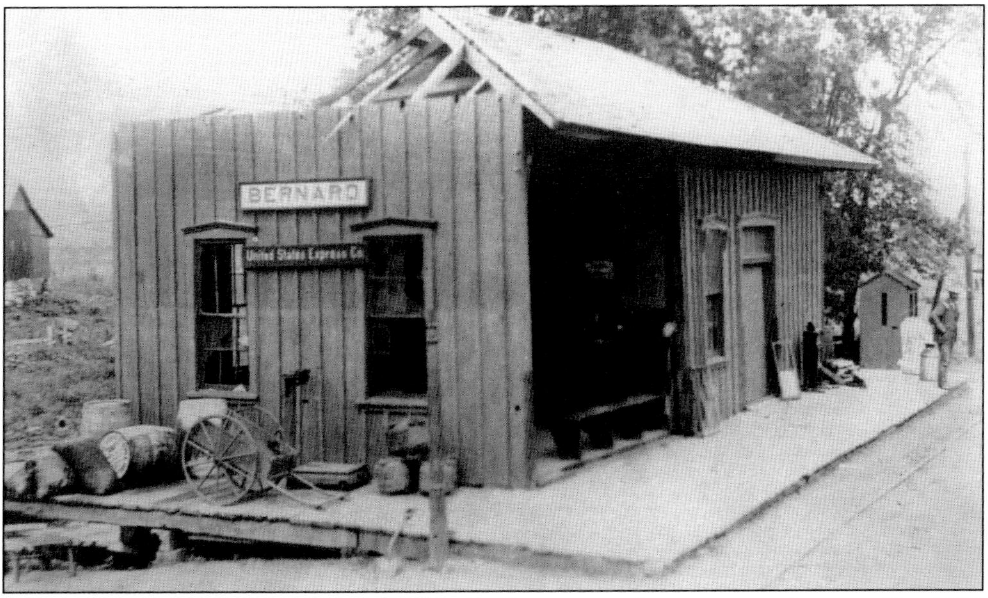

The Bernard depot had no bay at trackside to allow approaching trains to be seen. The 1907 tornado took part of the roof and broke many windows in the village.

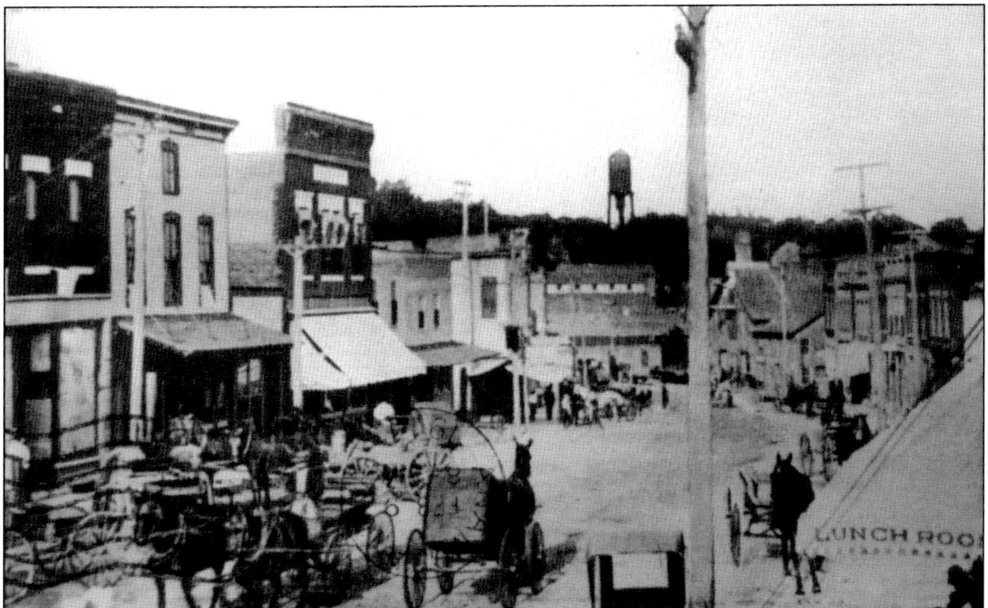

Even though the area had enjoyed economic and physical growth, the citizens of Cascade constantly reminded the Milwaukee Road of its lack of competence in satisfying the community's needs in the 1900s.

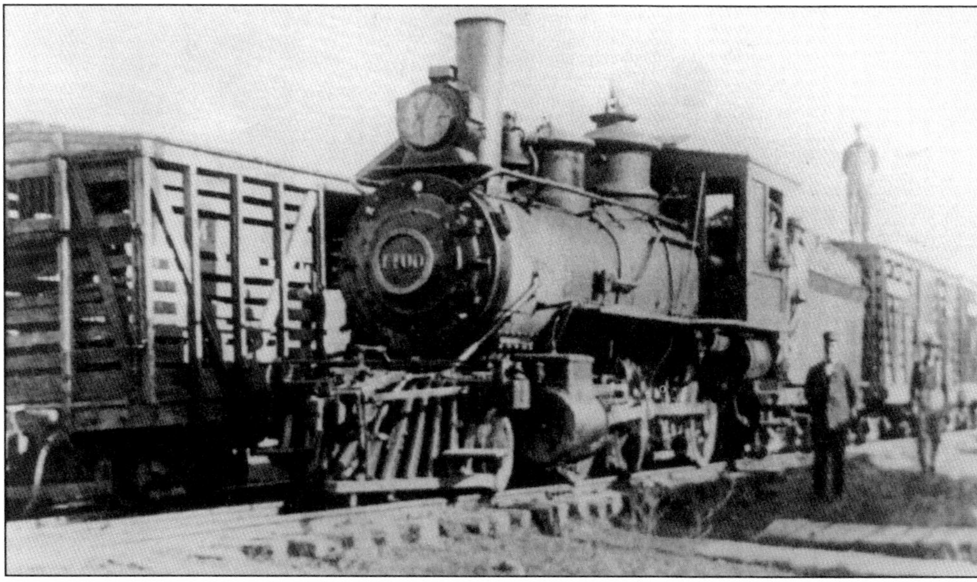

No. 1400, on the point of eastbound No. 126, is ready to leave Zwingle. Their switching duties finished, crew members stand still for a minute. Pictured here, from left to right, are Nathan Hunter (fireman, in the cab window), Charles Speilman (engineer, behind Hunter), Edward Gongware (conductor), William Cannon (brakeman, on top of stock car), and a farmer, Edward Akpock. (Higbe.)

Cascade Line.

		109	105	Mls.	Table 92	110	106			
		PM	AM			AM	PM			
----	Nos. 105 and 109 Mixed.	†7.15	†9.40	0	Lv....**Bellevue**....Ar	8.25	**5.20**	Nos. 106 and 110 Mixed.	----	----
----		**7.55**	10.45	11.4	"......La Motte......Lv	7.50	**4.20**		----	----
----		**8.10**	11.10	15.7	"....... Zwingle......."	7.38	**3.40**		----	----
----		**8.32**	11.35	22.0	".. Washington Mills.."	7.22	**2.50**		----	----
----		**8.45**	11.59	25.2	"....... Bernard......."	7.12	**2.30**		----	----
----		**9.03**	**12.15**	29.7	".......Fillmore ......"	7.00	**2.05**		----	----
----		**9.25**	**12.45**	35.6	Ar.....**Cascade**....Lv	†6.45	**†1.40**		----	----
		PM	PM			AM	PM			

To serve the businessmen of Cascade, the Milwaukee Road scheduled four trains at different times of arrival and departure. Train Nos. 109 and 110 were the fastest ever scheduled over the hilly railroad. One locomotive (of the three owned) was held in reserve or being shopped at Dubuque. The schedule could be handled by one locomotive if necessary.

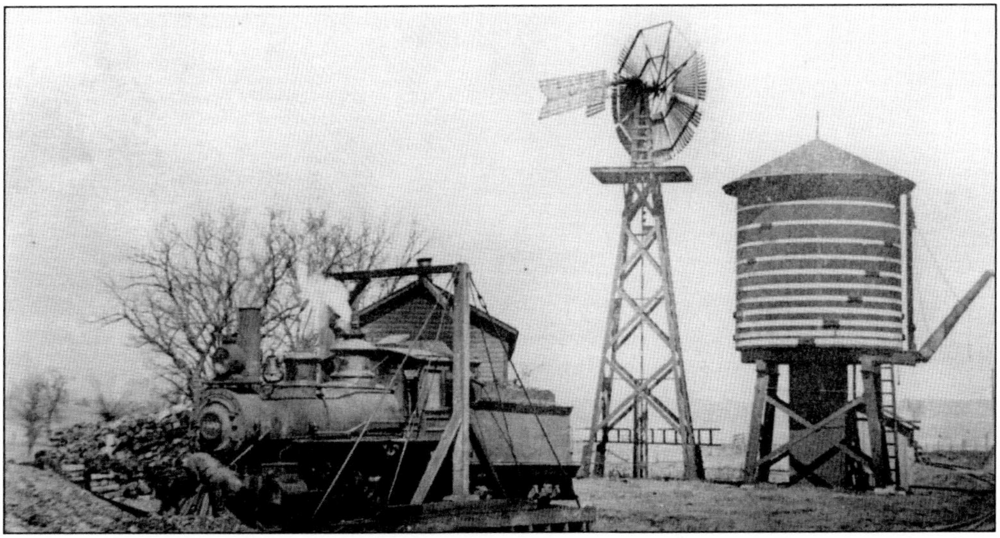

One engine crew member is at the front of the engine pushing the turntable in Cascade, while another is behind the locomotive, pushing. Once No. 1400 is turned to head east, it will get a drink of water and be ready to travel to Bellevue. (Wyrick.)

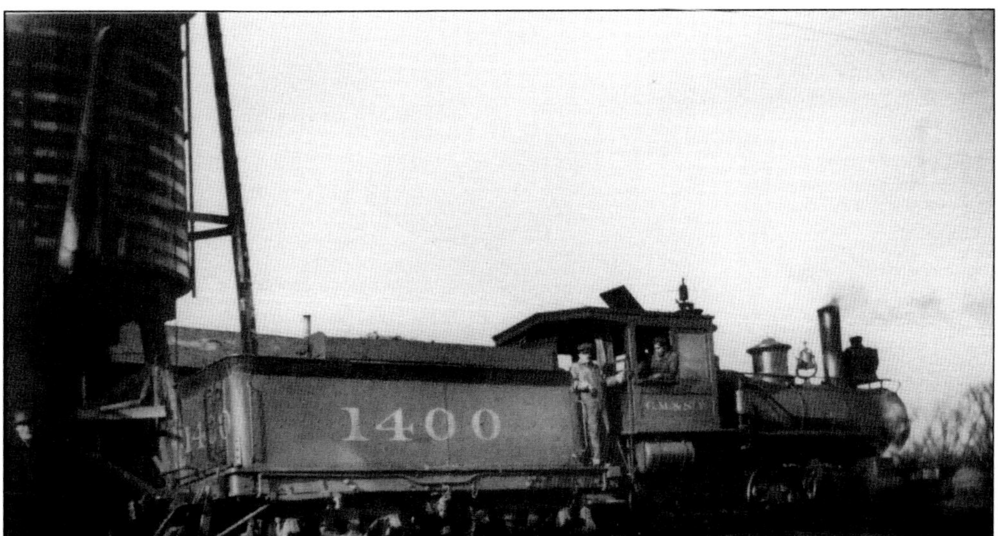

Brakeman Arthur Masters, standing on the tender platform, and fireman Nathan Hunter will back up No. 1400 to its train. Then it will whistle off and leave. (Wyrick.)

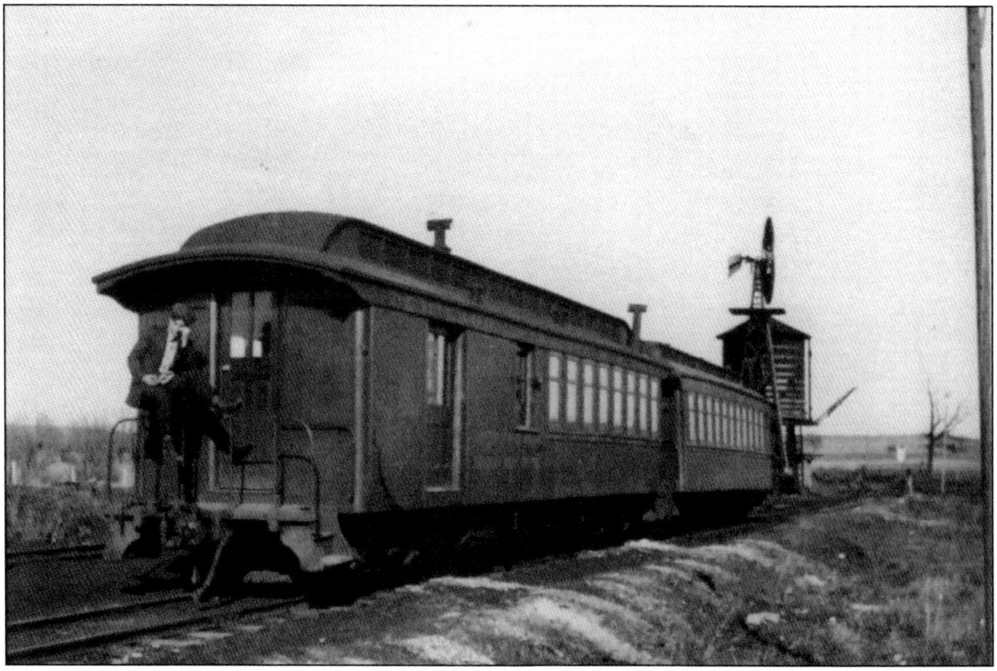

Nathan Hunter sits on the combine's brakewheel. In the background to the east, the windmill and water tank stand guard. Coach No. 12 is behind the combine. (Wyrick.)

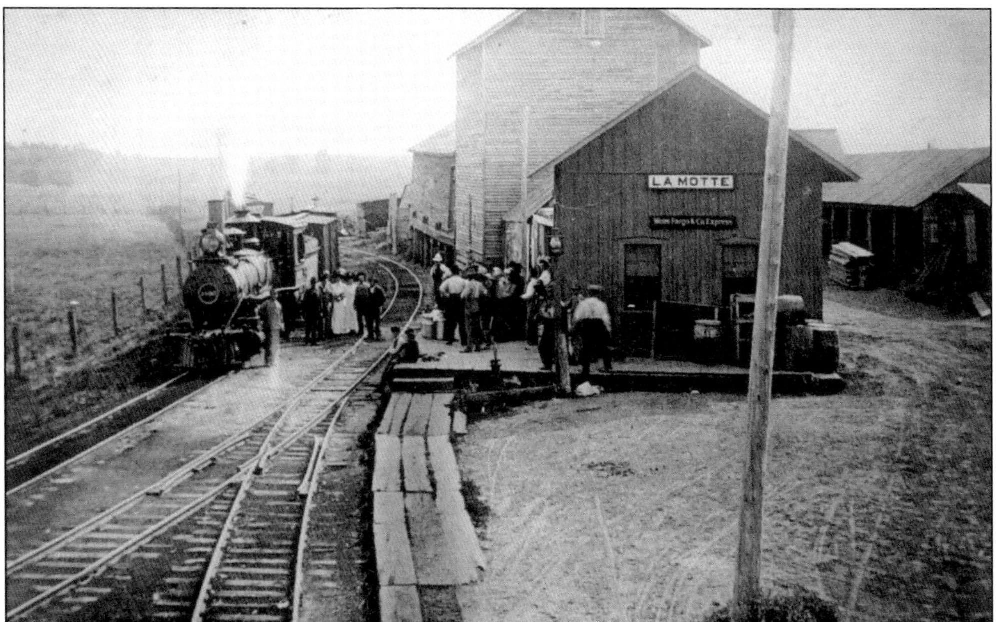

Sometime prior to 1920, when Zwingle was devastated by fire, No. 1400 readies to leave the little village. The depot, grain elevator, and stockyards—as well as the rest of the buildings pictured—would all be destroyed.

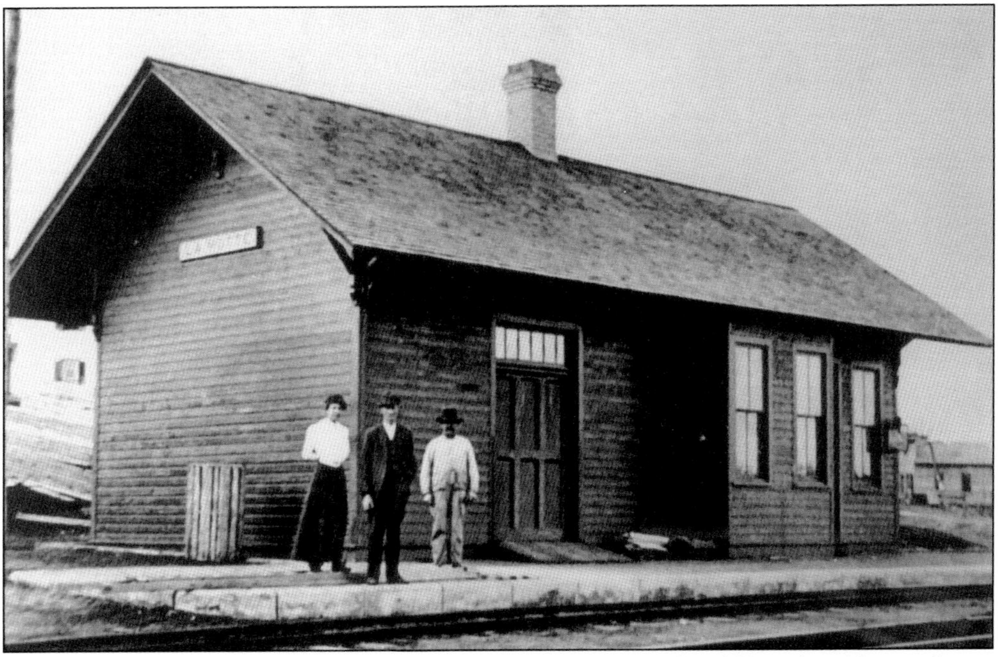

Three unidentified people stand by the new station in LaMotte. The old board-and-batten depot, large elevator, stockyards, and other buildings had burned to the ground in 1910.

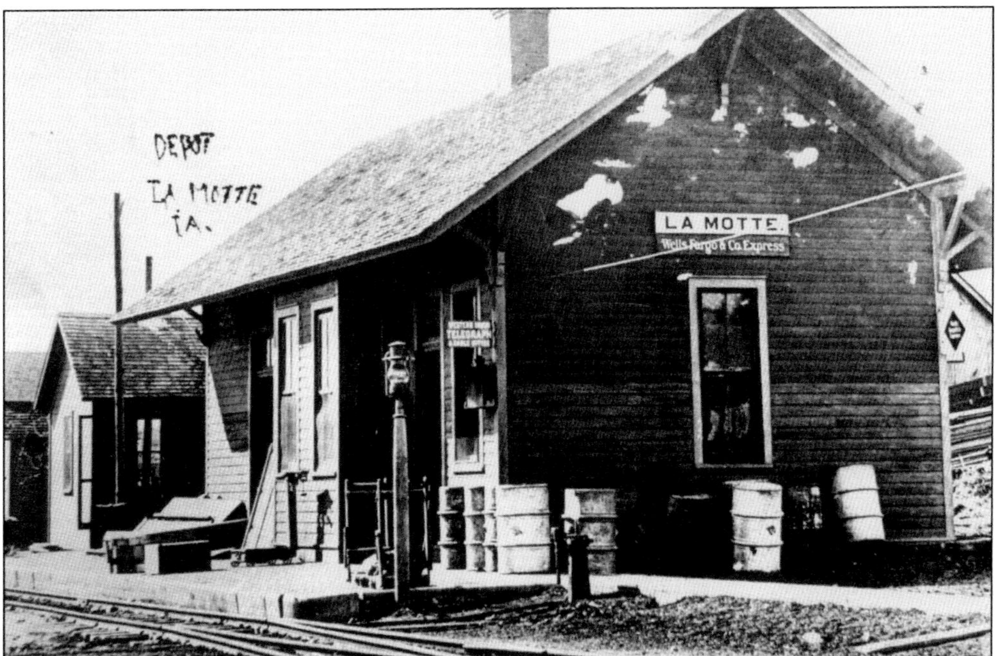

By 1911, the depot was back in business. A brick platform replaced the wooden one. (Nemmers.)

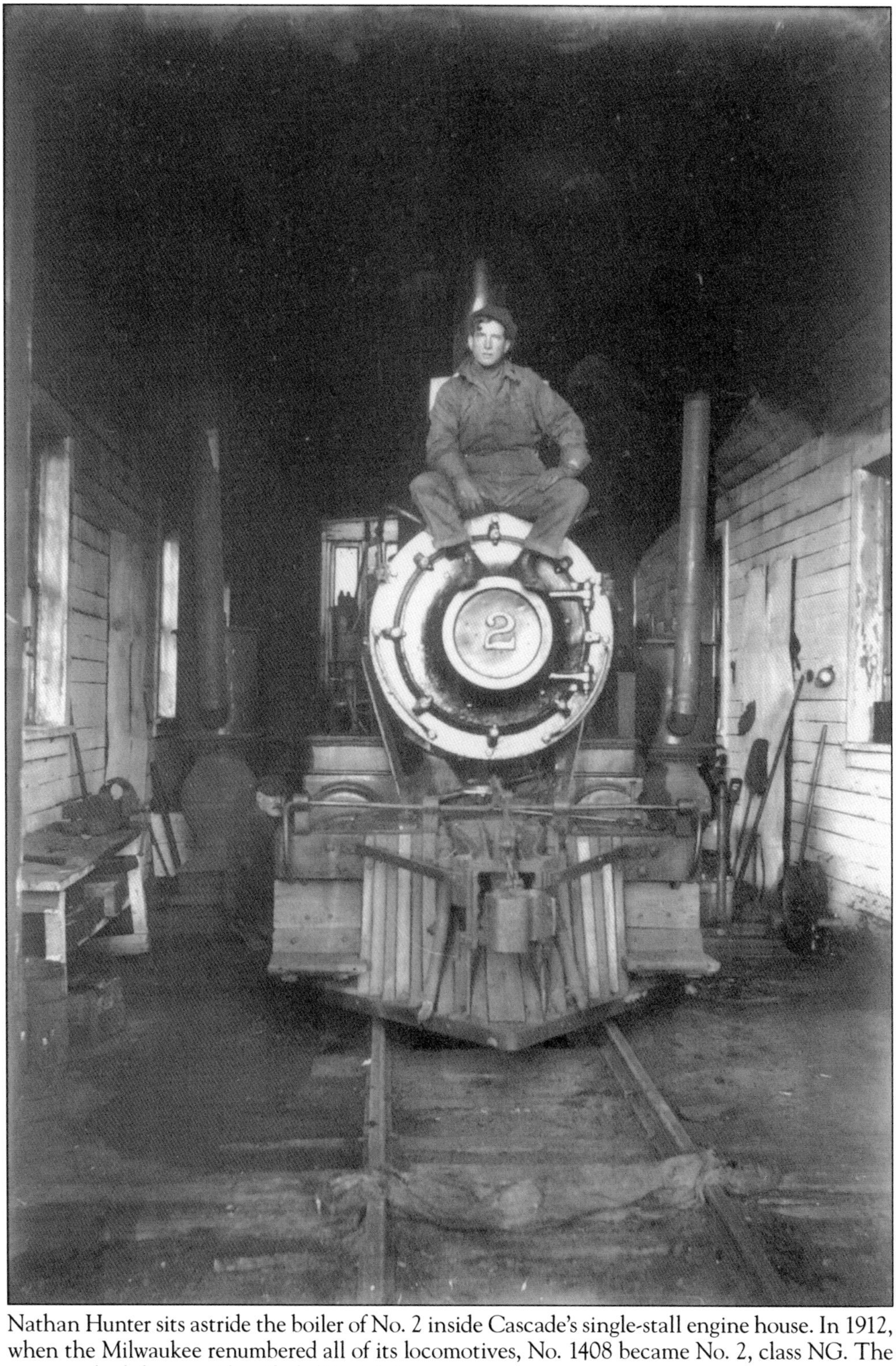

Nathan Hunter sits astride the boiler of No. 2 inside Cascade's single-stall engine house. In 1912, when the Milwaukee renumbered all of its locomotives, No. 1408 became No. 2, class NG. The man on the left is not identified. (Wyrick.)

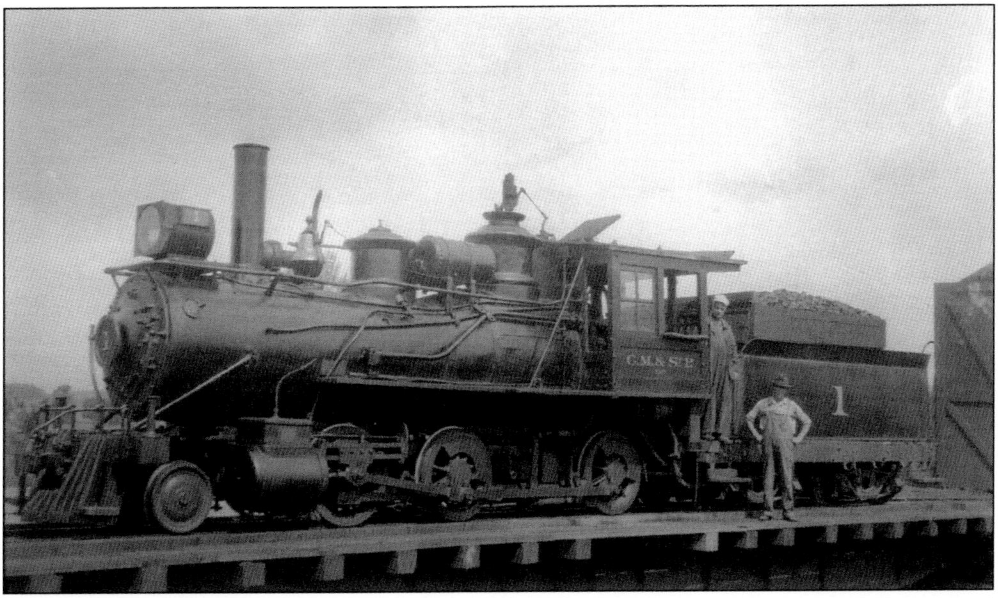

The Brooks Mogul 2-6-0 is pictured on the Cascade turntable in 1913. Originally numbered 1400, it was renumbered 1 in 1912. Engineer Richard Bogue stands on the tender platform. The man on the turntable is unidentified. (Campbell.)

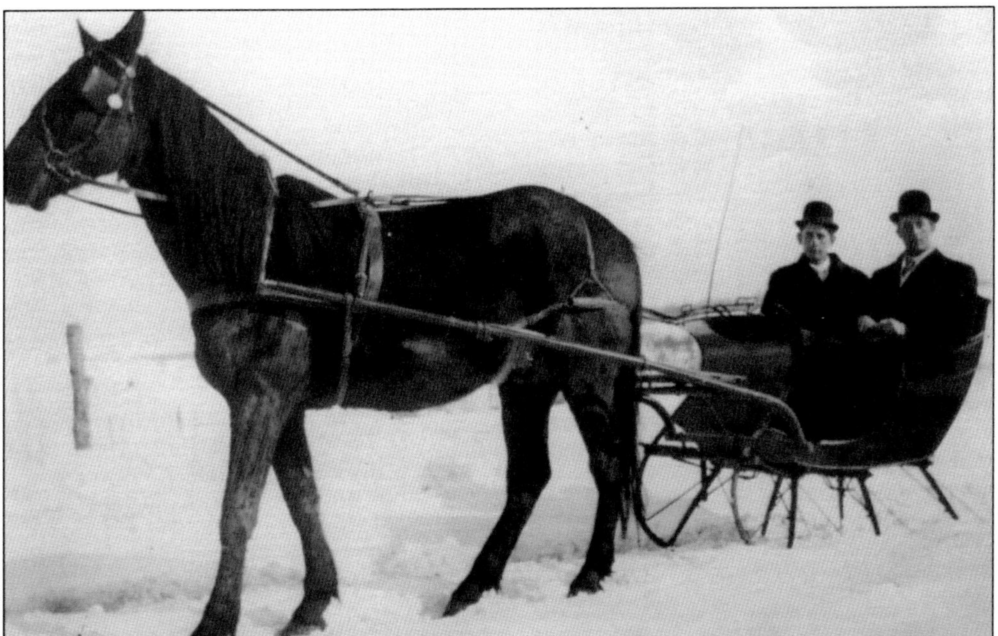

Despite modern conveyances such as trains and automobiles, many people such as these unidentified Cascade-area residents still preferred the more reliable horse and cutter in winter. (Talbert.)

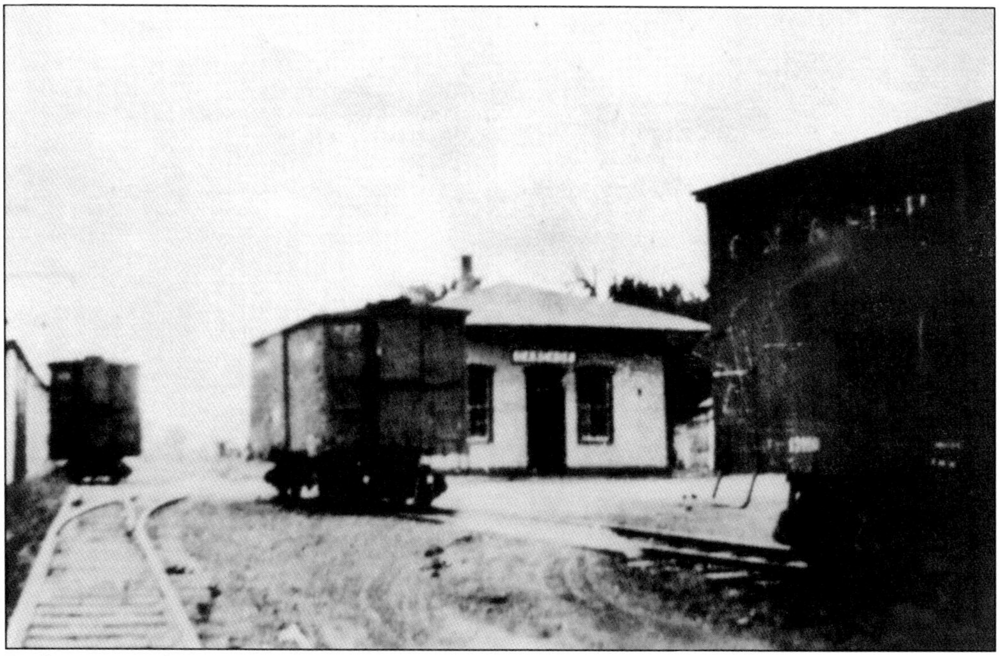

In this image, three narrow-gauge boxcars sit near the Cascade depot. Citizens of Cascade knew the world was gaining momentum, but the railroad they had so desperately desired was still operating with 1880s technology.

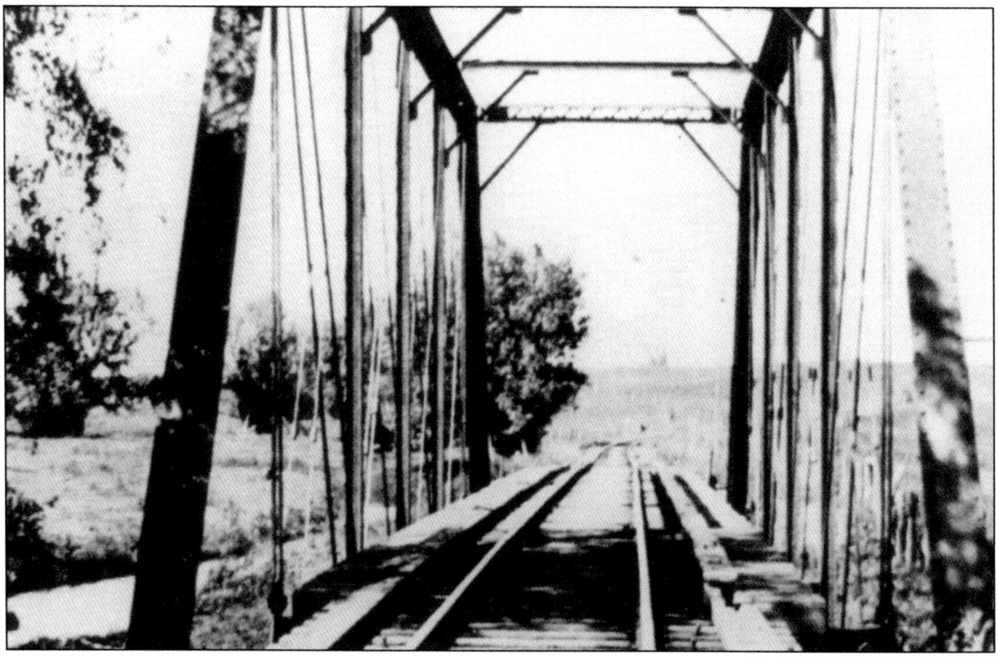

This steel bridge was located a half mile east of Zwingle. Once the Milwaukee Road had extended its rails to the northwestern United States and double-tracked its main line through central Iowa, little money was left for the narrow gauge. (Deppe.)

Three

BUSINESS AS USUAL

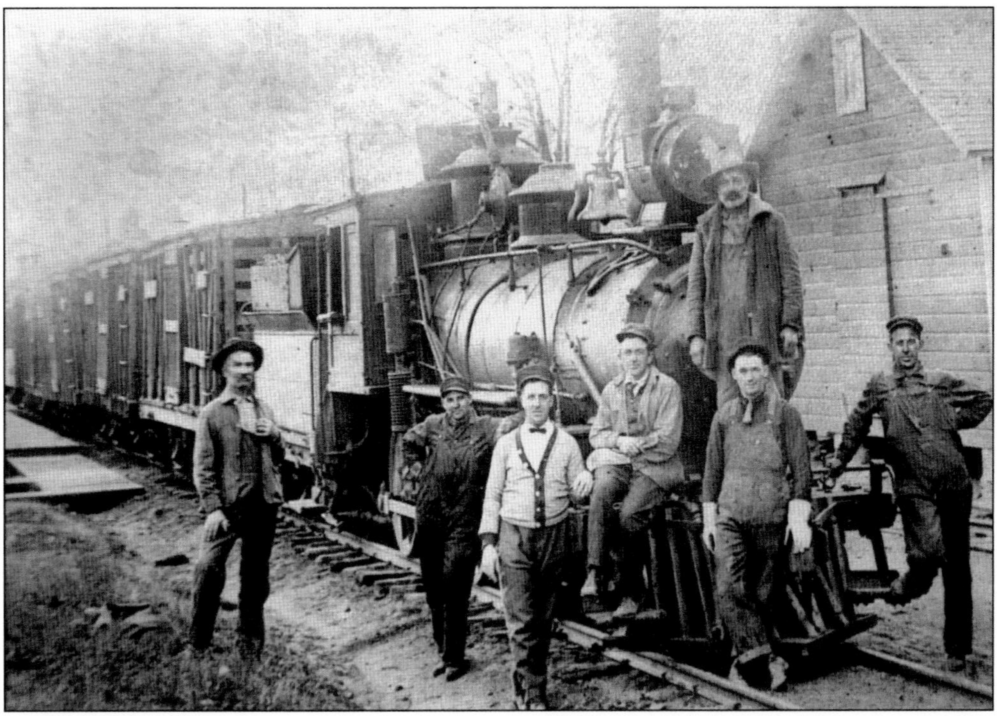

In this photograph, No. 2 readies to leave Cascade. Pictured here, from left to right, are ? Fagan, Benjamin Hunter (fireman), Edward Gongaware (conductor, in bow tie), Francis Leffert (sitting), William Cannon (brakeman), and unidentified. Townsman Michael Sager is standing on the pilot. Francis Leffert's son Carl took several of the photographs used in this book.

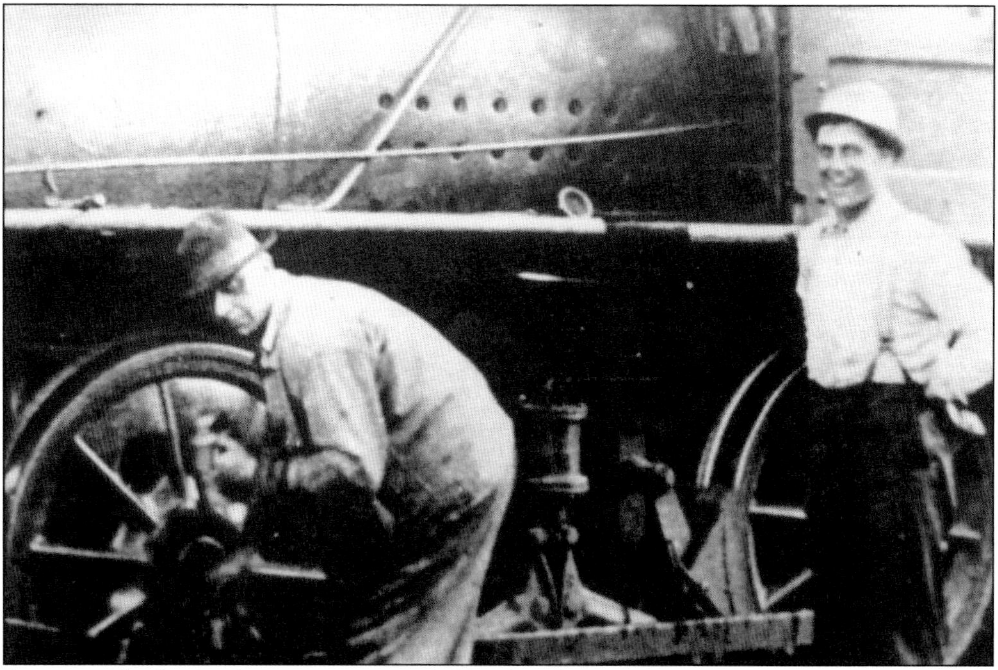

Engineer Charles Spielman appears startled by the photographer while looking up from oiling and inspecting his locomotive. Spielman was known for his touch on the whistle and could be identified by his slouched felt hat. The other man is unidentified.

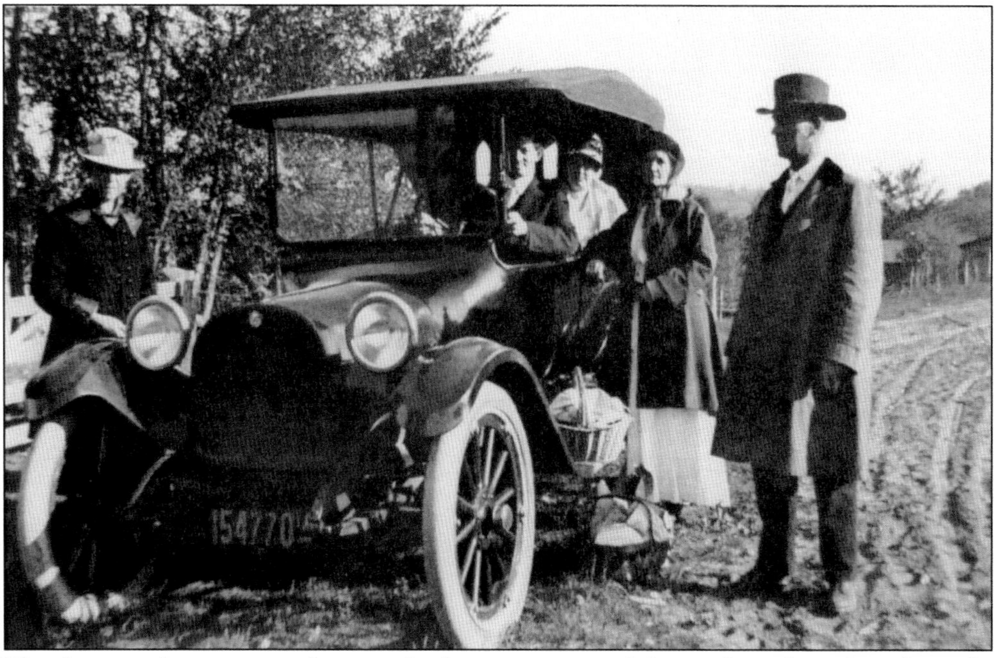

The driver and passengers of an overland touring automobile are dressed in their finest for a picnic. None are identified. The dirt road shows what could be expected after a snowmelt or a rainstorm.

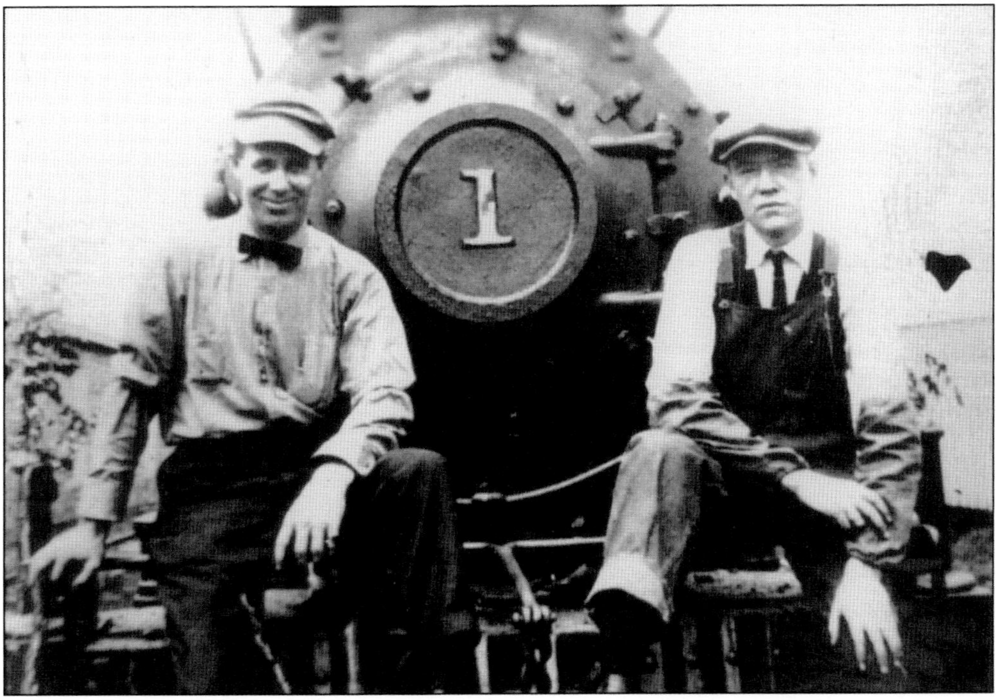

This photograph verifies the pride railroad men had in their jobs and the tools they used. Conductor Edward Gongaware (left) and brakeman Phillip Webber pose on the pilot of No. 1.

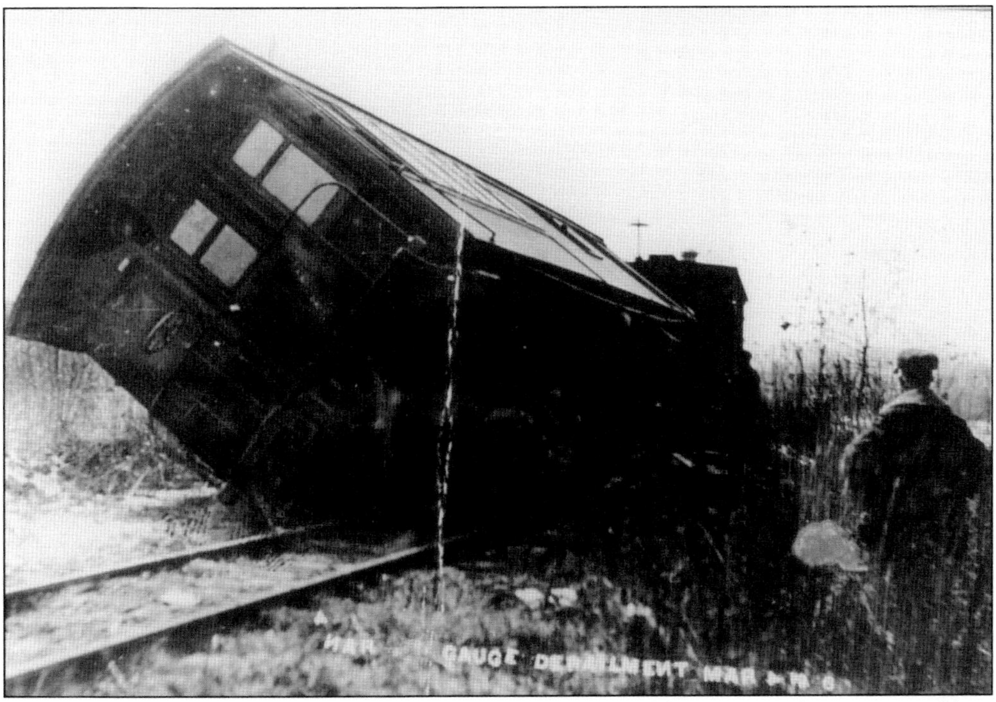

Included in the tall tales the narrow-gauge men told were several instances when a car would tip from the rails and balance on one side or the other. This photograph seems to prove it possible.

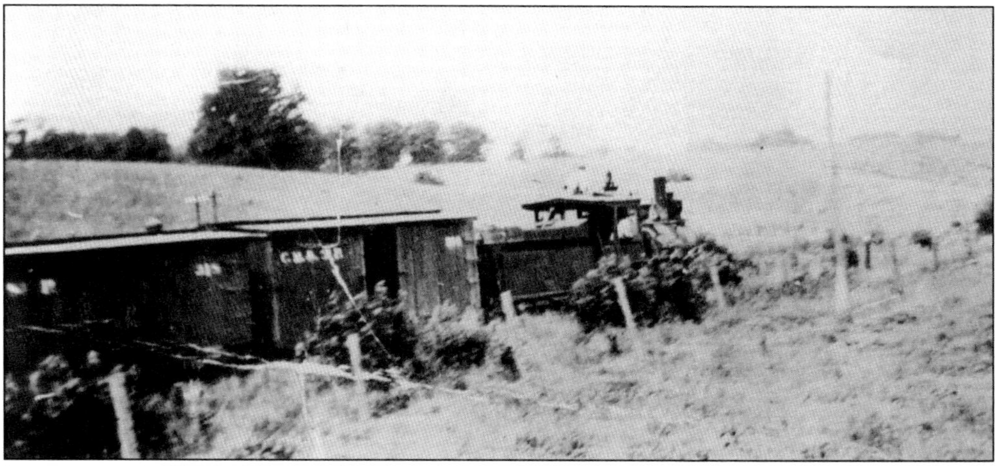

This scene shows the photographic ability of Marie Weber, who was on a picnic with several girlfriends. She captured the image when No. 1, the Brooks Mogul, passed on the point of a Sunday Extra headed for Bellevue. Her husband-to-be, Bill Cook, is perched on top of the cab. (Weber-Cook.)

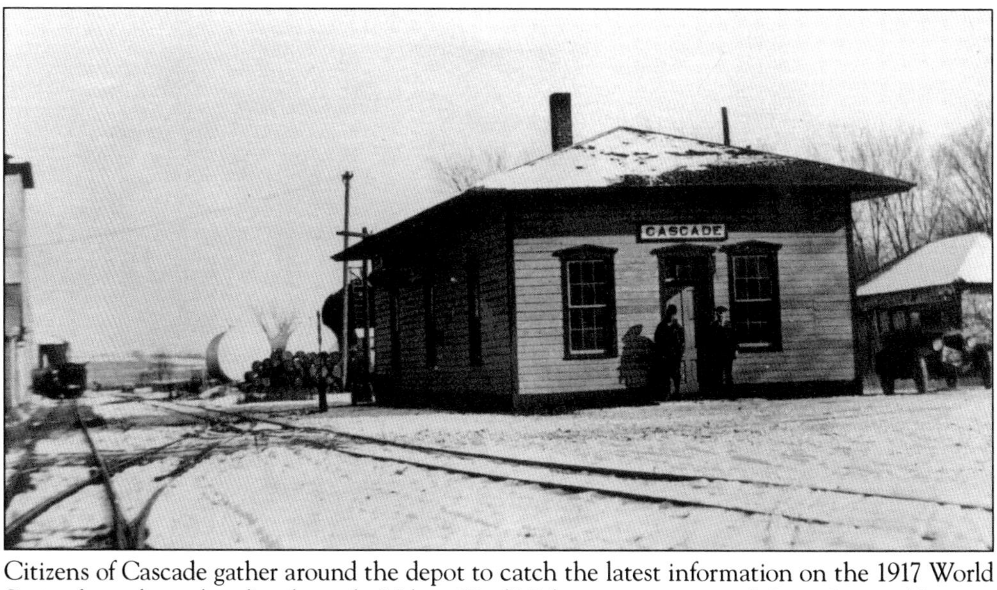

Citizens of Cascade gather around the depot to catch the latest information on the 1917 World Series from the railroad's telegraph. Urban "Red" Faber, a native son of Cascade, would go on to win three games for the Chicago White Sox. An unidentified man stands with Harry Care (right), the station agent in Cascade for years.

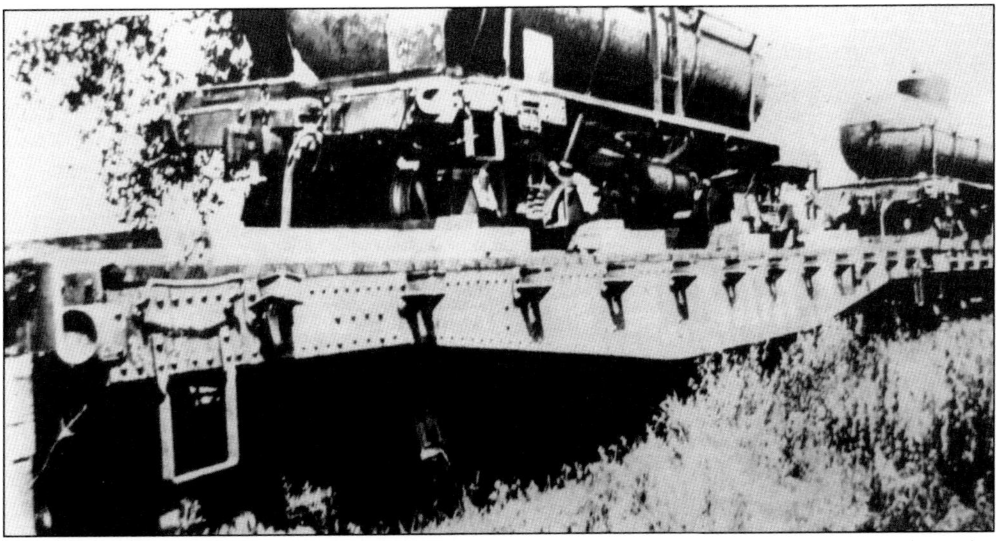

In 1916, the Milwaukee Road leased two 5,000-gallon tank cars to serve its customers along the three-foot rails. The cars arrived in Bellevue on standard-gauge flatcars equipped with rails.

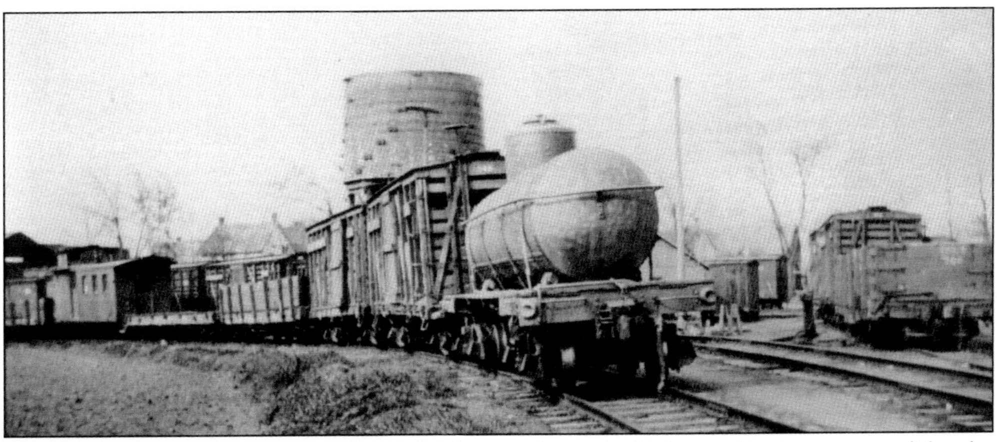

One of the two tank cars is on the end of a cut of cars in Bellevue. Both cars served for the next 20 years.

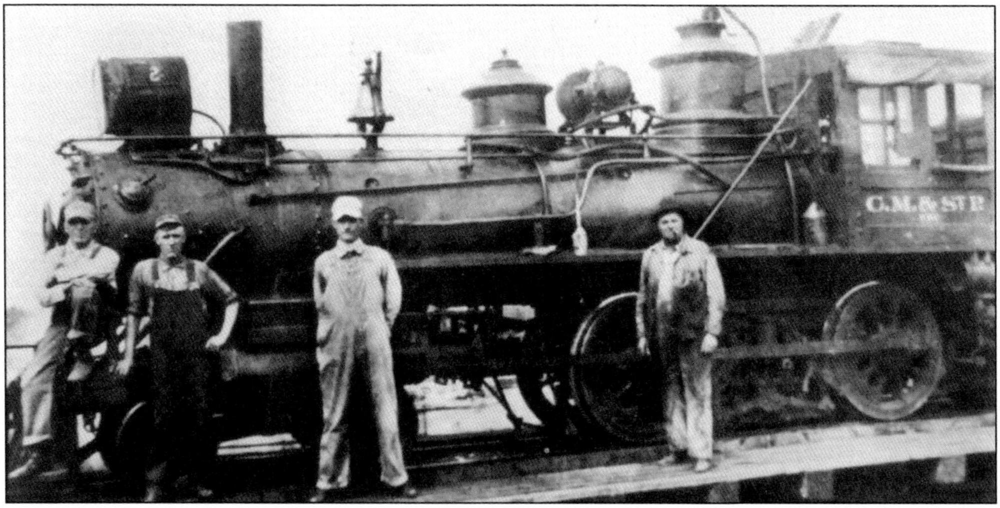

To keep No. 2 running, parts were cannibalized from No. 3, its look-alike that had worn out. Pictured here, from left to right, are Arthur Masters (brakeman), John Graham (roundhouse hostler), Arthur Lynch (fireman), and Charles Spielman (engineer). The 4-4-0 took on a long, lean look when its stack was shortened.

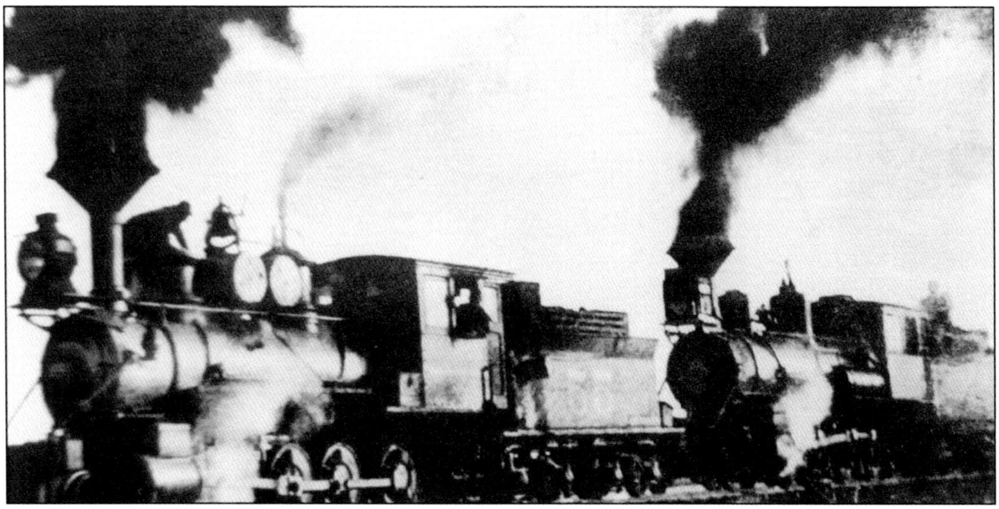

In this photograph of two narrow-gauge consolidation locomotives, No. 55 is on the point. Because the Iowa narrow gauge was short of power, in 1917 the United States Railway Administration ordered the Colorado and Southern to ship the Cooke-built 2-8-0 to the Milwaukee for Iowa service. Before a price could be agreed upon, the United States Railway Administration went out of business. The 2-8-0 was renumbered 4.

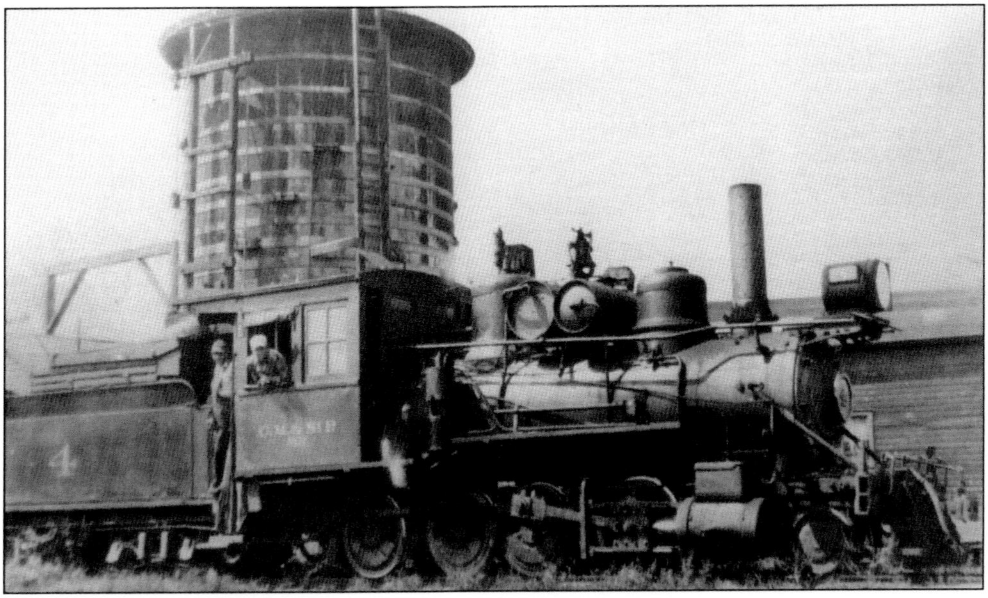

This Cascade scene shows No. 4, which was nicknamed the "big one," at work. It was the only eight-drivered narrow-gauge locomotive the Milwaukee owned. John Benzer (engineer) leans out the window while John Fuerste stands on the tender platform.

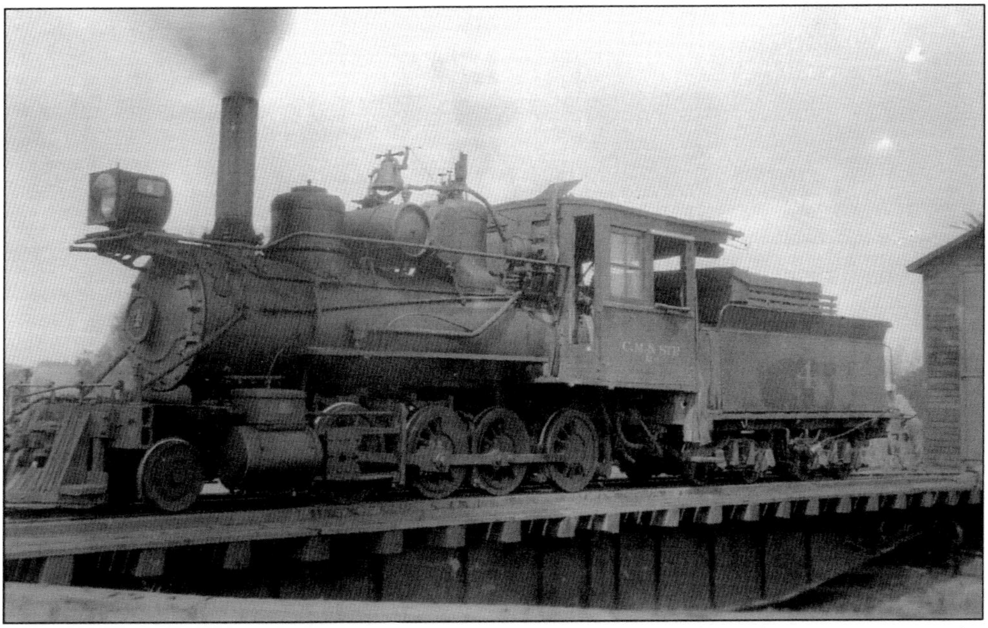

The Cooke consolidation, No. 4 is turned on the Cascade turntable. The equipment on the boiler gave the 2-8-0 personality. (Campbell.)

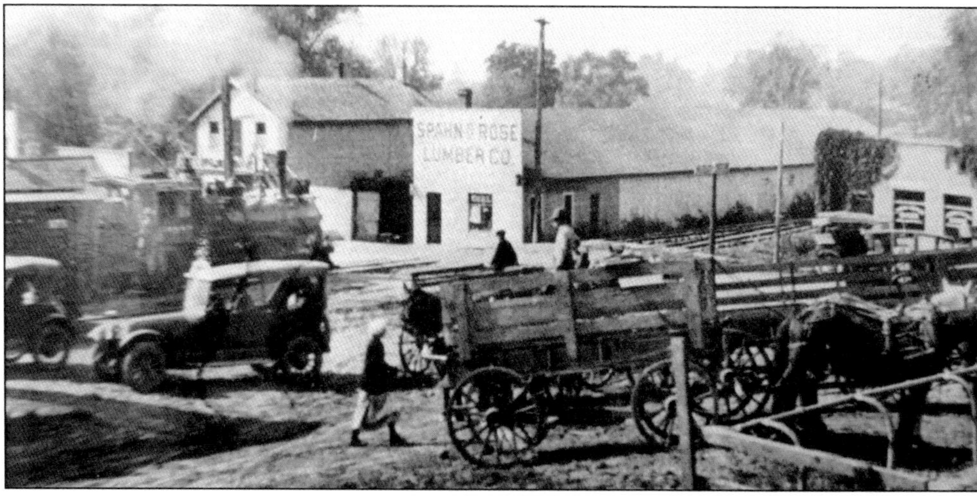

The last Pittsburgh 4-4-0 to operate on the narrow-gauge branch line, No. 2 leaves Zwingle sometime in the 1920s. The three automobiles in view are a harbinger of hard times to come for the little railroad.

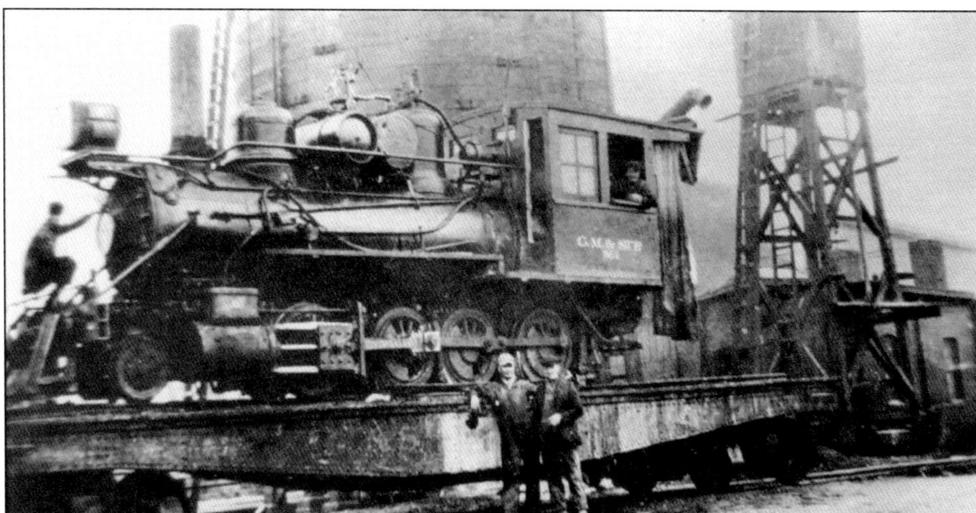

No. 4 and its carrier flatcar have been taken off the turntable at the Dubuque roundhouse and are ready to return to Bellevue. When the Dubuque shops closed, the narrow-gauge motive power was sent farther north to Marquette for back shopping. The men are unidentified.

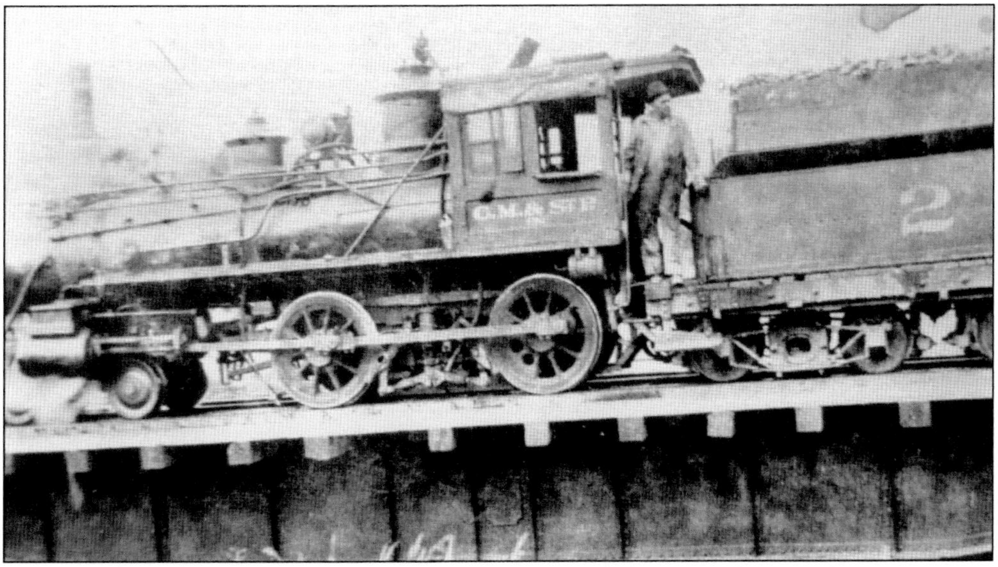

The Cascade gallows-type turntable was replaced around the start of the 20th century. Here Charles Spielman stands on the tender platform, considering the job of turning No. 2 by hand on the "armstrong" turntable.

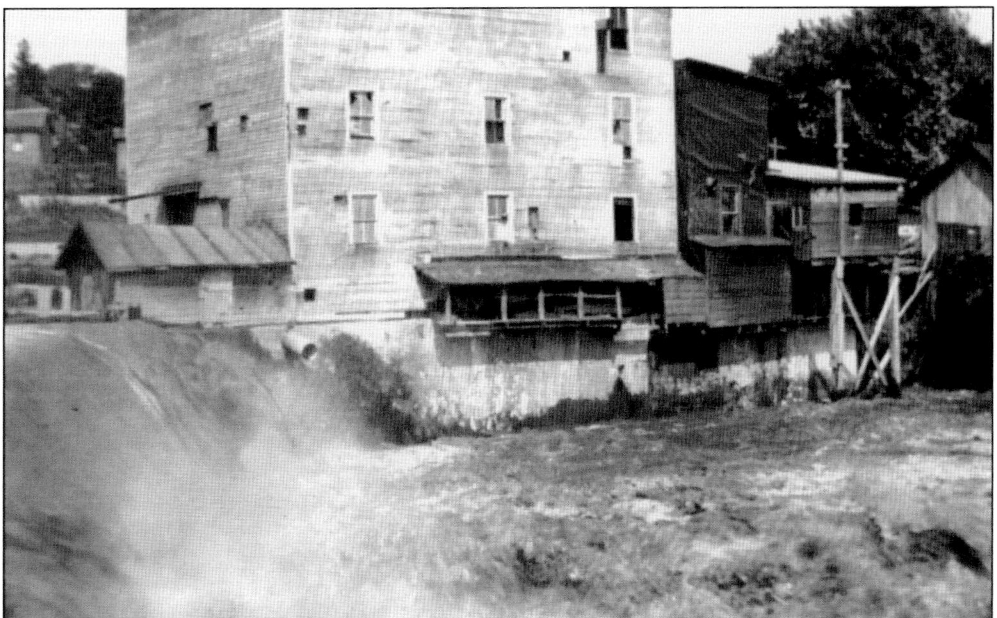

The falls that gave Cascade its name are seen during the 1925 flood. Two feed mills operated opposite each other for many years. (Wyrick.)

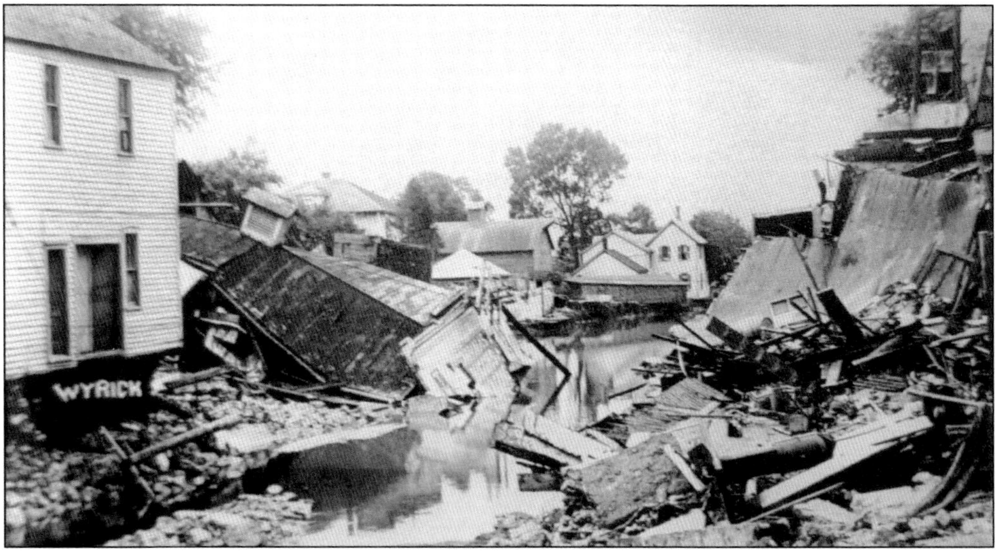

Photographer Claude Wyrick documents the devastation caused by the record snowfall quickly melting in the spring of 1925.

WESTWARD — BETWEEN BELLEVUE AND CASCADE SUBDSIVION — EASTWARD

SECOND CLASS 121 Mixed Daily Except Sun.	SECOND CLASS 106 Mixed Daily Except Sun.	Capacity of Siding in Cars: Passing Tracks	Capacity of Siding in Cars: Other Sidings	Distance from Bellevue	Time Table No. 16 In Effect 6:01 a. m., March 8, 1925 STATIONS	Office Closed Week Days	Distance from Cascade	Telegraph Calls	SYMBOLS See Special Rule, Page 8	SECOND CLASS 102 Mixed Daily Except Sun.	SECOND CLASS 106 Mixed Daily Except Sun.
L 5.10	L 8.10		116		BELLEVUE		35.7	BU	RBWCTJ	A 2.25	A 3.15
• 6.05	• 9.05		27	11.4	11.4 LA MOTTE	5:00PM to 8:00AM	24.3	AM	WD	• 1.25	• 2.15
• 6.30	• 9.30		17	15.7	4.3 ZWINGLE	5:00PM to 8:00AM	20.0	WI		• 1.01	• 1.50
• 7.05	• 10.05		14	22.6	6.9 WASHINGTON MILLS	No Office	13.7		CWD	• 12.25	• 1.15
• 7.25	• 10.25		35	25.2	3.2 BERNARD	5:00PM to 8:00AM	10.5	BR		• 12.11	• 1.00
• 7.45	• 10.45		30	29.8	4.6 FILLMORE	No Office	5.9			• 11.50	• 12.40
8.10	11.10		54	35.7	5.9 CASCADE	5:00PM to 8:00AM		CD	RBWCTD	L 11.25	L 12.15
3.00	3.00				Schedule Time					3.00	3.00
12.0	12.0				Average Speed per Hour					12.0	12.0

SPECIAL RULES

EASTWARD TRAINS ARE SUPERIOR TO WESTWARD TRAINS OF THE SAME CLASS

Trains must not exceed maximum speed of 20 miles per hour.

All eastward trains reduce speed to 10 miles per hour descending Washington Mills and LaMotte hill, and westward trains descending Sylvia Hill.

All regular branch freight trains will carry passengers.

This timetable, which became effective on March 8, 1925, shows four scheduled freight/ passenger trains daily except Sundays. While it may seem that the Milwaukee was improving service, the narrow gauge was still operating by 1880 rules. The trains could not exceed 20 miles per hour.

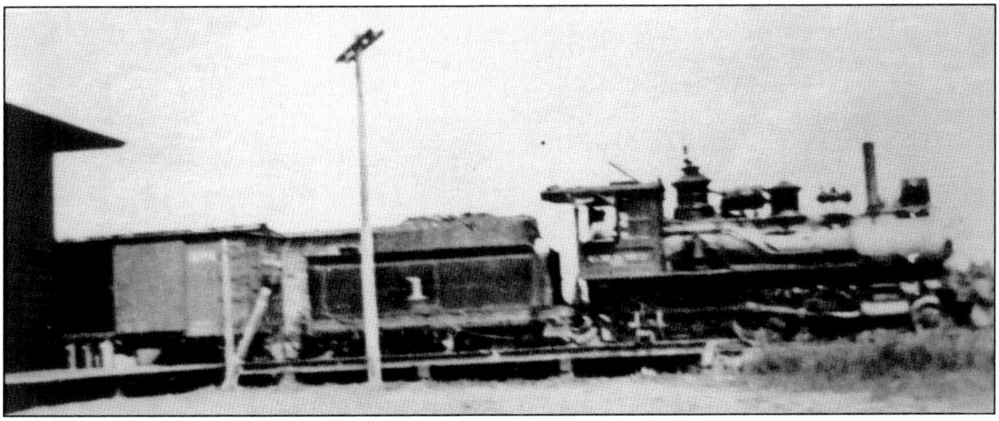

The Brooks Mogul is ready to whistle out of Cascade. One of the two Pittsburgh 4-4-0 engines, No. 2, did yeoman service. It was obvious at the time that more motive power was needed to help the 2-6-0 and the 2-8-0.

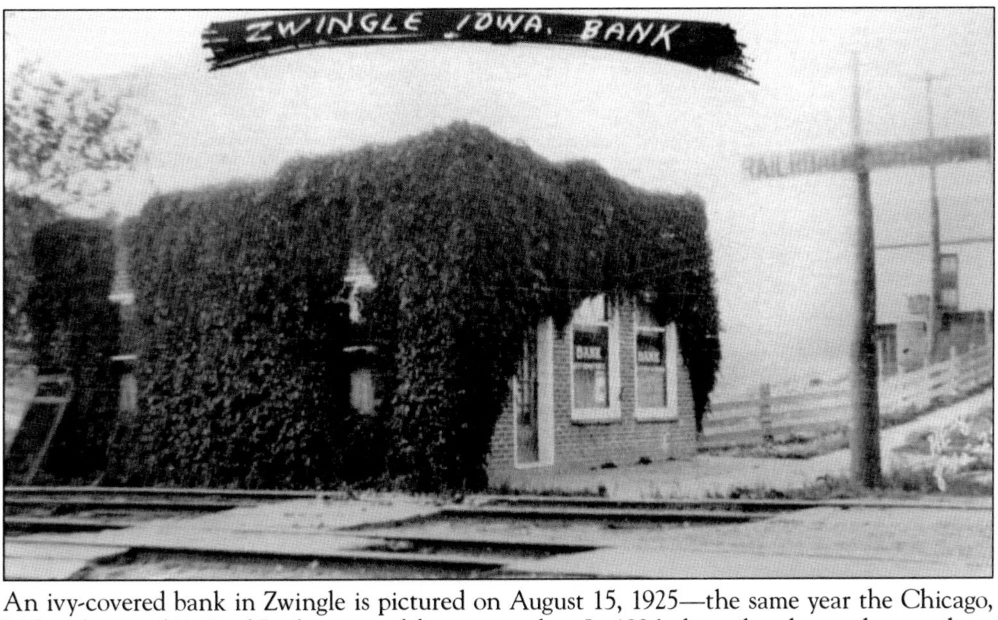

An ivy-covered bank in Zwingle is pictured on August 15, 1925—the same year the Chicago, Milwaukee, and St. Paul Railway voted for receivership. In 1926, the railroad agreed to purchase another locomotive for the Iowa narrow gauge, and the following year, the Chicago, Milwaukee, St. Paul, and Pacific Railroad emerged from reorganization. (Neiers.)

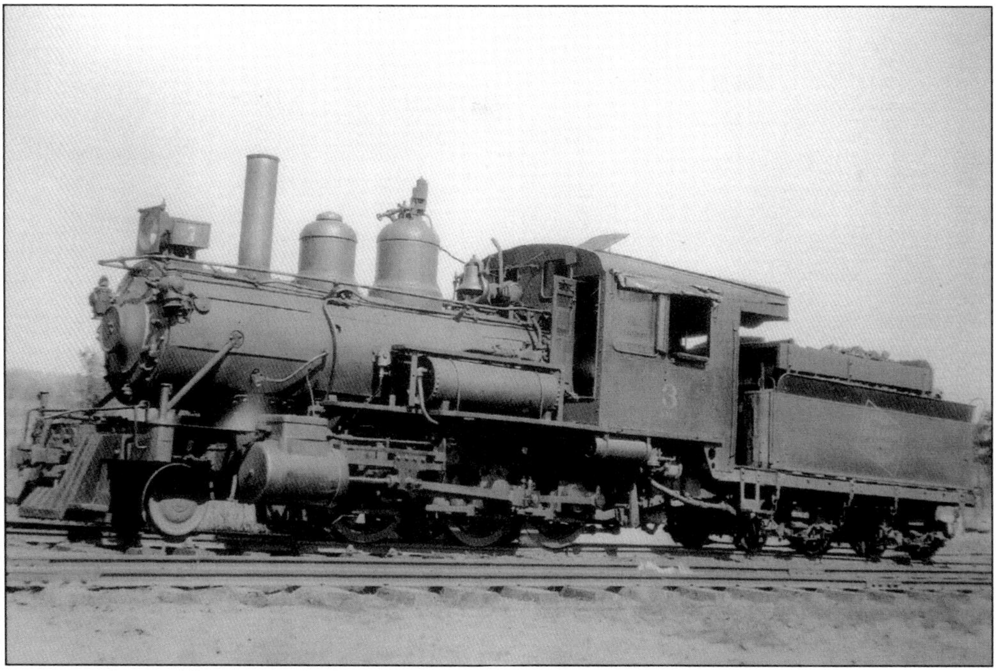

In 1926, this Baldwin outside-frame 2-6-0 was purchased secondhand from the Catskill and Tannersville Railroad. It was numbered 3, and for a while, the four locomotives were numbered 1, 2, 3, and 4. (Campbell.)

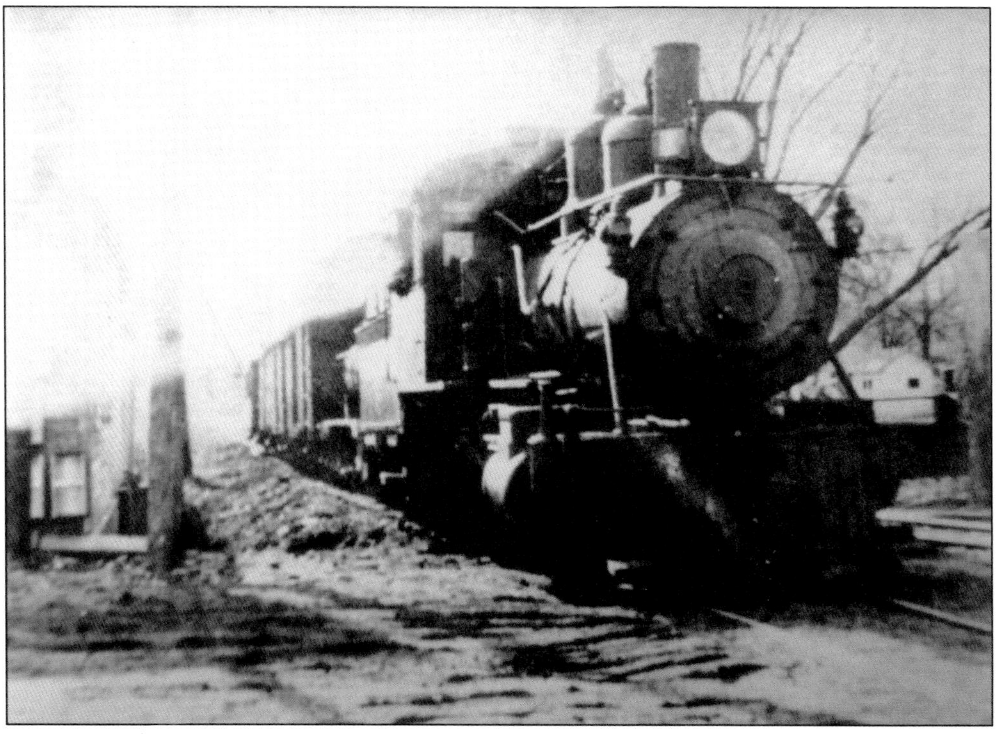

No. 3 passes through Zwingle as it heads west. The squared-off headlight was a Milwaukee variance.

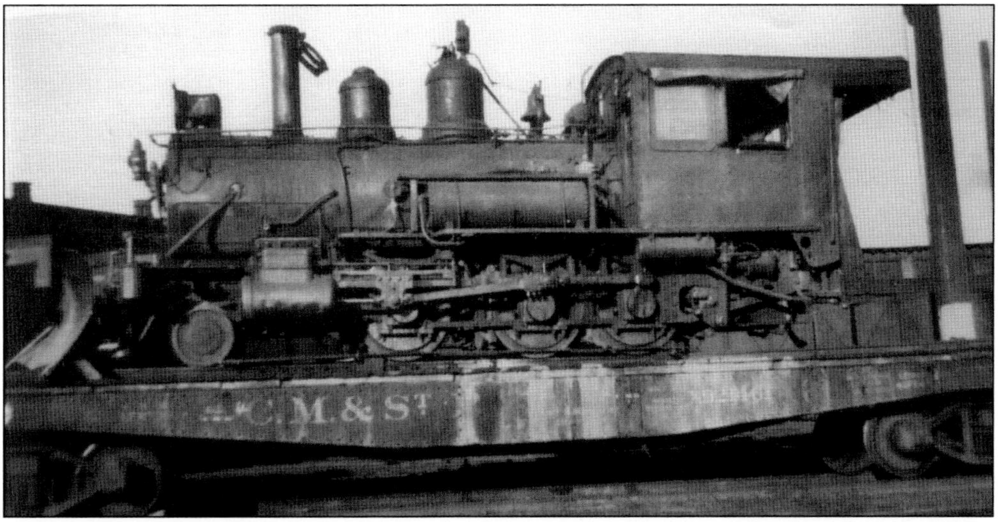

The Baldwin-built 2-6-0, pictured here in Marquette, was an outside-frame locomotive. It was larger and more powerful than the other steam engines. The snowplow on the pilot helped to a small degree in the winter but was not much help in some of the deep cuts on the branch line. (Adney.)

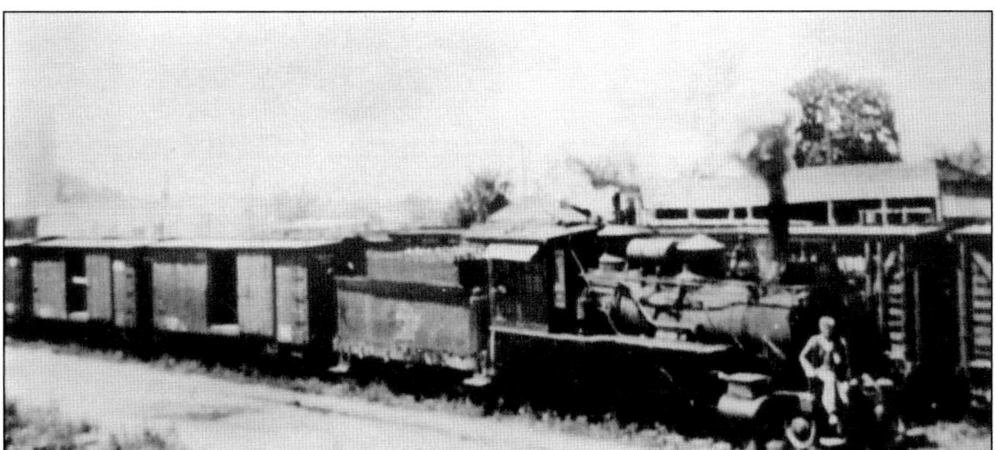

No. 1 is on the point of a Bellevue-bound train. Before leaving, it will couple onto the stock cars on the next track. The new Milwaukee logo is on the tender.

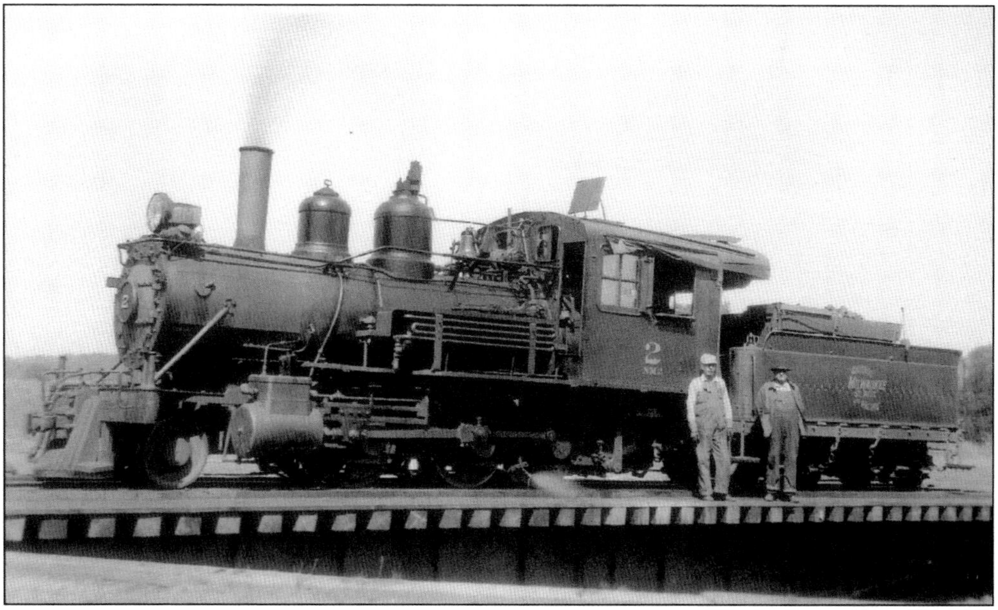

When the second Pittsburgh 4-4-0 quit, another Baldwin No. 2 outside-frame locomotive was purchased in 1928. The quickest way to distinguish No. 2 from No. 3 if the numbers were not visible was by their headlights. No. 2 had a round headlight, while No. 3 had a Milwaukee-type squared-off headlight. (Campbell.)

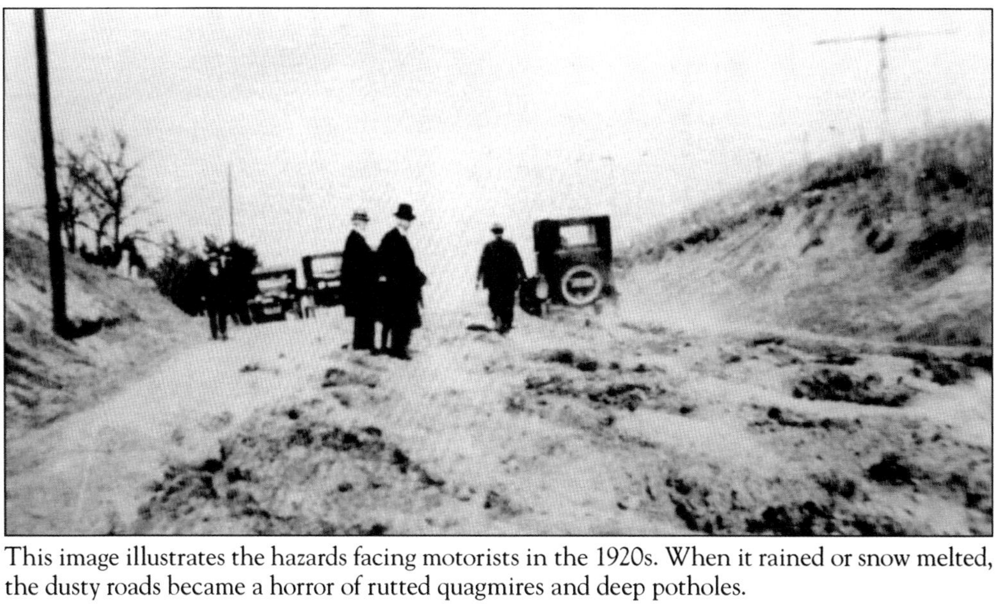

This image illustrates the hazards facing motorists in the 1920s. When it rained or snow melted, the dusty roads became a horror of rutted quagmires and deep potholes.

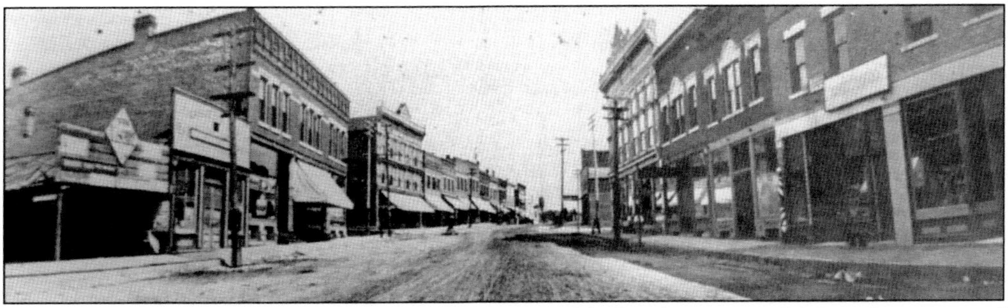

Cascade's main thoroughfare, Highway 151, is pictured before being paved. Main Street proved not much better then the country road. Paving was welcomed by the citizens but forecast a dim future for the little railroad.

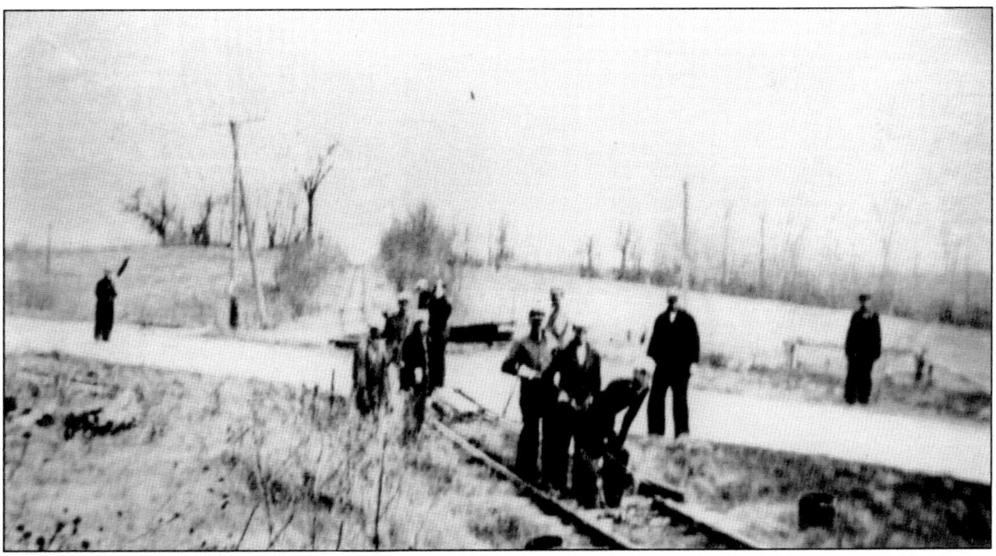

Highway 151 is seen here, with the narrow-gauge line heading to the eastern horizon. Going to Dubuque was a lot easier after the road had been paved. (Deppe.)

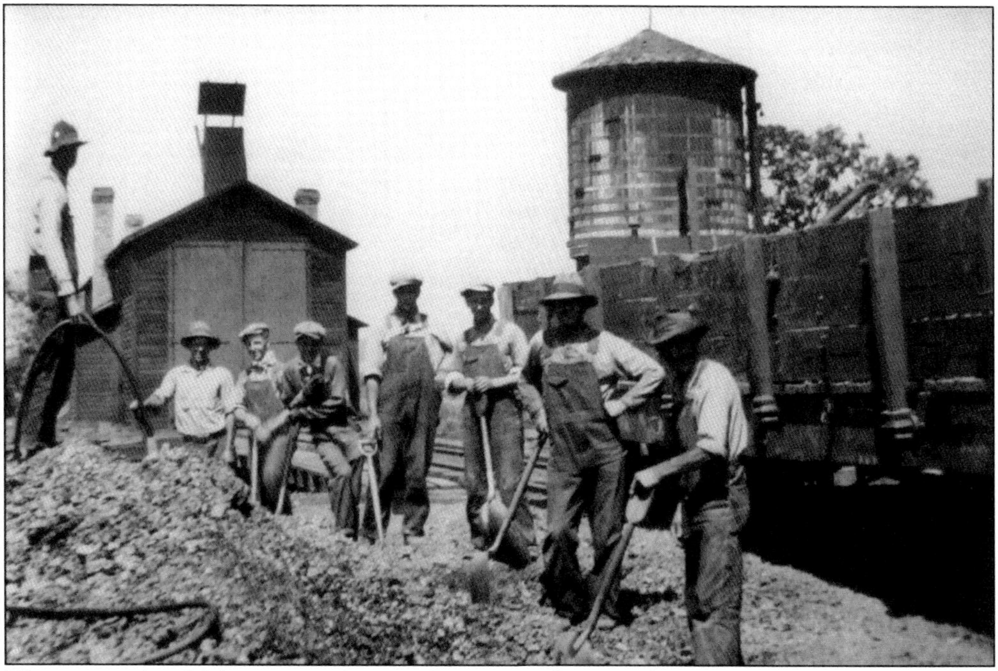

This image, dated July 2, 1928, shows eight men working in the Cascade yards. The only crew member identified is Robert Homer, on the far right.

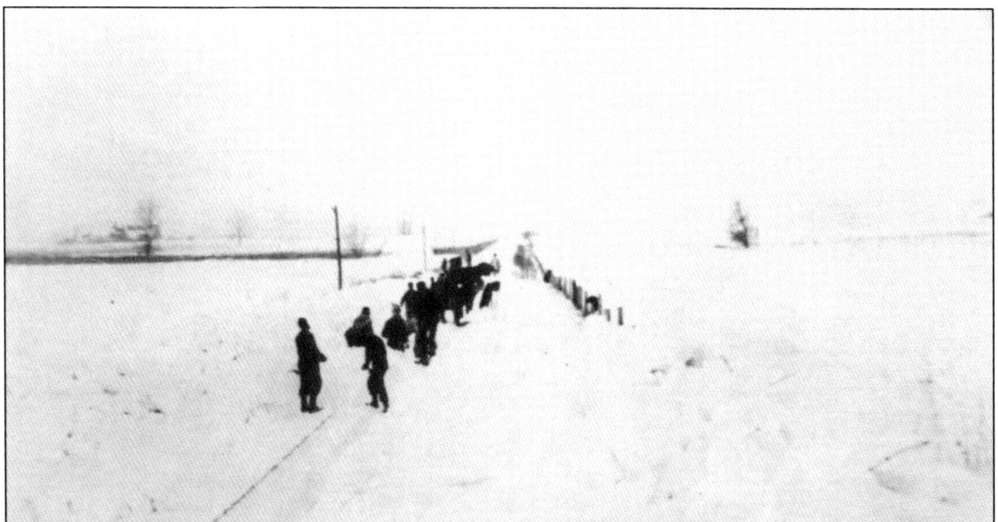

Many men were hired to shovel cuts free of drifts and places where the locomotives could not clear the way. Pay was around 30¢ an hour with time and a half over eight hours. (Deppe.)

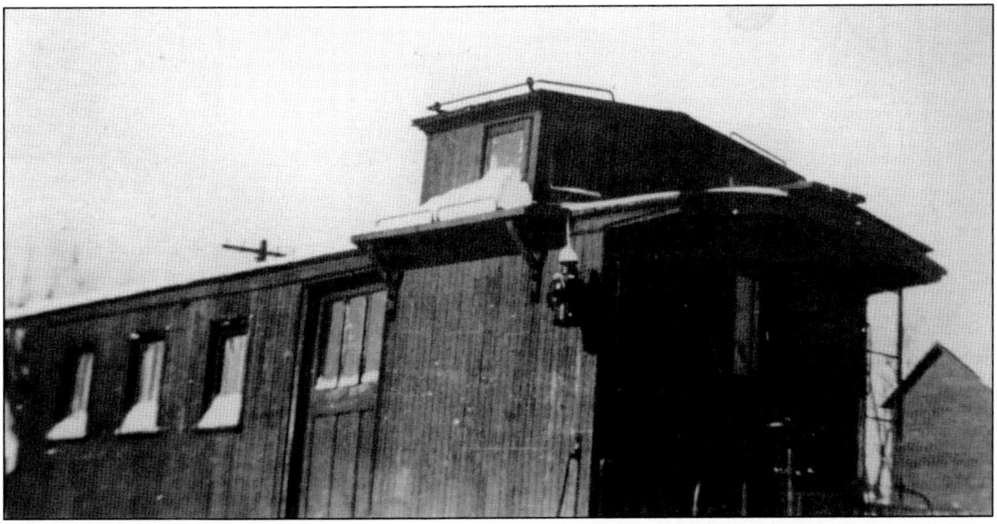

The narrow gauge had but one caboose. It has a different cupola here than on page 20. The Milwaukee did not allow crew members to walk across the roof of the cupola in the early 20th century. A walkway around either side was built to get to one end or the other. (Bogue.)

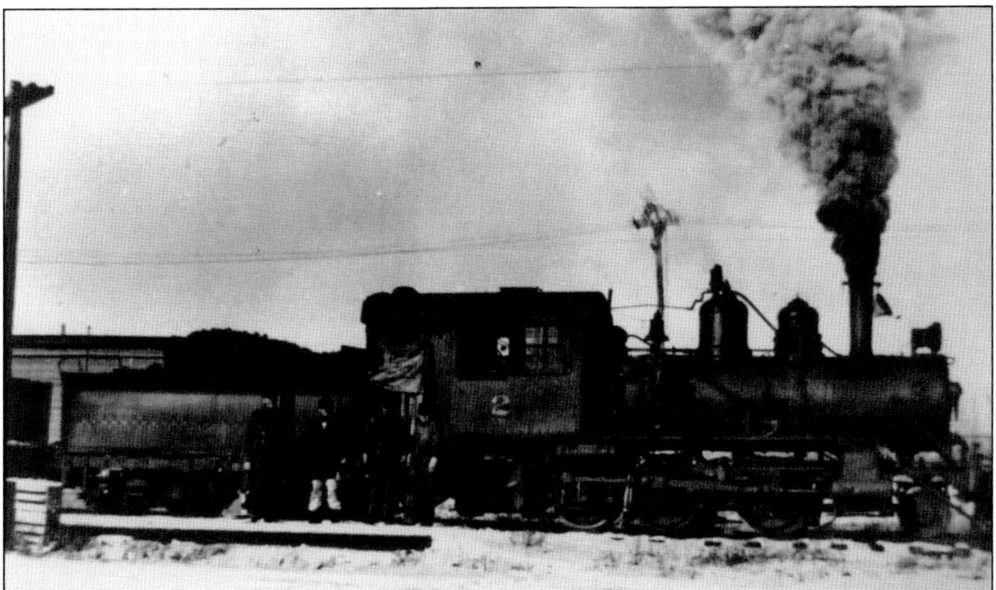

Baldwin Locomotive No. 2, acquired to replace the 4-4-0 No. 2, belches smoke into a gray, cold morning in Cascade. Shown here, from left to right, are Walter Graham (conductor), Richard Sullivan (brakeman), Charles Spielman (engineer), and Michael Galvin (brakeman).

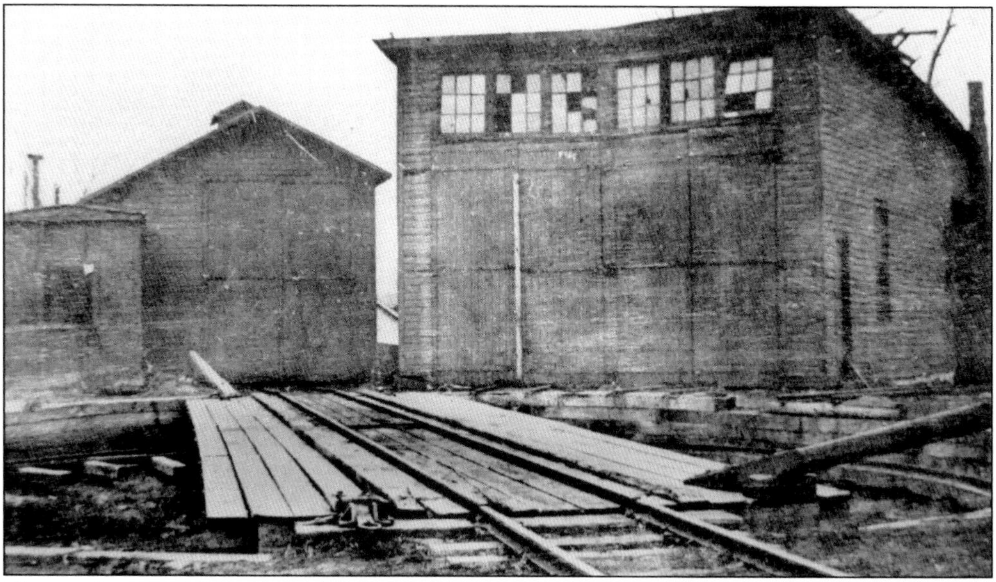

This is the narrow gauge's Bellevue roundhouse. A third, unattached stall was added in the early 20th century when a third locomotive, the Brooks Mogul, was to be purchased. Additional sheathing on the interior walls made the smaller building much warmer in winter. (Deppe.)

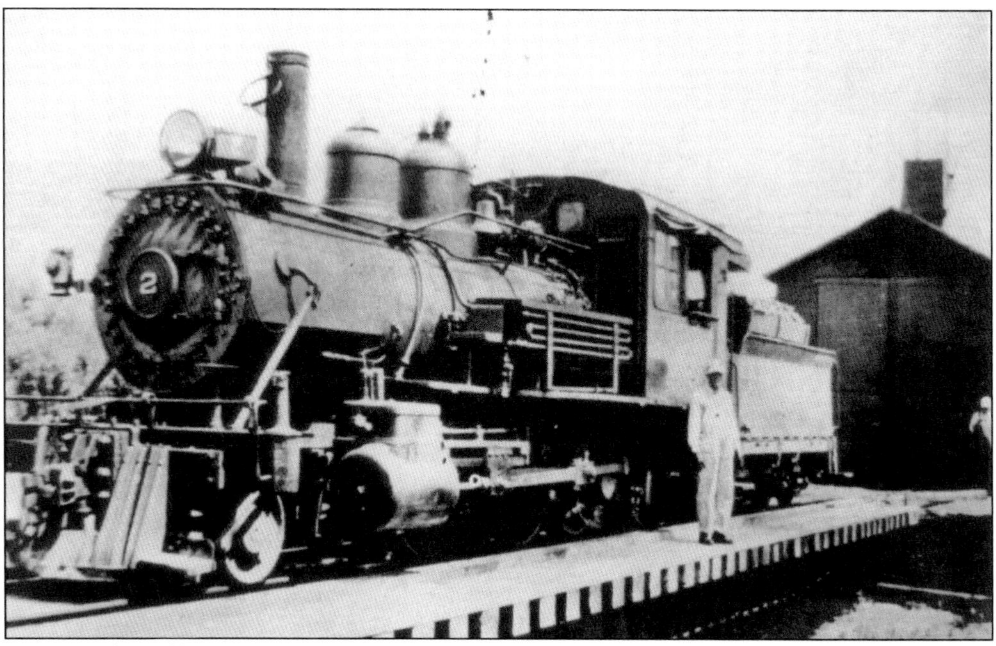

Compare the Baldwin No. 2's boiler, shown here, with that of the 4-4-0 No. 2 on page 40. (Leffert.)

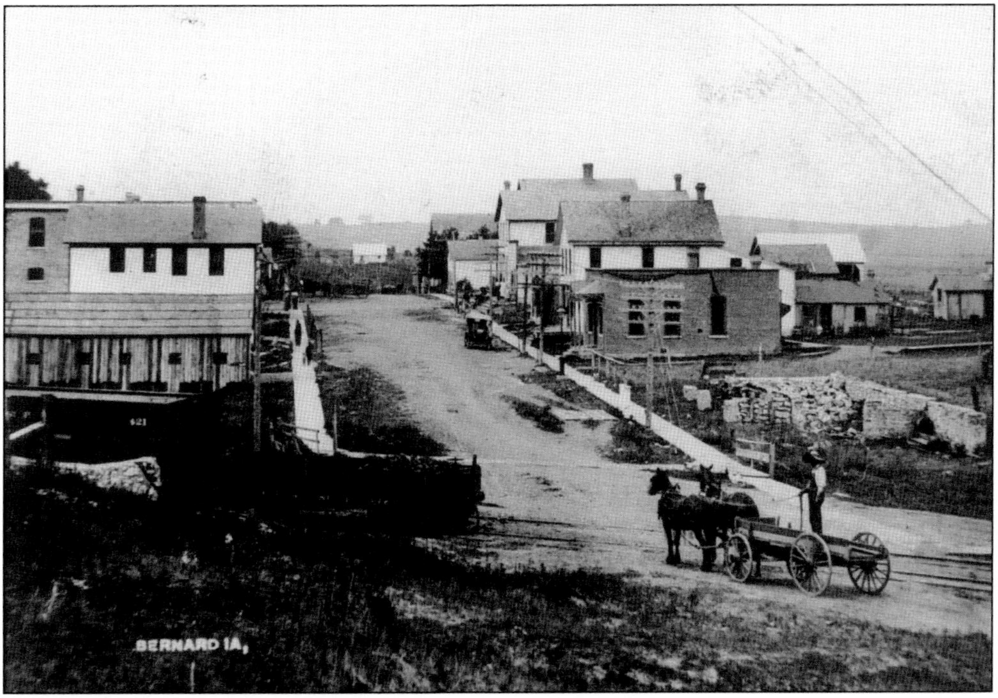

The main source of motive power was horses, as shown here. The automobile and hard-surfaced roads would eventually win out over the little railroad. Still, the trains brought prosperity to small communities such as Bernard, above.

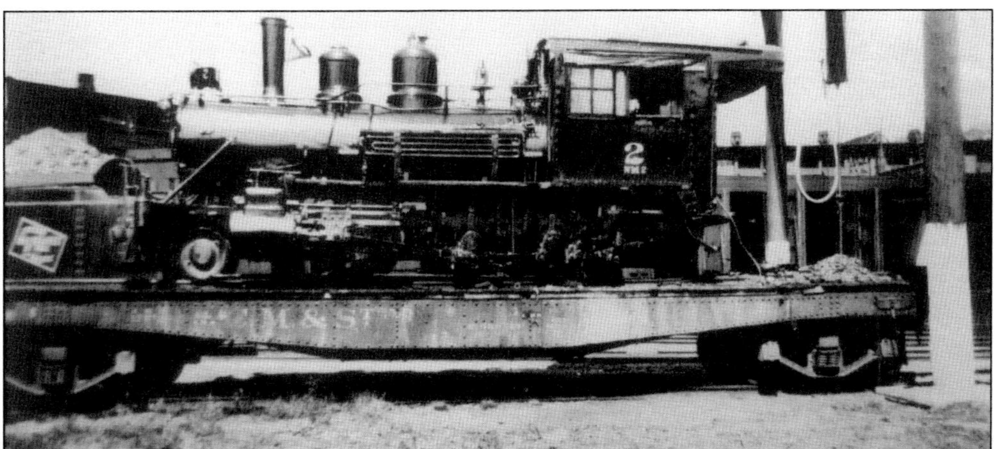
This image shows the fireman's side of No. 2, an outside-frame 2-6-0, on a flatcar at Marquette. The engine is ready after back shopping for the 70-mile trip to Bellevue. (Adney.)

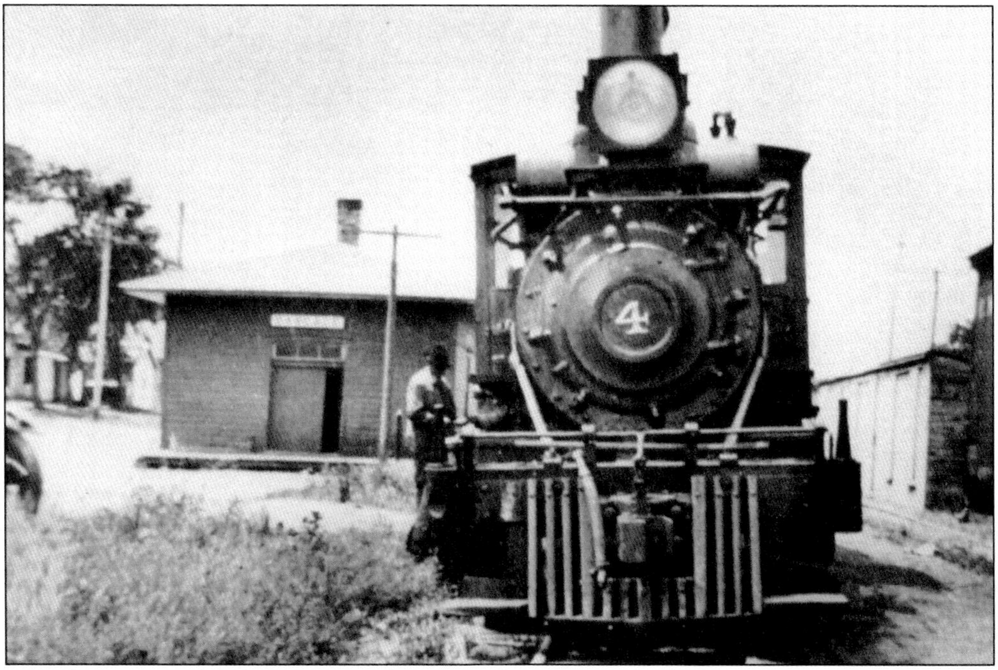

After being turned, fed, and watered at Cascade, No. 4 is checked by Charles Spielman. The 2-8-0 will soon pull its train eastward to Bellevue on the Mississippi River.

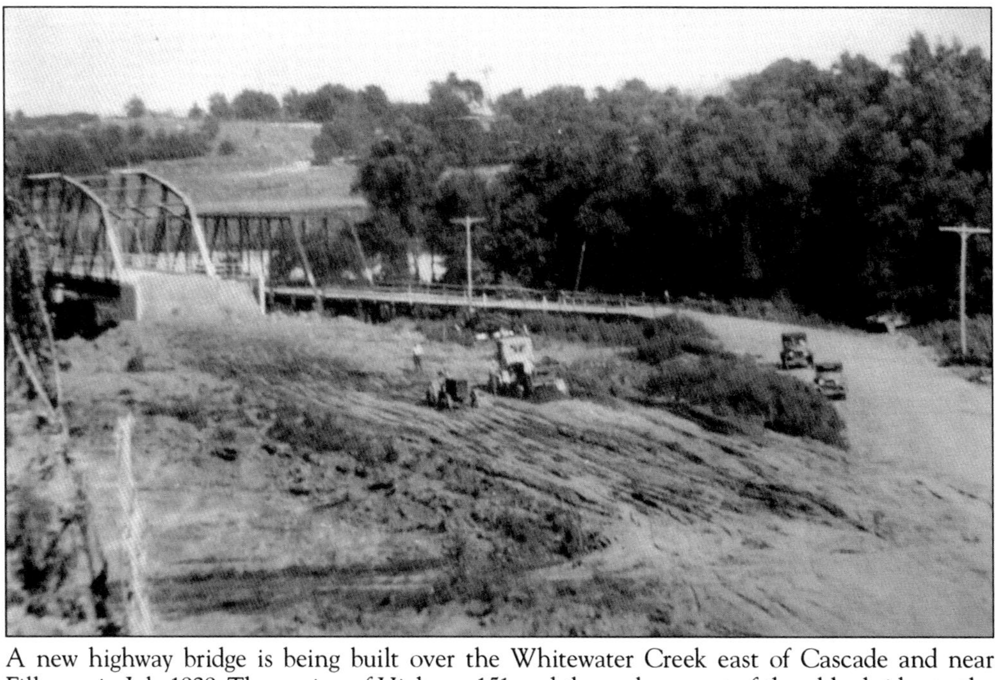

A new highway bridge is being built over the Whitewater Creek east of Cascade and near Fillmore in July 1929. The paving of Highway 151 and the replacement of the older bridge to the right were two more nails in the little railroad's coffin. The grove of trees on the right obscures the narrow gauge's bridge and right-of-way.

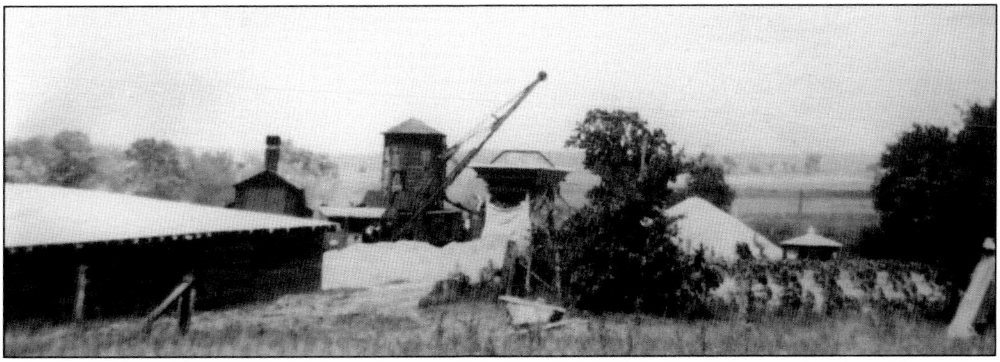

The Cascade single-stall engine house and water tank appear in the background of this July 2, 1928, image. At the center, a crane and dry mixer for paving materials are visible on the camera side of the water tank. It is ironic that the railroad hauled most of the equipment and materials for the highway and that the yards were used for mixing. The shed on the left stored cement.

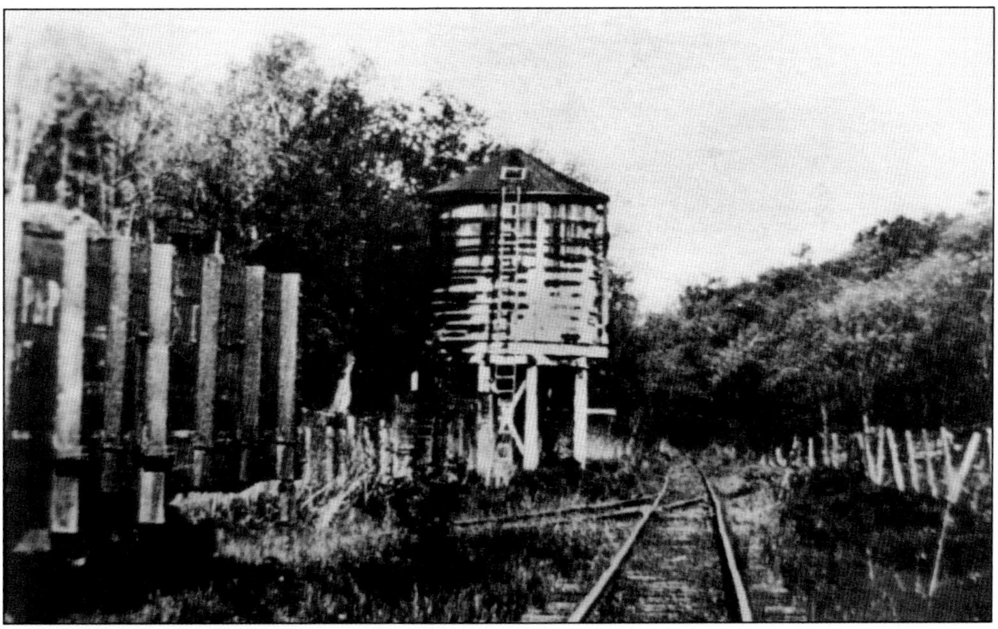

As a youth, Carl Leffert took many photographs with his box camera. Here he shows the tank at Washington Mills, where a gondola sits on the siding to the left. (Leffert.)

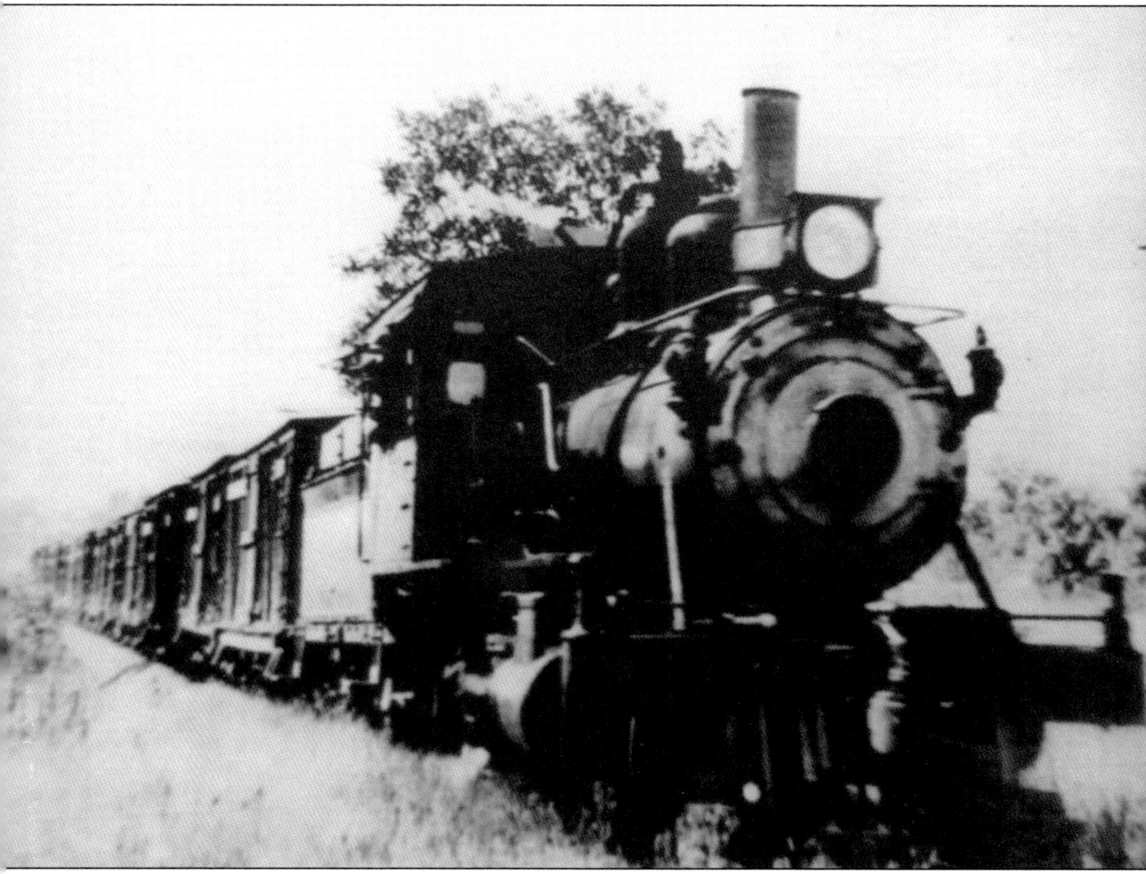

No. 3 pulls a train of stock cars through eastern Iowa. This locomotive, a class NM 2 Baldwin 2-6-0, replaced a Pittsburgh class NG 4-4-0 when it quit.

Four

Hard Times

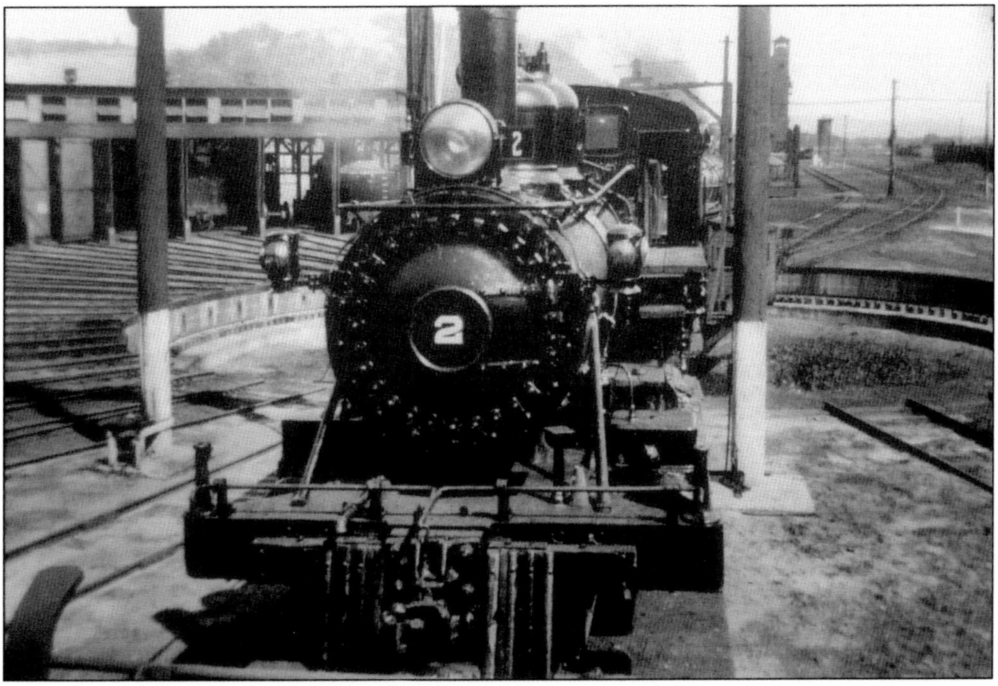

No. 2, the last steam power acquired for the Milwaukee narrow gauge, readies to leave Marquette for Bellevue after being back shopped. (Adney.)

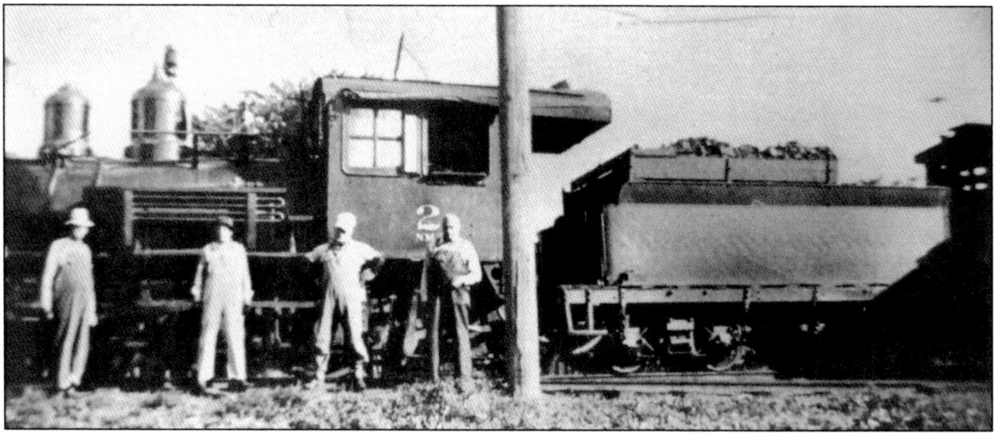

Its shiny sand and steam domes reveal that No. 2 has recently been back shopped. Pictured here, from left to right, are unidentified, Richard Sullivan (brakeman), Richard Bogue (engineer, wearing white cap), and Charles Spielman (engineer).

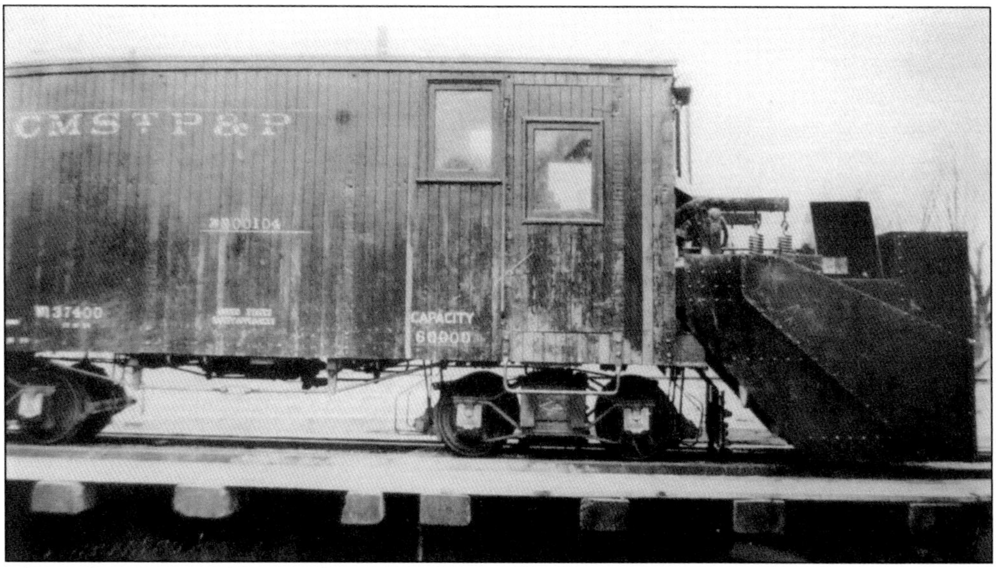

The Milwaukee Road's one-of-a-kind snowplow was produced by the Klauer Manufacturing Company in Dubuque. It was patterned after Klauer's Sno-Go street plows. This new railroad-style Sno-Go appears on the Bellevue turntable sometime after December 2, 1929, when it was delivered. (Streuser.)

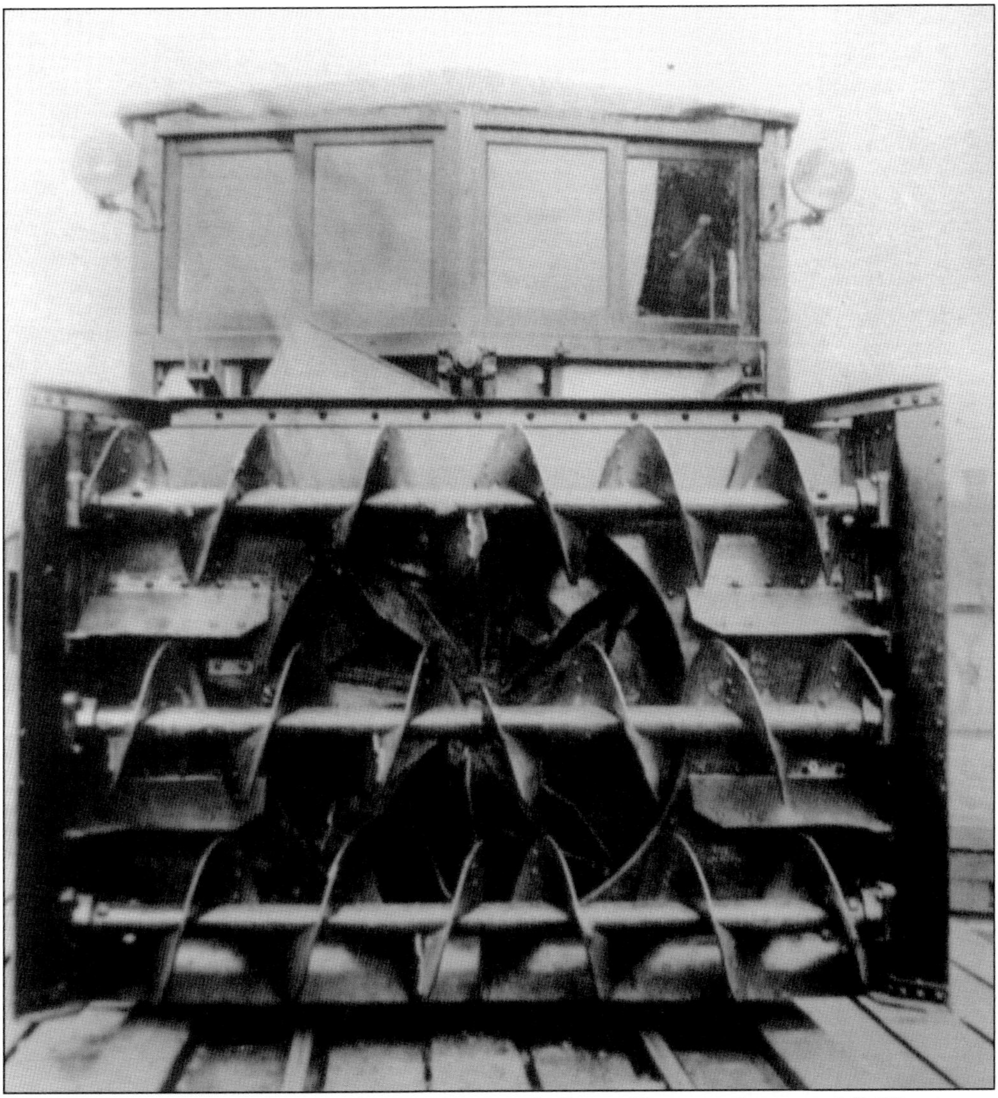

Less than a month after delivery, the Sno-Go was challenged by a two-foot snowfall. This image clearly shows how the plow worked. One of its two Climax engines turned the augers that pulled the snow to the center, where it was thrown to either side by the second Climax engine powering the blower, which turned at 1,000 revolutions per minute. (Streuser.)

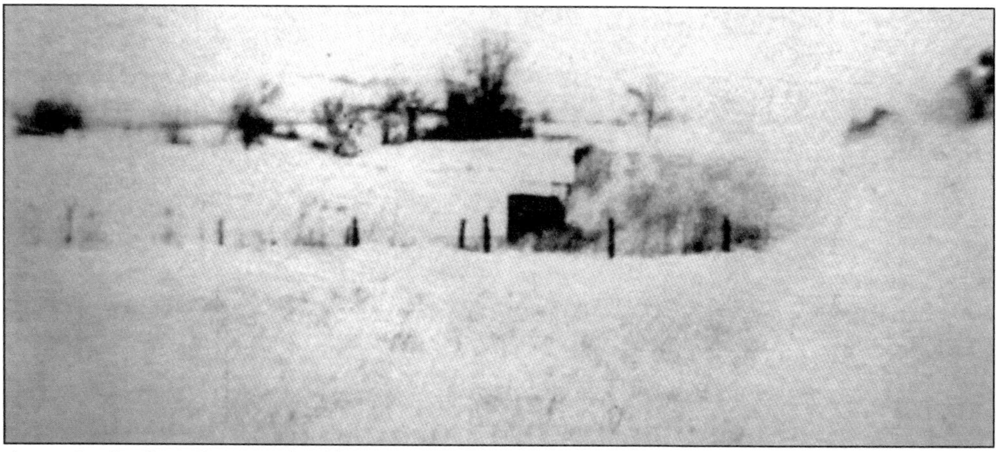

At work, the Sno-Go is pushed by a steam locomotive about one mile west of Bernard, headed toward Cascade. The engine's smoke can be seen in the upper right-hand corner, above the snow cloud from the plow. (Otting.)

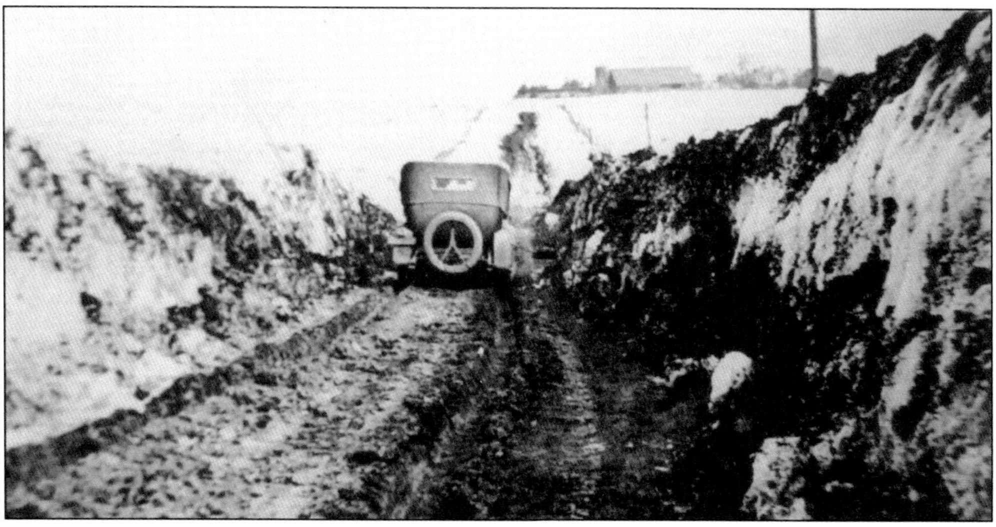

A Wills-Knight battles snow on a typical early-1930s road. Paving was truly a godsend for the automobile, although it proved to be eventual death for the little railroad. (Otting.)

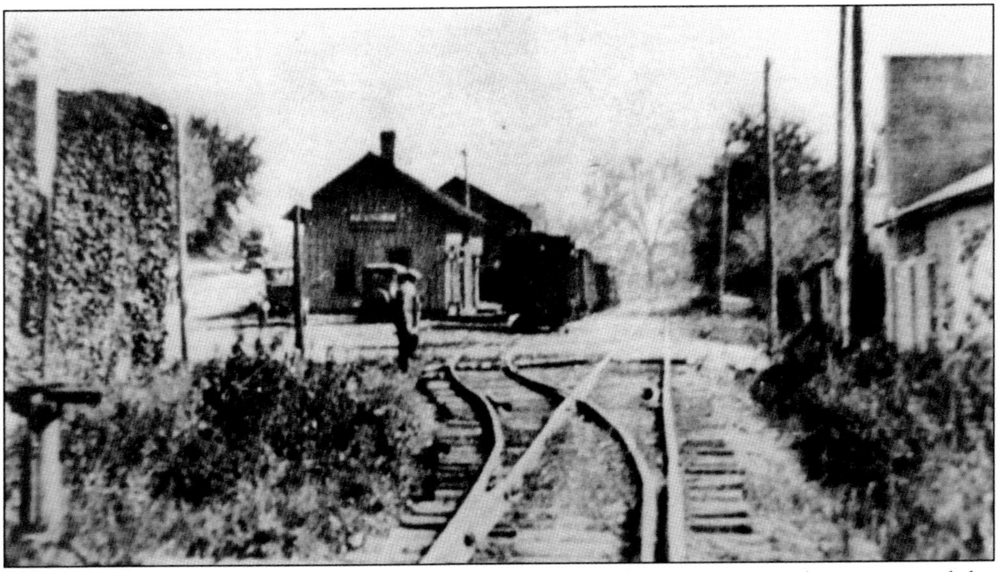

In this view looking east along the branch line, Zwingle's depot appears with two automobiles parked on its west end, to the left of the boxcars on the siding. Highway 61 crosses the tracks beyond the switch.

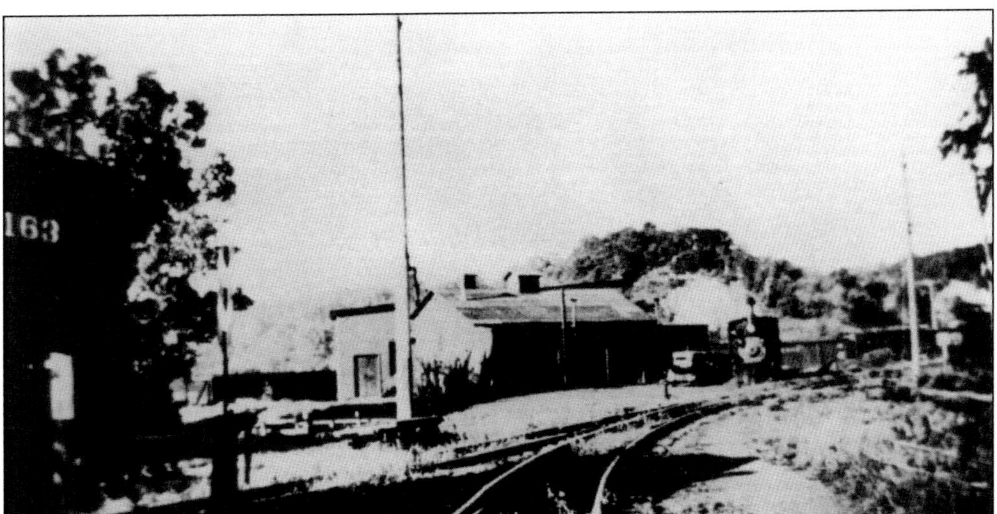

This southwestward view in Bellevue shows No. 4, the 2-8-0 Cooke consolidation passing on its right, and the two-stall roundhouse standing behind the 60-foot-long engine house addition.

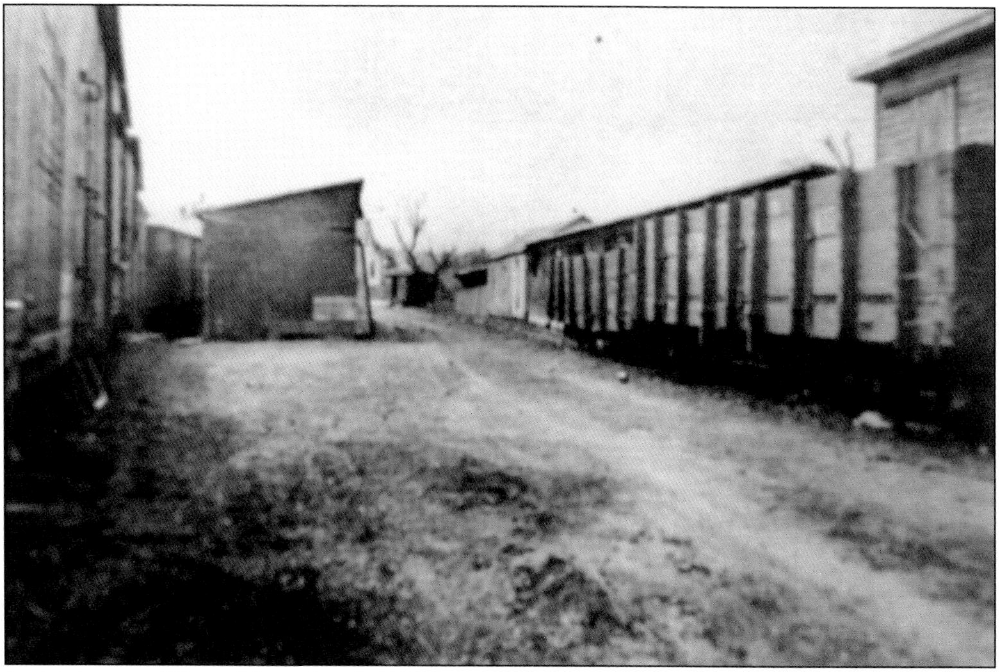

In this image of Cascade's yards, a freight house appears in the foreground, while in the distance, lumber and coal sheds are partially obscured by the gondolas on the right. (Bogue.)

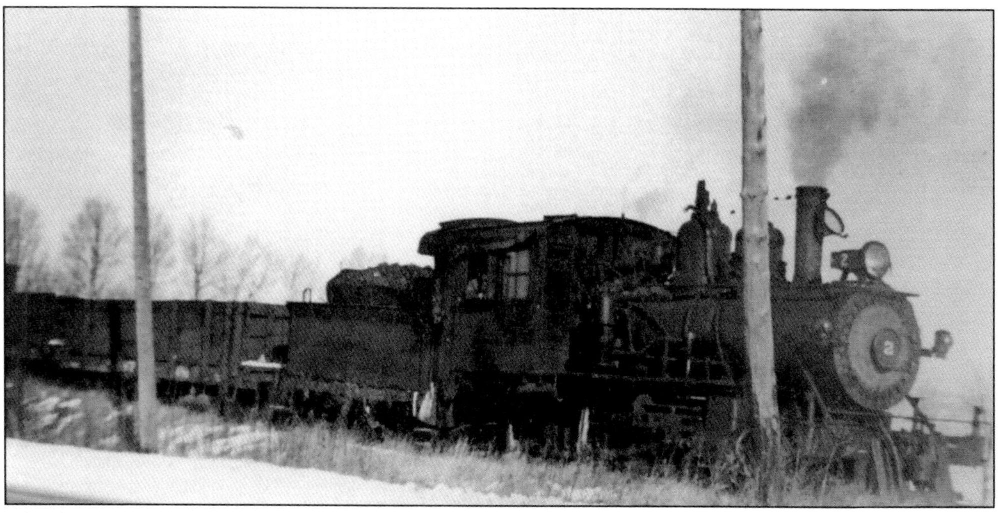

Charles Spielman is at the throttle of outside-frame 2-6-0 No. 2. as it approaches a grade crossing on Highway 151, heading toward Cascade. This photograph was taken after 1929, when paving of the stretch of road had been completed.

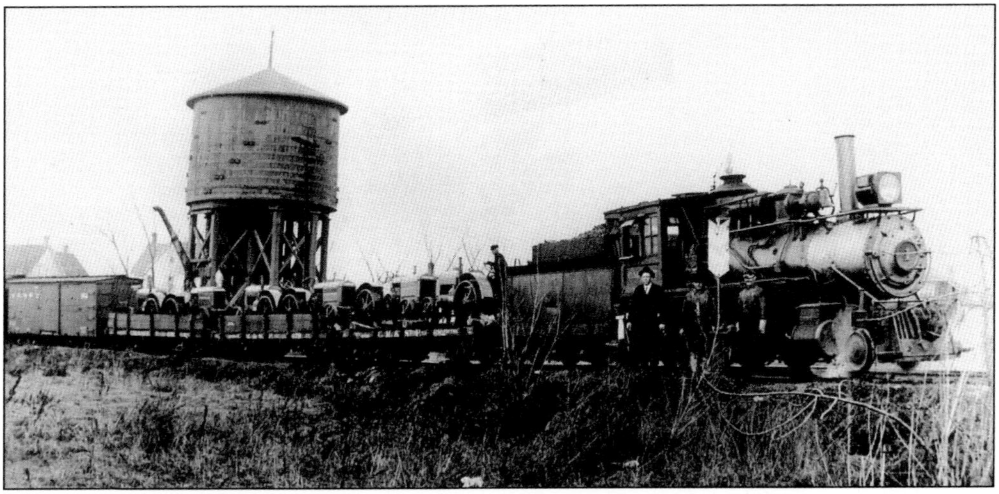

No. 1, the Brooks Mogul, is on the point of a train ready to leave Bellevue. Six brand-new McCormick 10-20 tractors, introduced in 1915, would make a half dozen farmers happy, although teams of horses would still be used until after World War II. Still, the Milwaukee accountants calculated that the branch line had lost $66,000 for the year 1931. (Streuser.)

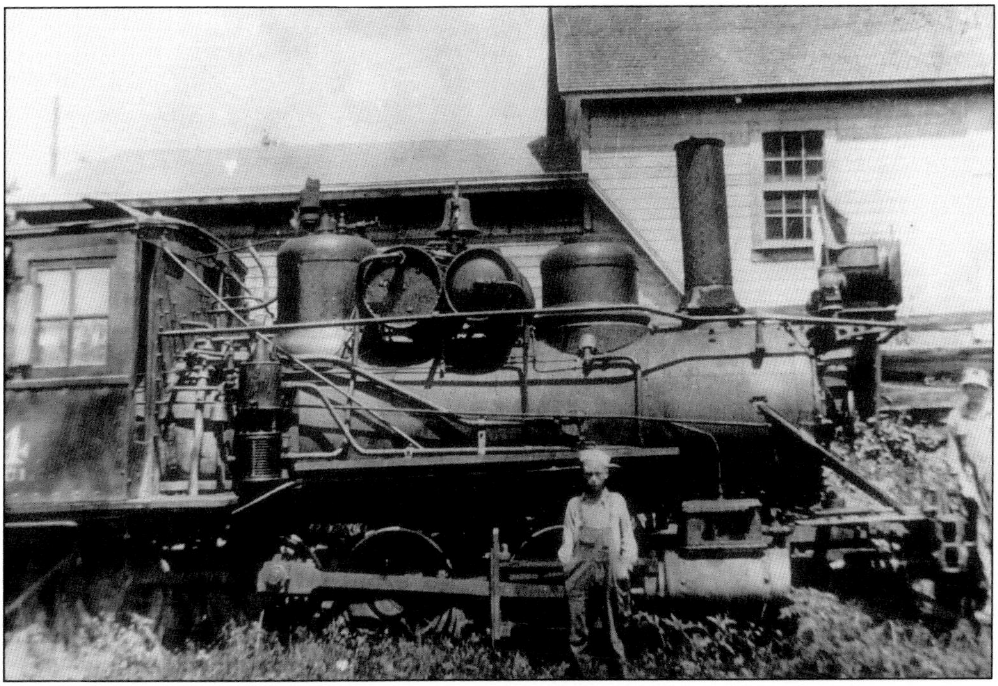

Wearing a white cap, Carl Leffert poses in front of the Cooke consolidation's first driver in Zwingle. His father was employed by the Milwaukee Road. Donald Datisman stands on the pilot to the right.

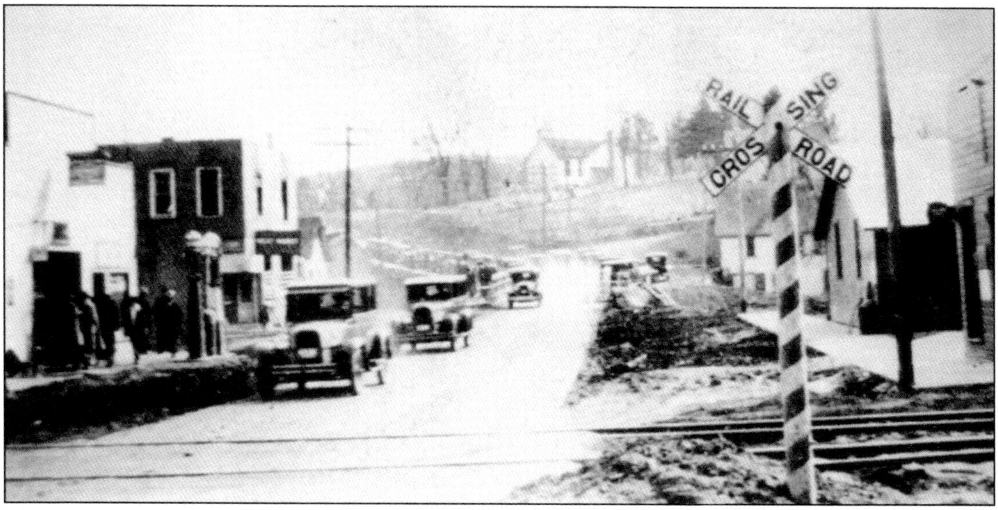

More and more automobiles were appearing in Zwingle and surrounding towns during the early 1930s, competing with standard-gauge railroads as well as the northeastern Iowa three-foot-wide line. (Kemerer.)

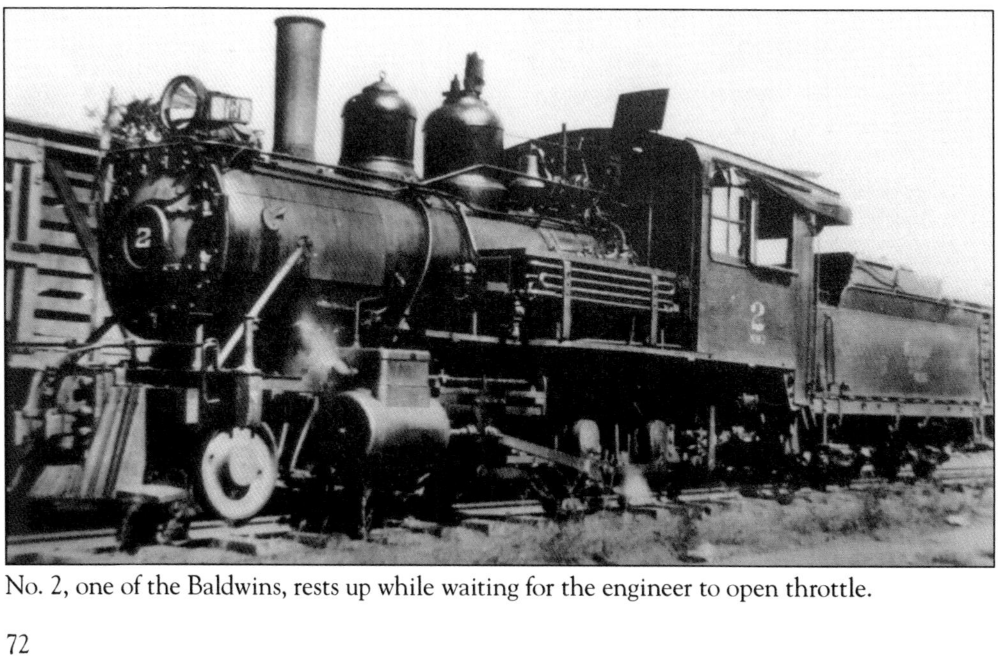

No. 2, one of the Baldwins, rests up while waiting for the engineer to open throttle.

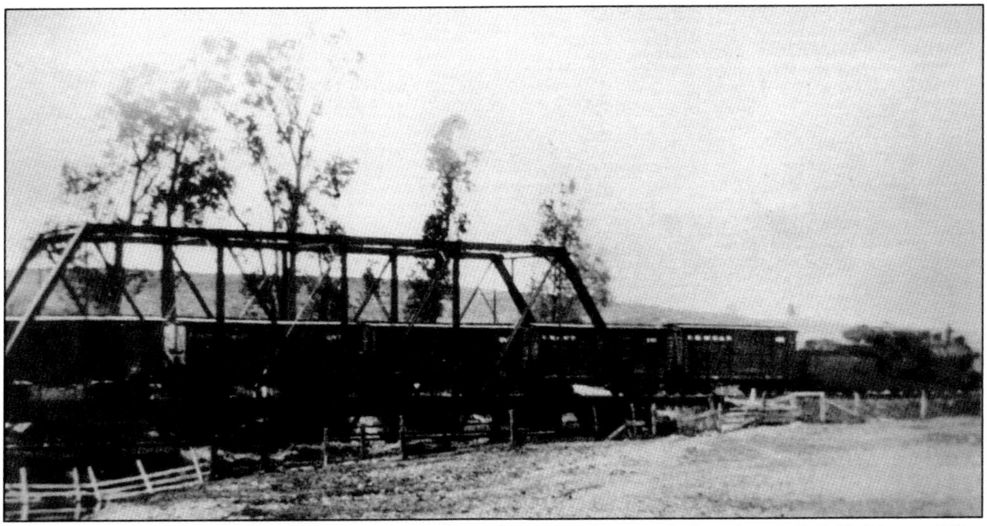

This bridge near Zwingle carries the weight of a mixed train behind a 2-6-0 Baldwin. The bulk of the work went to the two outside-frame locomotives when the other locomotive developed severe problems.

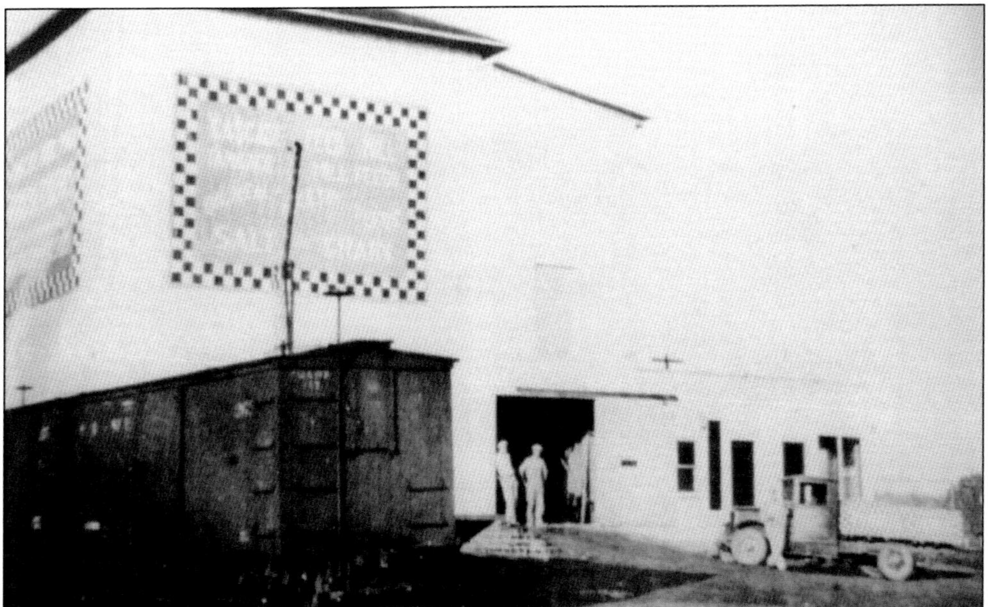

In this 1930s image, boxcars sit in front of George Wassenaar's feed mill in Cascade. Seen here are Earl Loes (left), Ralph Garfield (center), and Francis Loes, leaning against the International truck. (Neiers.)

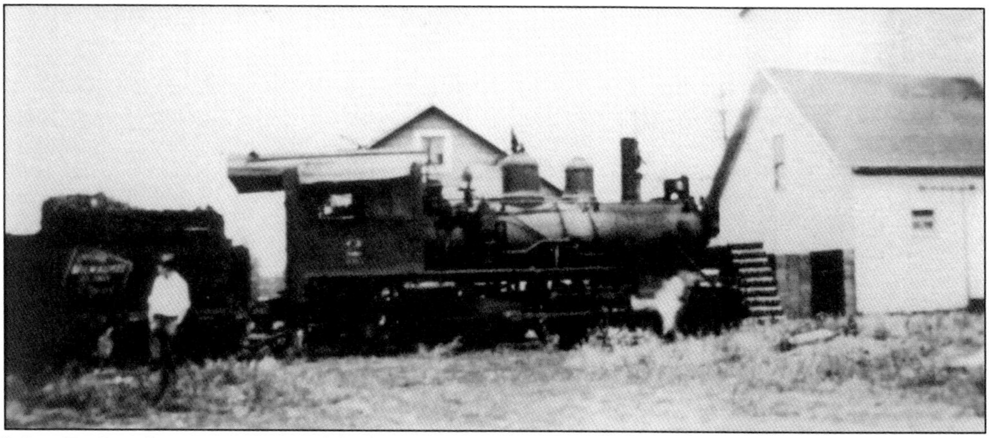

John D. Smith was 14 years old when he took train No. 81 to Cascade and No. 82 back to Bellevue. His father, a Milwaukee Road engineer, suggested he experience the little branch line before it was abandoned.

Dubuque & Illinois Division — 2-26-33

Bellevue-Cascade

Narrow Gauge

READ DOWN — READ UP

		81 Mix. Ex. Sun.	Miles	Table 47	82 Mix. Ex. Sun.			
		AM			PM			
......	......	7 00	0	Lv .... **Bellevue** .... Ar	2.30	See table 27, page 28, for connections at Bellevue.		
......	......	8.00	11	.........La Motte.........	1.30			
......	......	8.25	16	.........Zwingle..........	1.00			
......	......	8.55	22	......Washington Mills▲.....	12.20			
......	......	9.20	25	..........Bernard..........	12.05			
......	......	9.40	30	..........Fillmore▲.........	11.40	......	......	......
......	......	10.15	36	Ar......... **Cascade** Lv	11.15	......	......	......
		AM			AM			

February 1933 saw a change in time schedules for the branch line. Still, it took 3 hours and 15 minutes to travel the length of the track—the same as in 1880 when the line first opened.

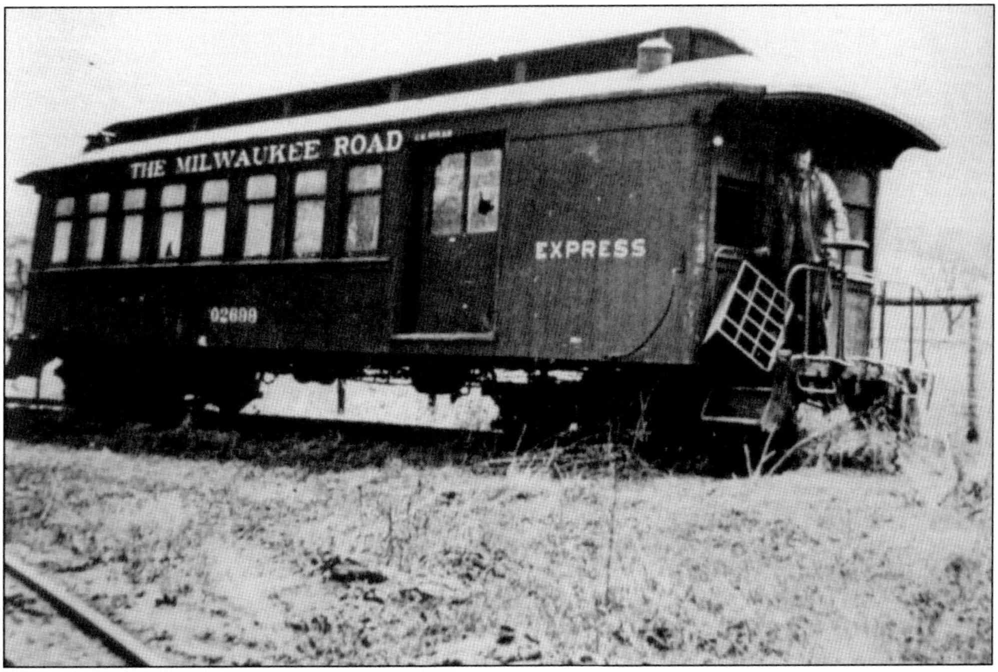

According to an equipment list compiled by Ted Schnepf, the combine pictured, Milwaukee No. 02699, was No. 8 when the Milwaukee Road began business in the 1880s. Lester Deppe stands on the platform.

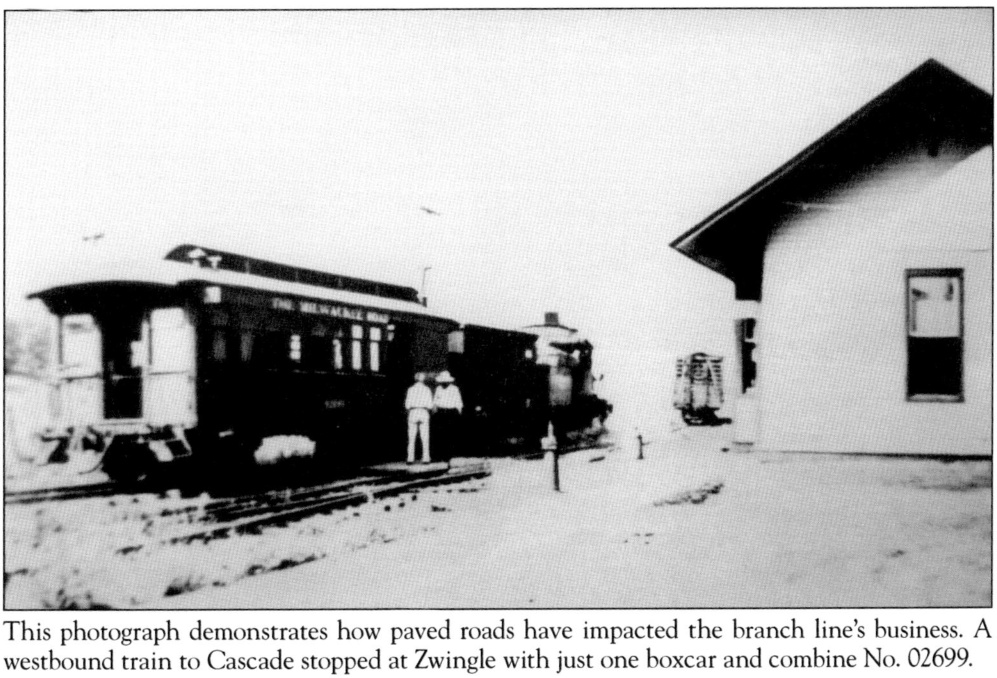

This photograph demonstrates how paved roads have impacted the branch line's business. A westbound train to Cascade stopped at Zwingle with just one boxcar and combine No. 02699.

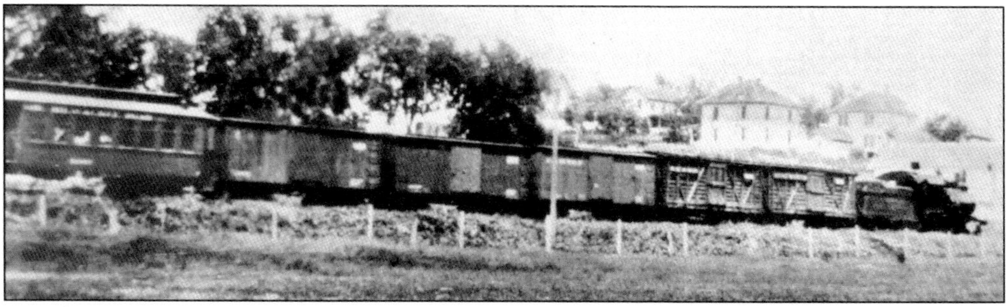

On a lazy summer day in the early 1930s, a Baldwin-built 2-6-0 drifts into Zwingle on the point of two stock cars, three boxcars, and combine No. 02699.

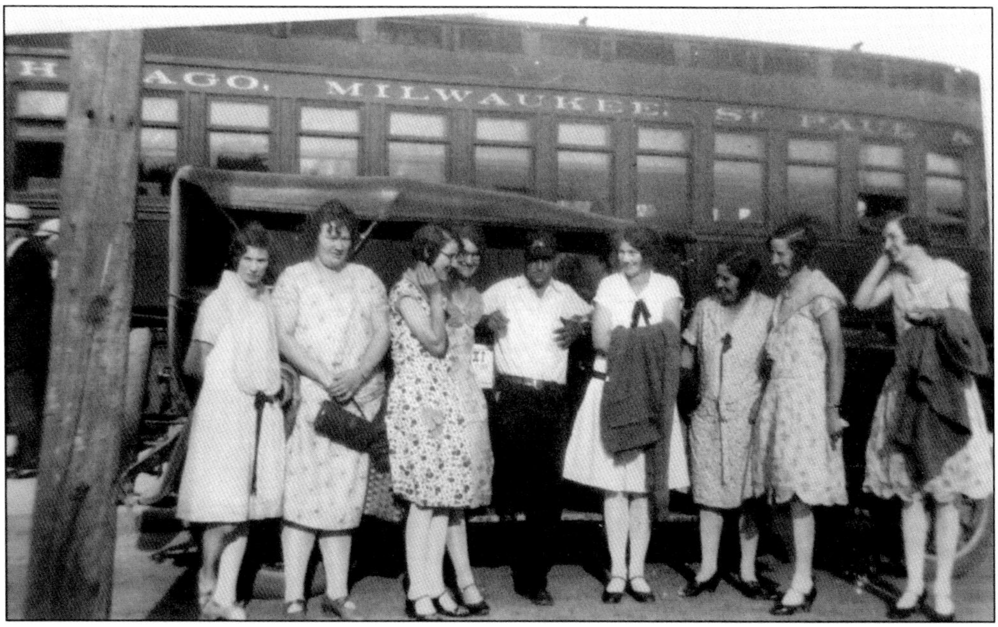

The narrow gauge was always good copy for the local newspapers, as evidenced by this photograph. These ladies traveled from Cascade to Bellevue for a day's shopping. Pictured here, from left to right, are two unidentified women, Rose Moorman, Clara Moorman (Rollinger), an unidentified taxicab driver, Frances Moorman (Koppes), Frances Kurt (Burlage), Margaret Kurt, and Ann Kurt (Luber). The passenger coach in the background is a standard-gauge car. (Rose Moorman.)

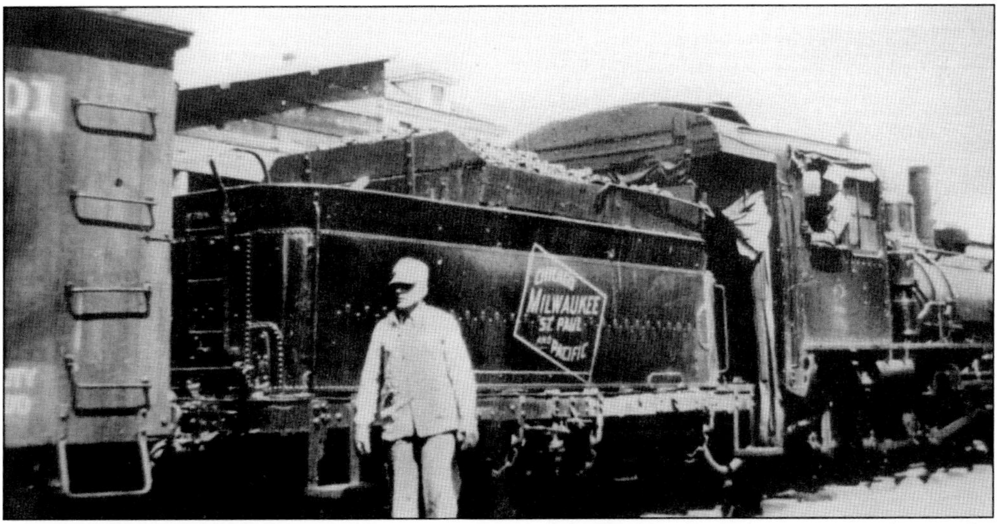

Brakeman Richard Sullivan, who began working on the Milwaukee Road as a call boy, walks past the tender of No. 2 while Richard Bogue leans out the cab window. (Kemerer.)

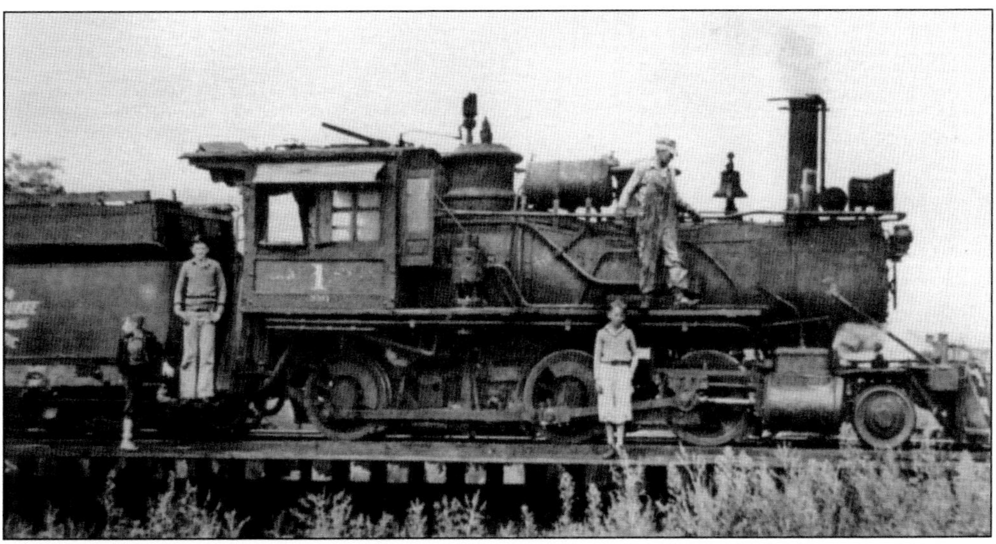

Three unidentified boys pose with No. 1 as the engineer walks along the boiler.

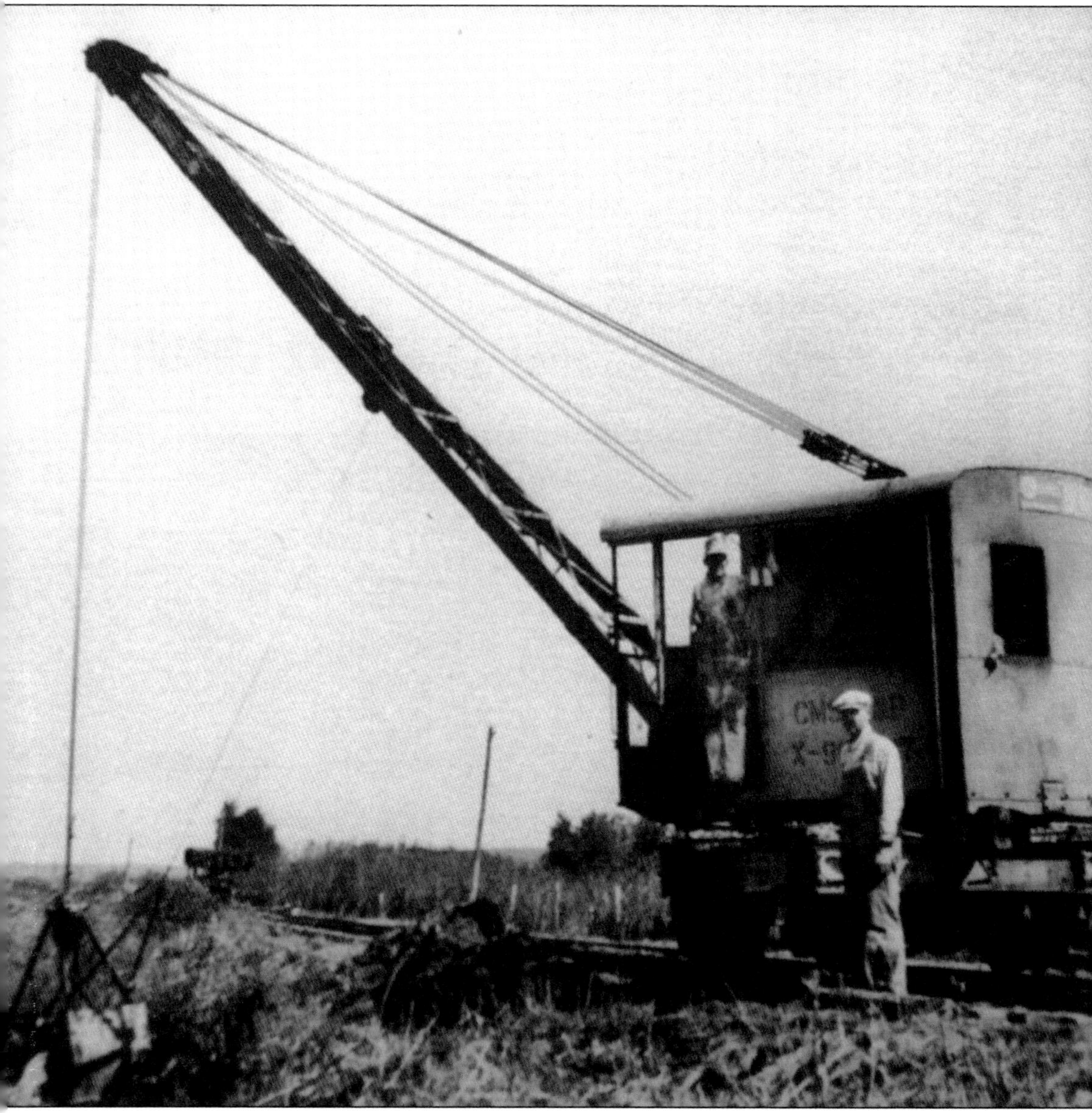

An unidentified crew cleans the track ditches east of Cascade. The dual-gauge crane was purchased by the Milwaukee Road from the Cullen-Frestedt Company of Chicago in 1929. (Schnepf.)

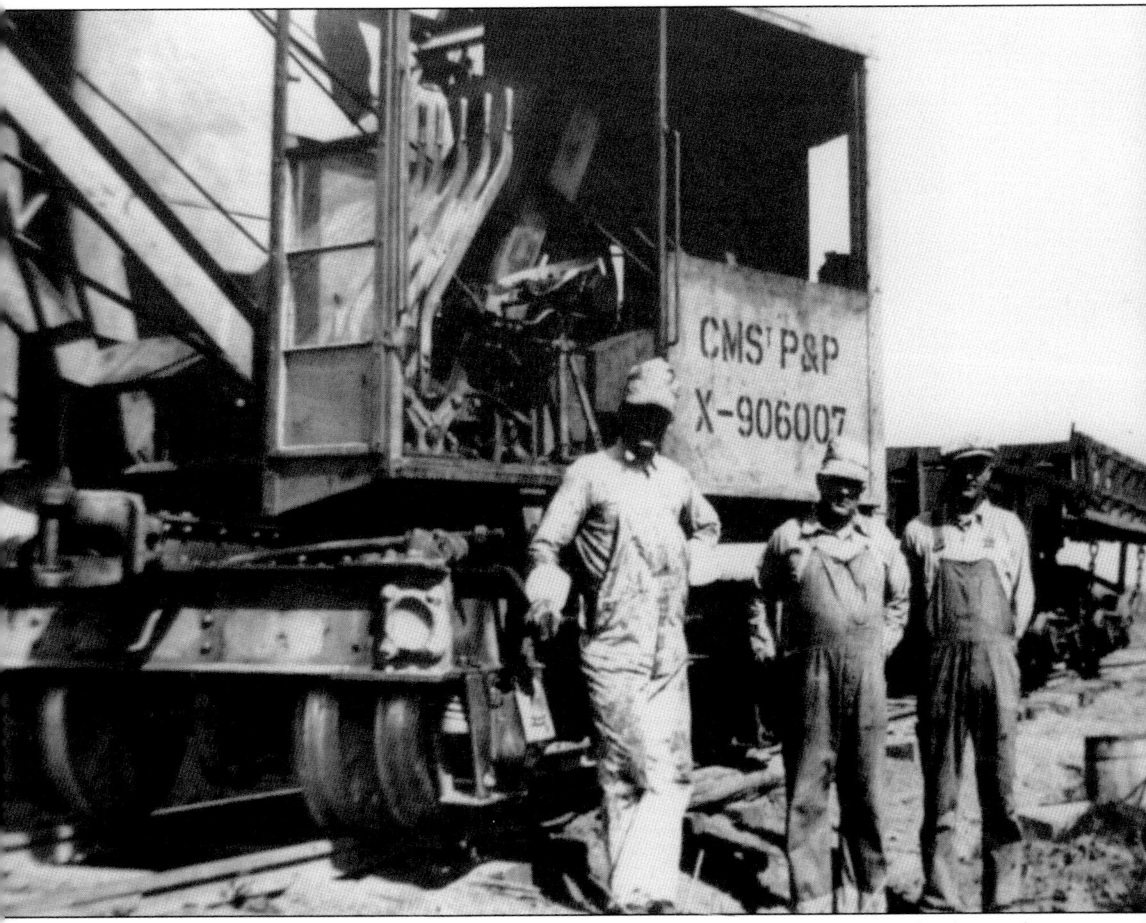

Visible in this photograph are the dual-gauge wheels, with the narrow-gauge wheels on the rails. The primary purpose of the crane was to transfer freight between narrow-gauge and standard-gauge cars. A mechanical dump car is behind the crane. (Schnepf.)

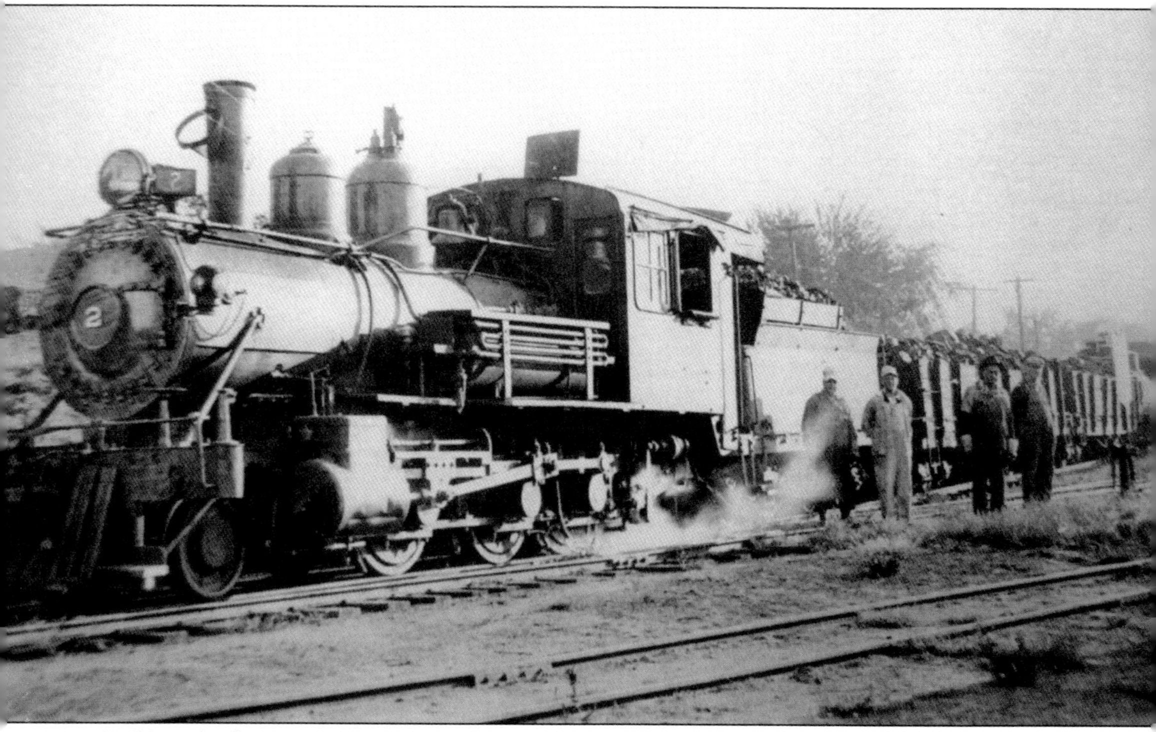

Baldwin-built No. 2 prepares to leave Bellevue with two gondolas full of coal, a leased tank car, and a combine serving as a caboose. Pictured here, from left to right, are unidentified, Edward Green (fireman), Charles Spielman (engineer), and unidentified. (Streuser.)

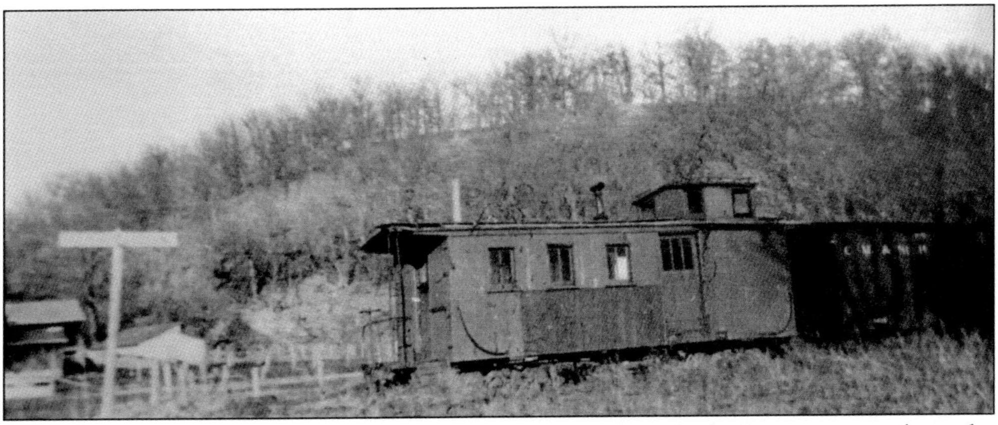

The narrow gauge's only caboose trundles after its train through the Iowa countryside in the snowless winter of 1930.

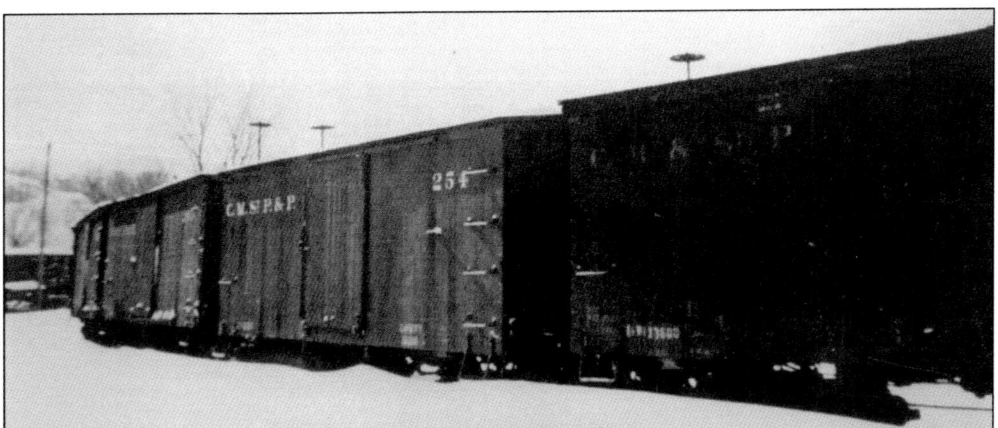

A string of boxcars pulls to a stop in Bellevue, arriving from Cascade and points in between. (Deppe.)

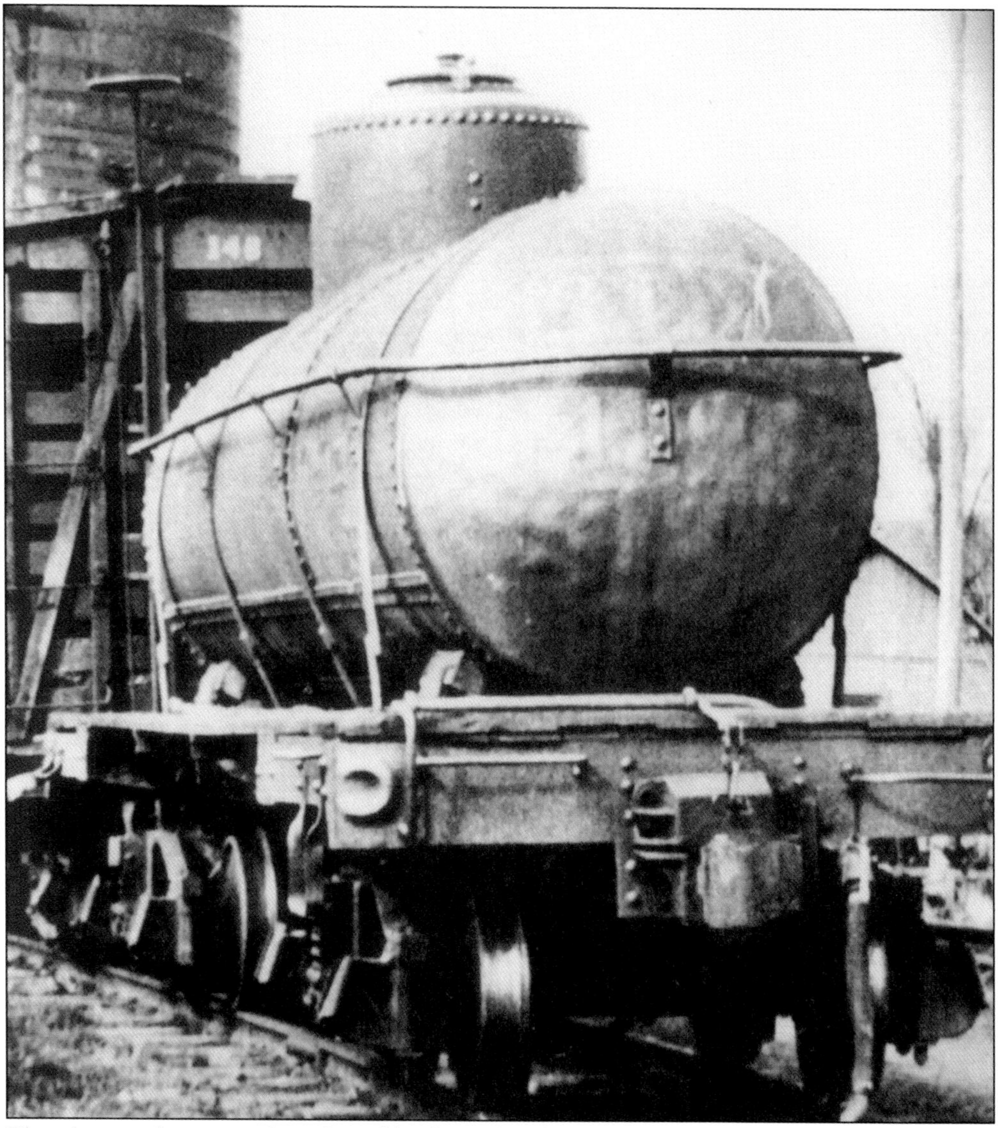

This close-up shows a tank car leased by the Milwaukee Road. Each one carried 5,000 gallons of gasoline to the ever-thirsty, ever-increasing number of automobiles and tractors.

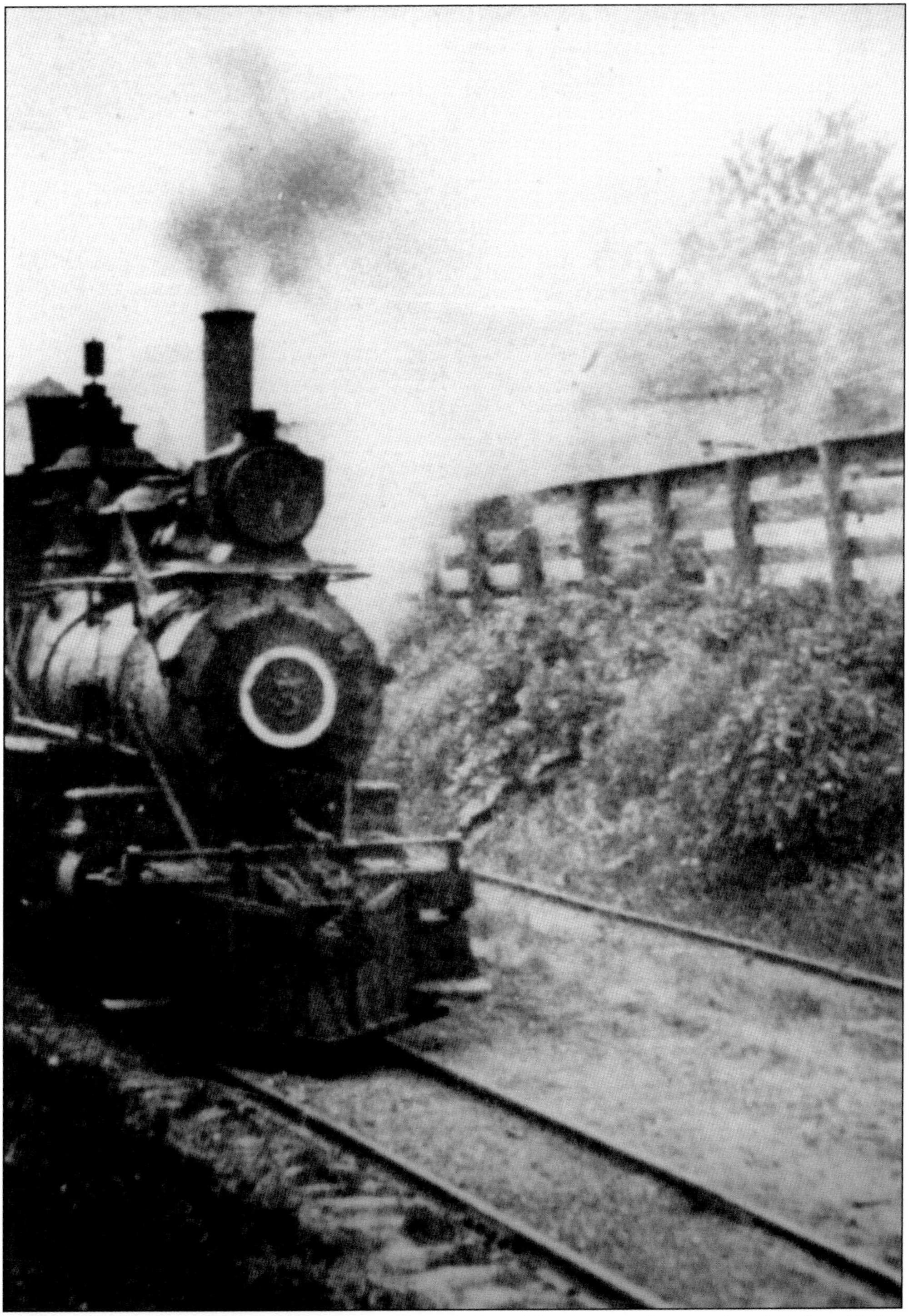

When it first arrived on the narrow-gauge branch line, No. 3 sported a round carbide headlight. Here it drifts into Zwingle shortly after its arrival.

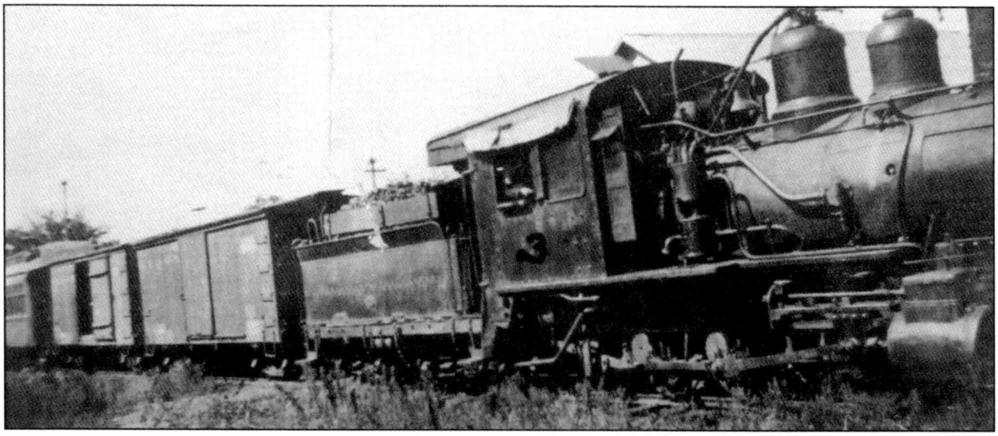

No. 3, its cab number enhanced with ink, chugs through the Iowa countryside with two boxcars and a combine serving as a caboose.

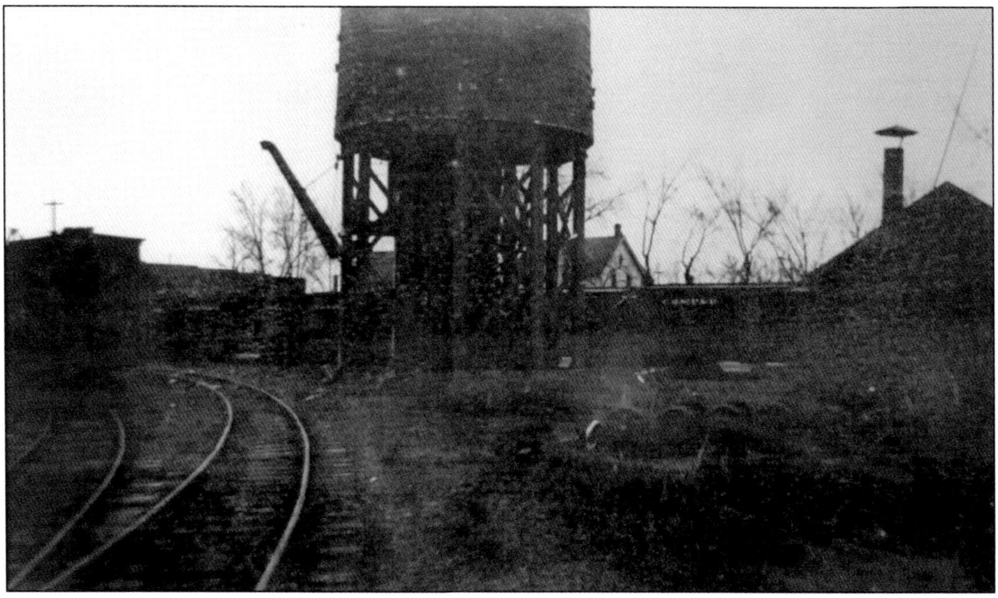

The narrow gauge's Bellevue water tower dominates this eastward view. The interchange tracks beyond the tower hold cars to be emptied or filled.

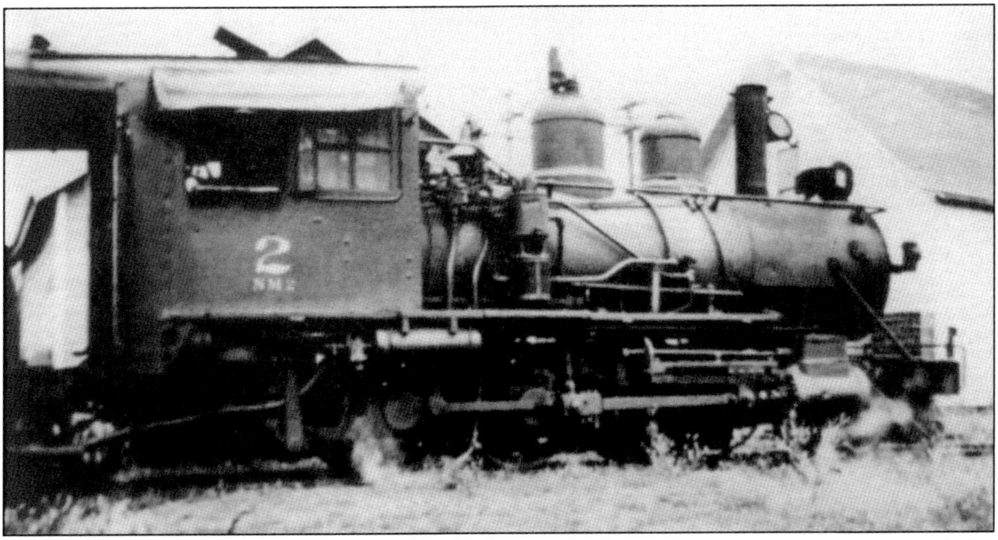

Turned and serviced, No. 2 is ready for the trip to Bellevue. It is pictured just west of the grain elevator. (Smith.)

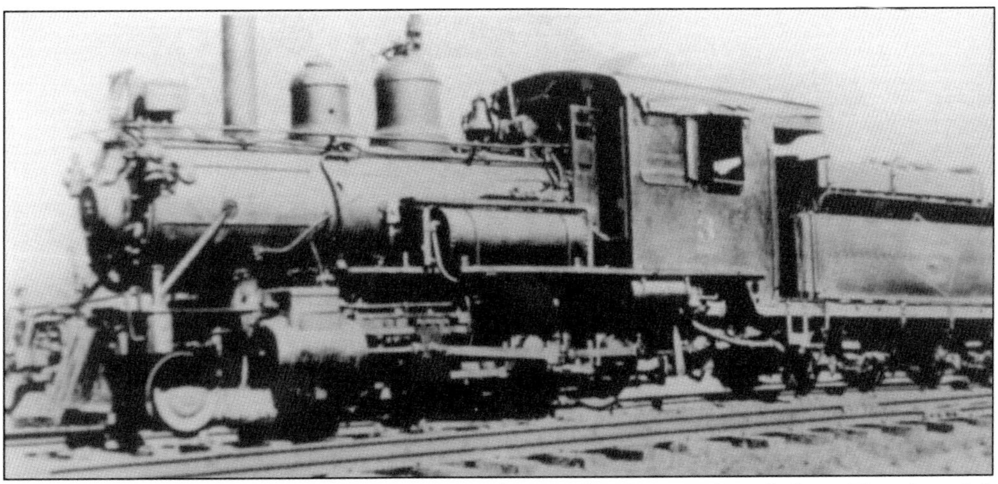

The Iowa winters uncovered No. 3's one weakness: the design of its firebox. Nos. 2 and 3 were originally built for use in the southern part of the United States. Iowa's wide variety of temperatures, from summer to winter, affected the hot flue sheets and caused leaks. A required overhaul by the Interstate Commerce Commission proved unsatisfactory when the boiler water foamed on its first trip after the extensive and expensive repair job.

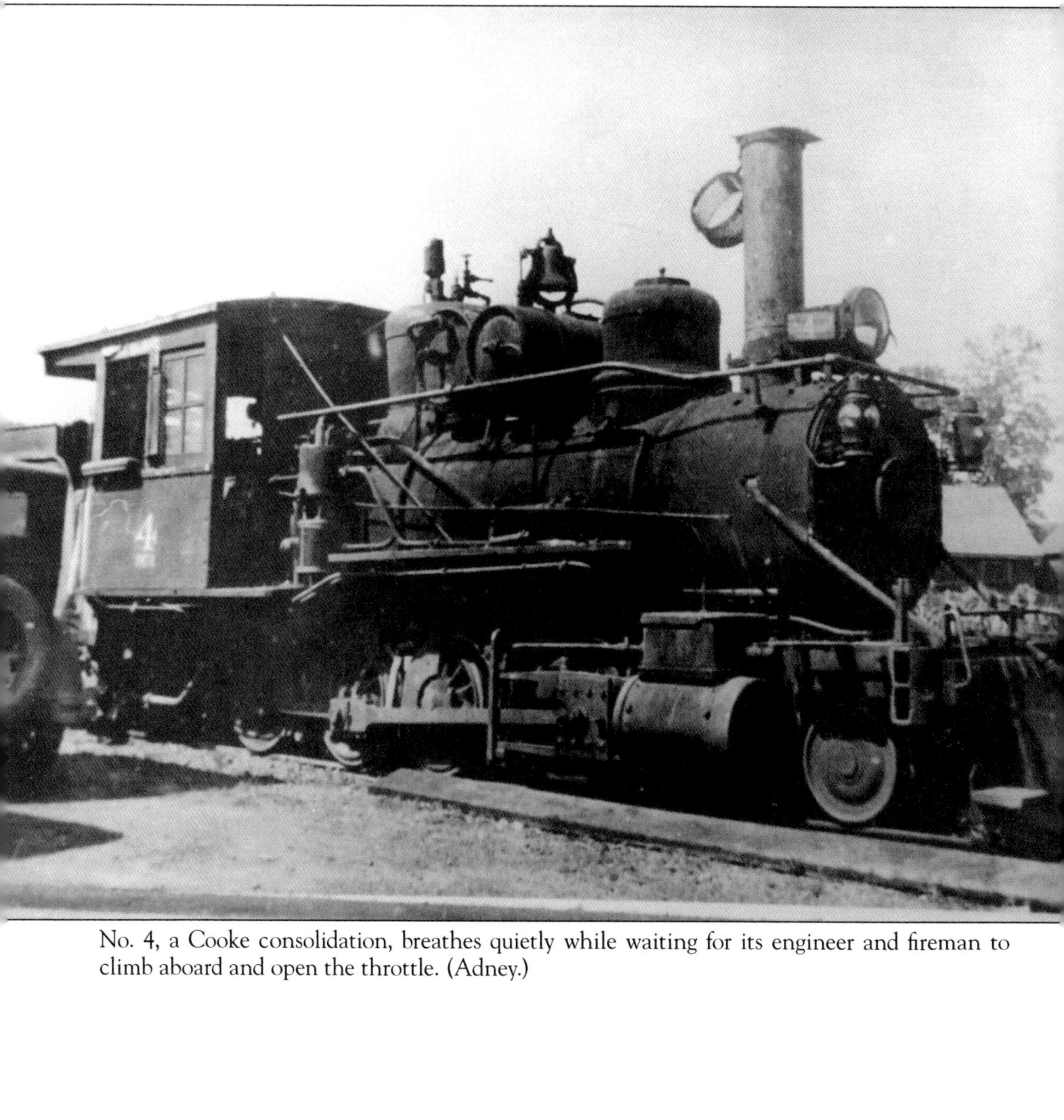

No. 4, a Cooke consolidation, breathes quietly while waiting for its engineer and fireman to climb aboard and open the throttle. (Adney.)

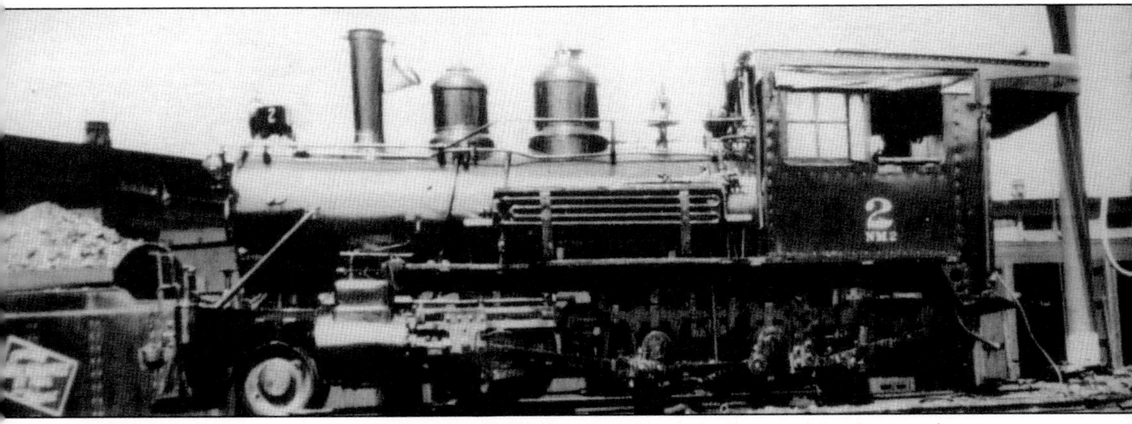

After back shopping at the Marquette roundhouse, No. 2 looks spick-and-span despite its headlight number being inserted upside down. (Adney.)

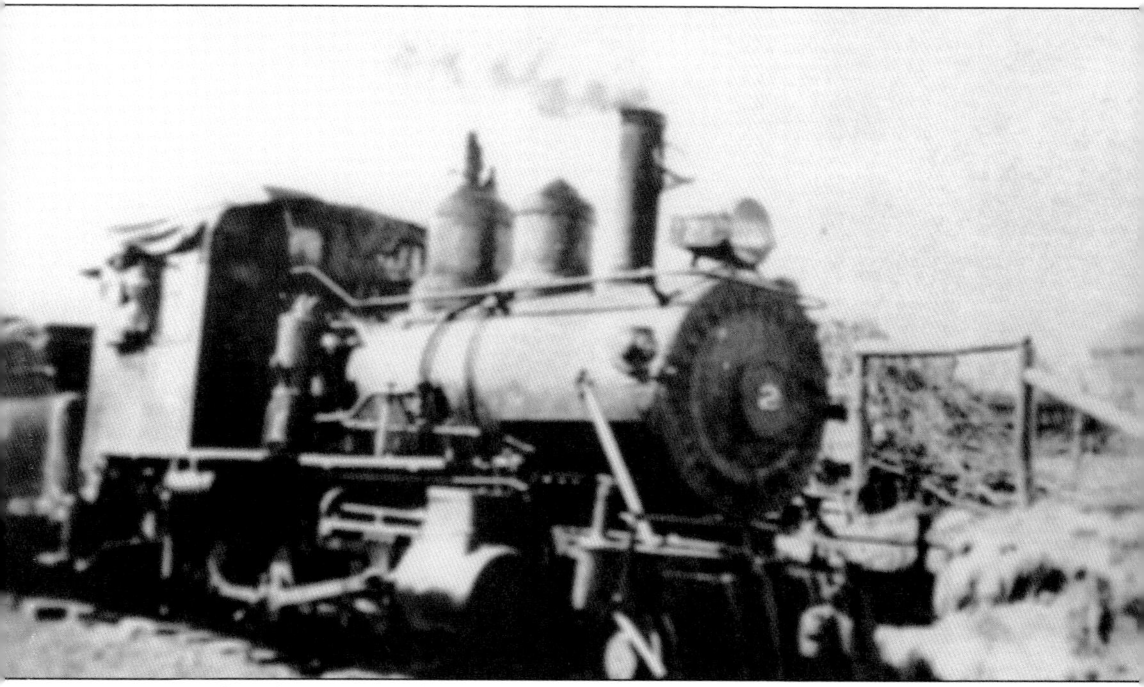

No. 2, seen here leaving Cascade around 1932, proved to be the workhorse of the steam engines.

Five

The Bellevue and Cascade Railroad

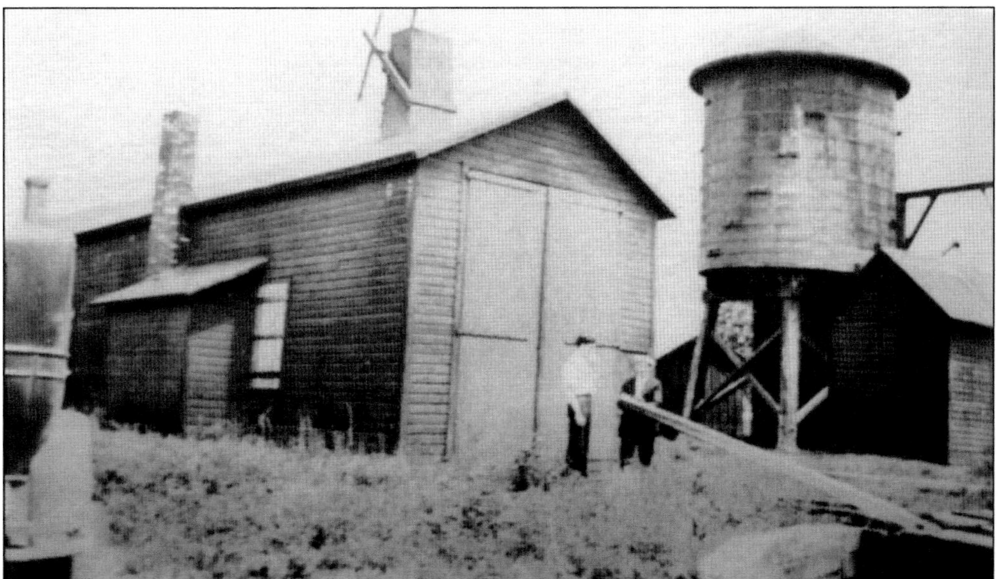

Interested in buying the little branch line, Earl Bradley had William King (left) and Samuel Goldish look over property. King, a master mechanic, and Goldish, a Minnesota businessman who would operate the railroad, are examining the Cascade locomotive facilities.

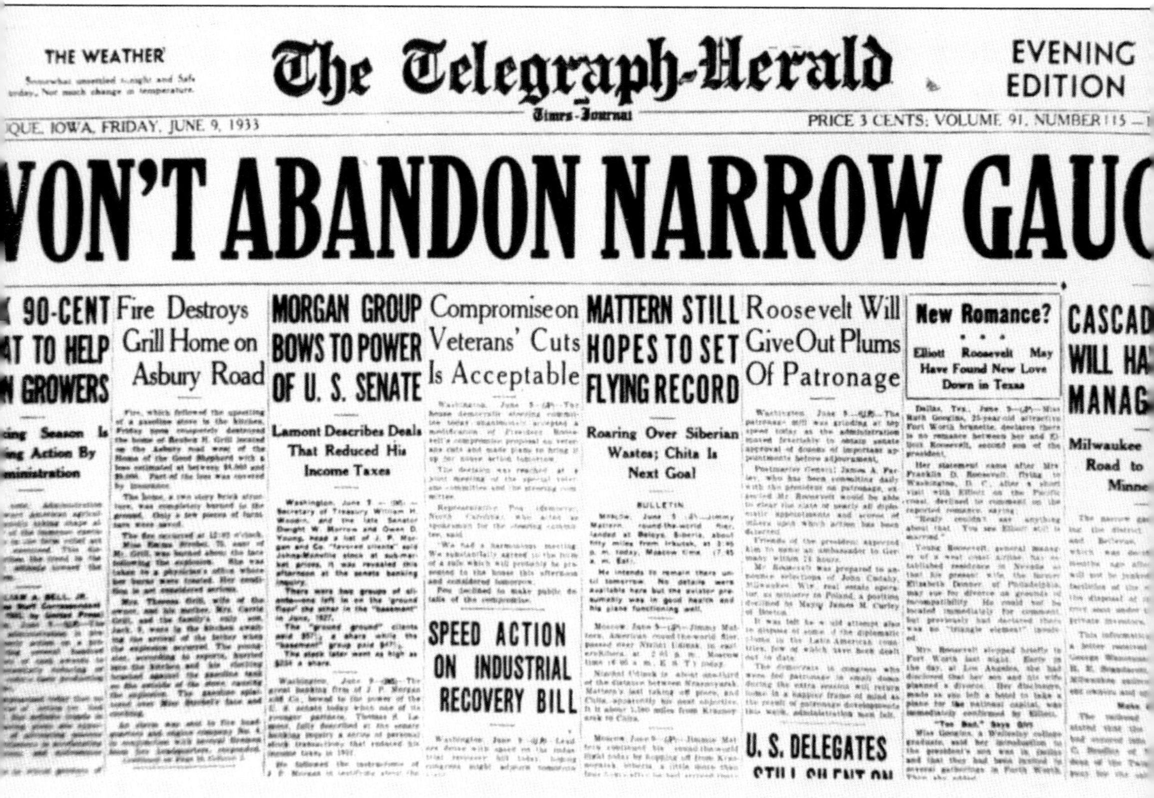
THE WEATHER

Somewhat unsettled tonight and Saturday. Not much change in temperature.

The Telegraph-Herald

Times-Journal

EVENING EDITION

...QUE, IOWA, FRIDAY, JUNE 9, 1933

PRICE 3 CENTS; VOLUME 91, NUMBER 115

...VON'T ABANDON NARROW GAU...

... 90-CENT ...AT TO HELP ...N GROWERS

...ing Season Is ...ing Action By ...ministration

Fire Destroys Grill Home on Asbury Road

MORGAN GROUP BOWS TO POWER OF U. S. SENATE

Lamont Describes Deals That Reduced His Income Taxes

Compromise on Veterans' Cuts Is Acceptable

SPEED ACTION ON INDUSTRIAL RECOVERY BILL

MATTERN STILL HOPES TO SET FLYING RECORD

Roaring Over Siberian Wastes; Chita Is Next Goal

Roosevelt Will Give Out Plums Of Patronage

U. S. DELEGATES STILL SILENT ON

New Romance?

Elliott Roosevelt May Have Found New Love Down in Texas

CASCAD... WILL HA... MANAG...

Milwaukee Road to Minne...

The only other time the gauge made the headlines on page one of the Dubuque paper had

The first time the little railroad made headlines, newspapers reported the fatal accident of February 22, 1907. The second time was in 1933, after the Milwaukee Road filed for abandonment but was instead sold to a Minnesota firm. This was big news in a time when businesses were going broke every other day.

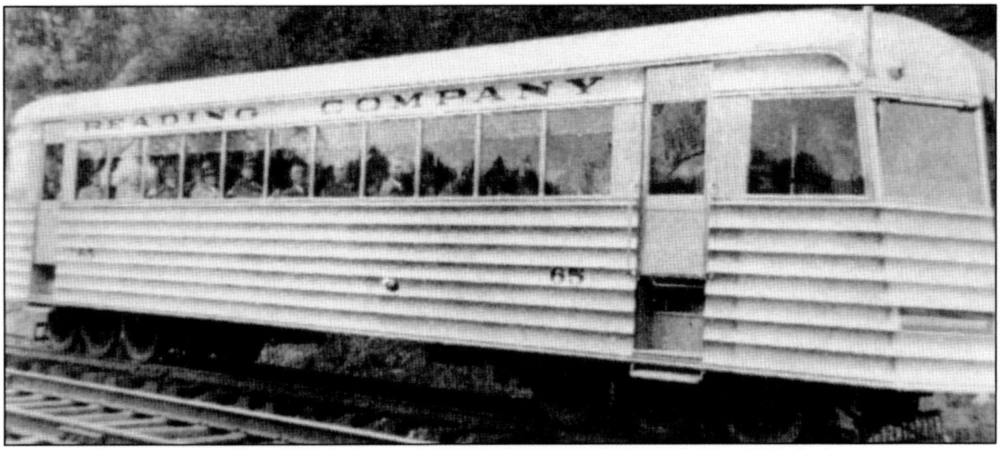

Experiments in France led to the innovation of the Michelin rubber-tired railroad truck, as seen in this image of a powered passenger car so equipped. The Reading Railroad only had one such car. The Texas and Pacific also owned one unit.

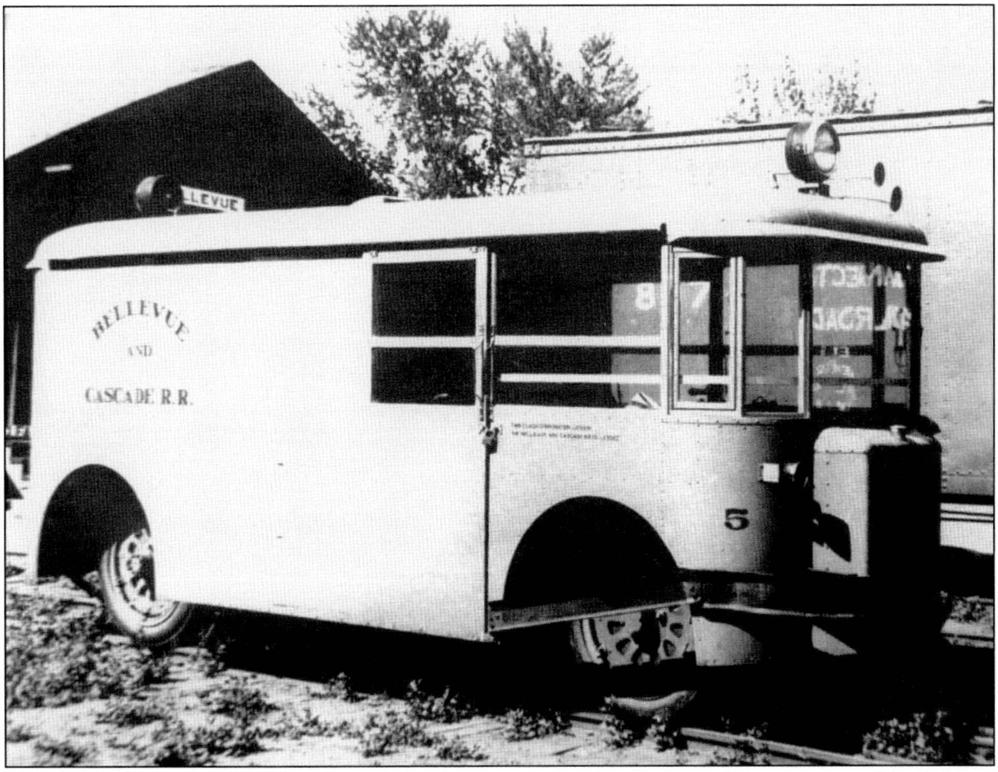

The new owner's experimental power, seen here, was a bright yellow unit quickly dubbed "the Canary." The milk truck locomotive that ran on flanged rubber tires was one of the first innovations Earl Bradley implemented. However, No. 5 could only move one or two freight cars at a time.

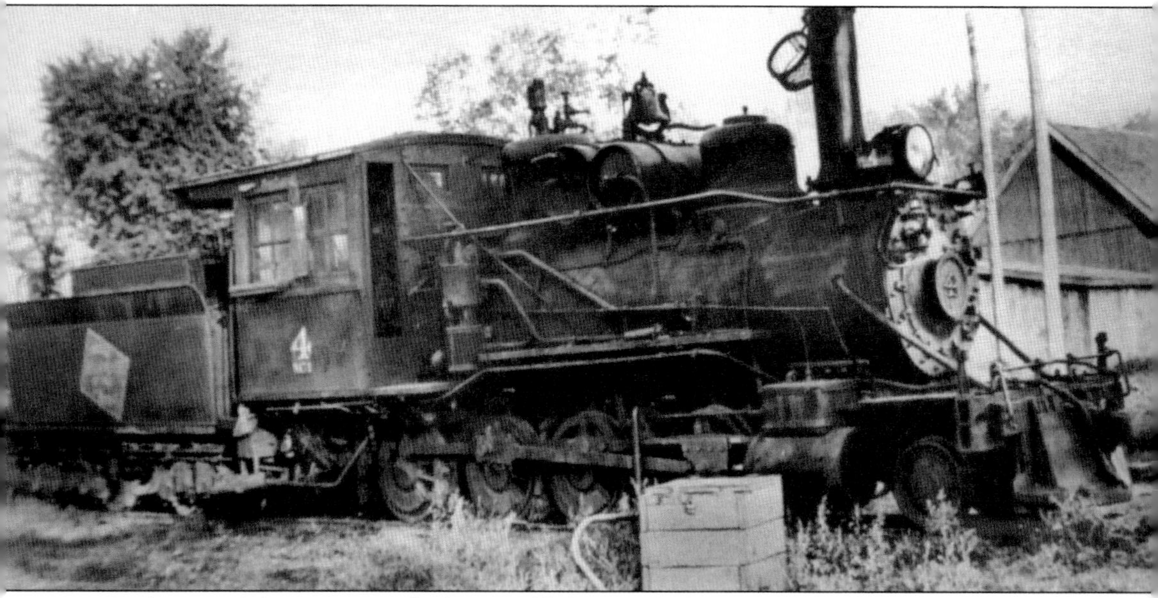

Cooke consolidation No. 4, which was sold along with the railroad, sits on a siding in Bellevue. One of the cylinders had cracked, and because the cylinders were incorporated in the frame casting, it could not be repaired. (Adney.)

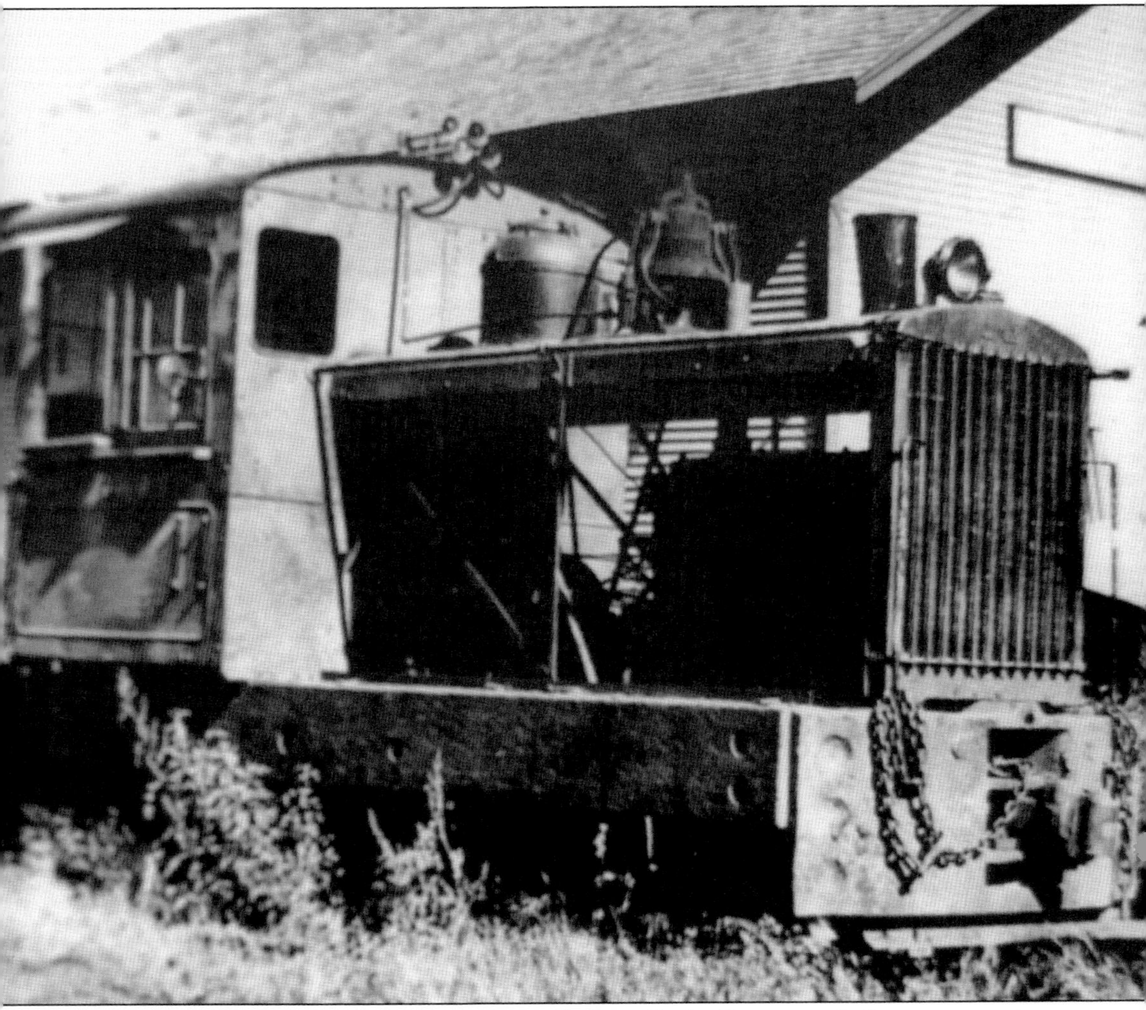

"The Ox," a Plymouth switch, was acquired from S. J. Groves and Sons contracting firm in Minneapolis after Earl Bradley took over the Bellevue and Cascade and business picked up. (Leffert.)

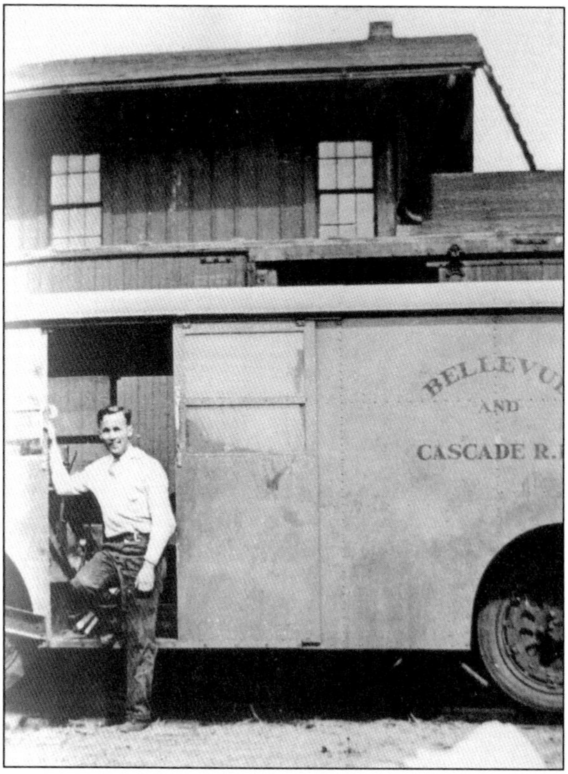

Arne Hackman stands at the door of the Canary on the west side of the Bellevue station. Even though stops were made at every depot along the branch lines to allow people to look over No. 5, the motor unit still made the one-way trip to Cascade in two and a half hours. (Bradley.)

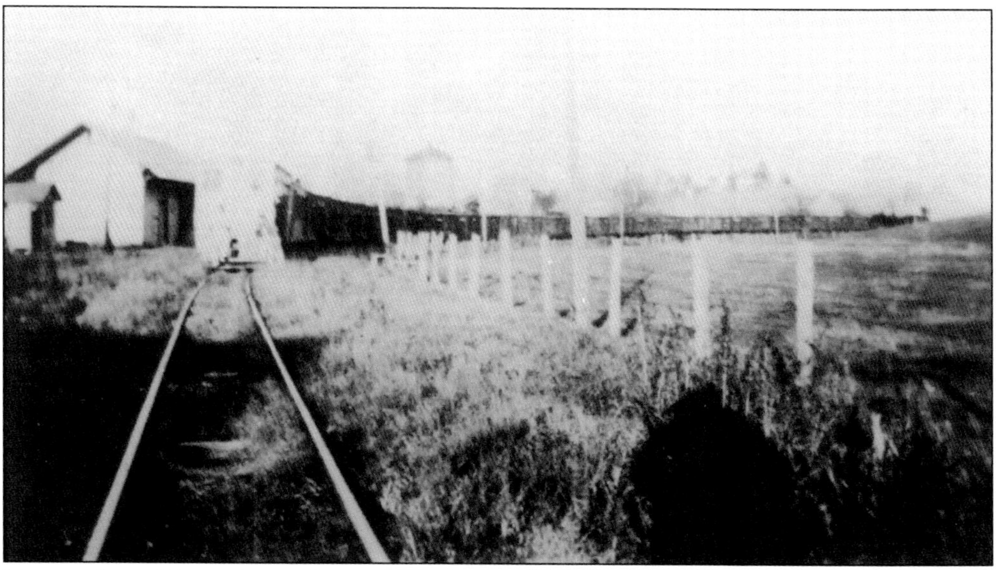

Here at least 24 stock cars have three pieces of motive power moving them. Two steam locomotives, Nos. 1 and 2, are on the point pulling and the Ox is pushing as the train struggles through LaMotte. (Bradley.)

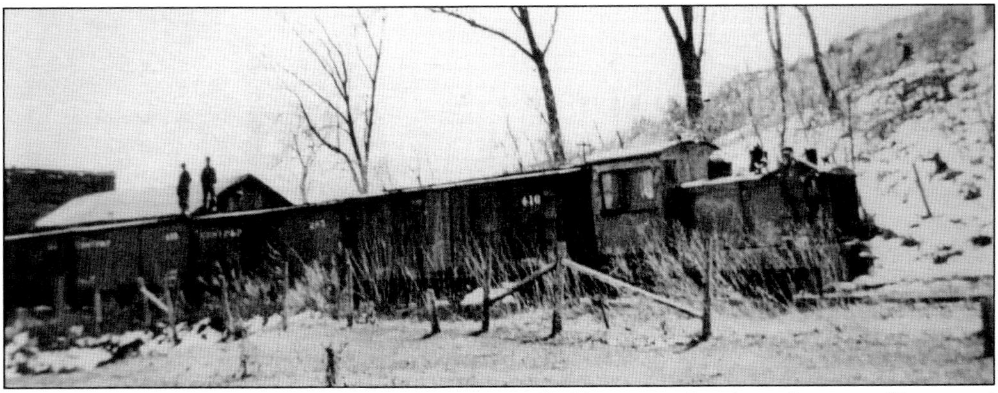

The Ox, westbound at Washington Mills, was so-called because of its deep, four-toned horn and its ability to move more cars than the Canary. (Deppe.)

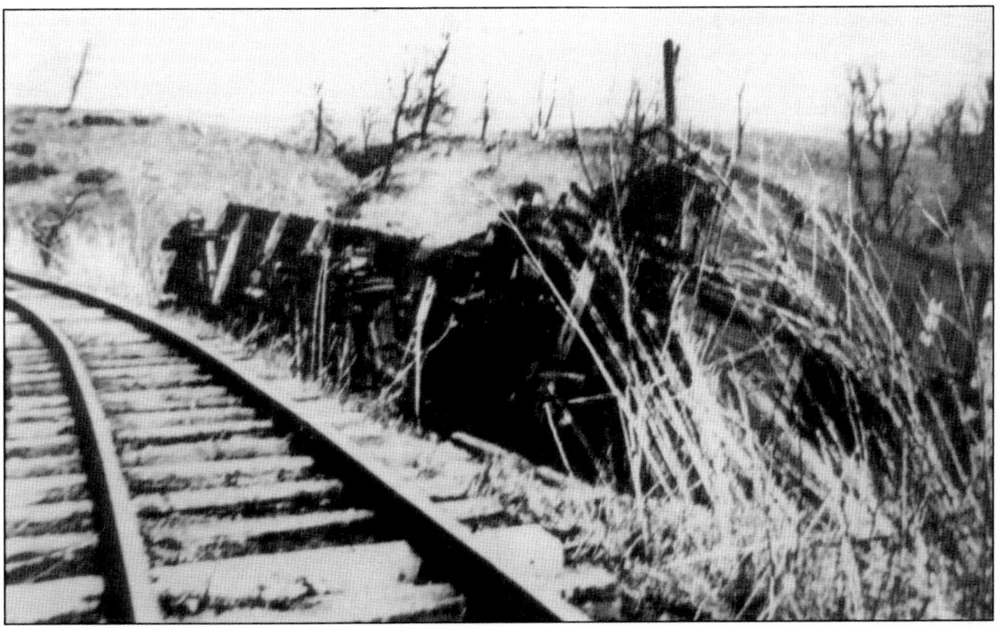

This image shows the aftermath of an inexperienced engineer's speedy approach to the bridge over Lytle's Creek at Washington Mills. His two-car train was deposited along the tracks. The freight was recovered, but because the Bellevue and Cascade had not acquired the Burro crane, the boxcars remained there. (Bogue.)

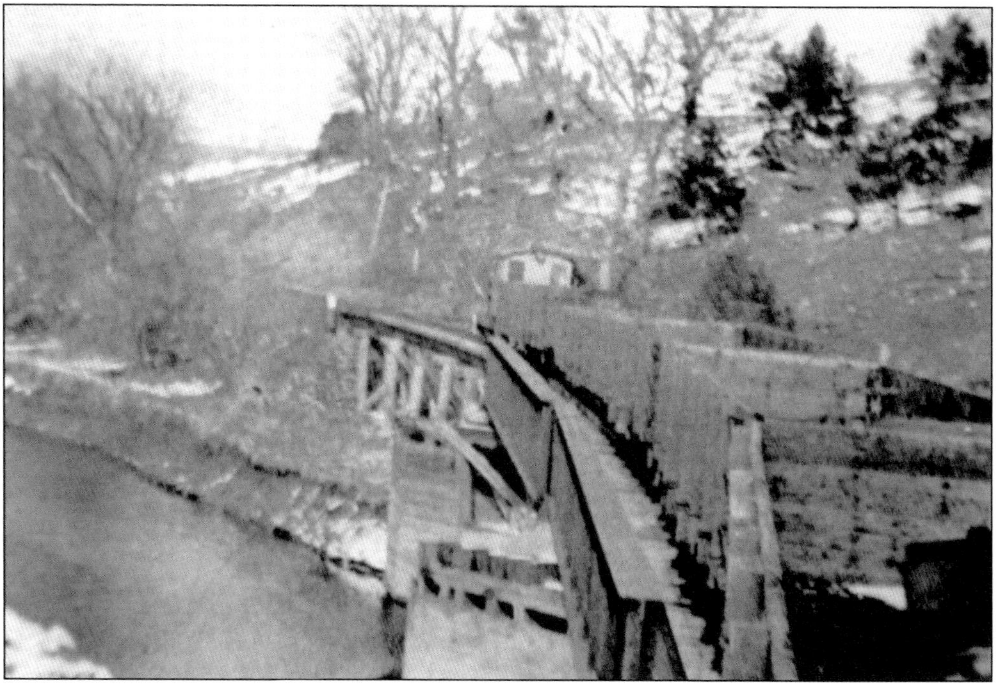

On the point of four gondolas and the caboose, the Ox crosses Lytle's Creek at Washington Mills. (Bogue.)

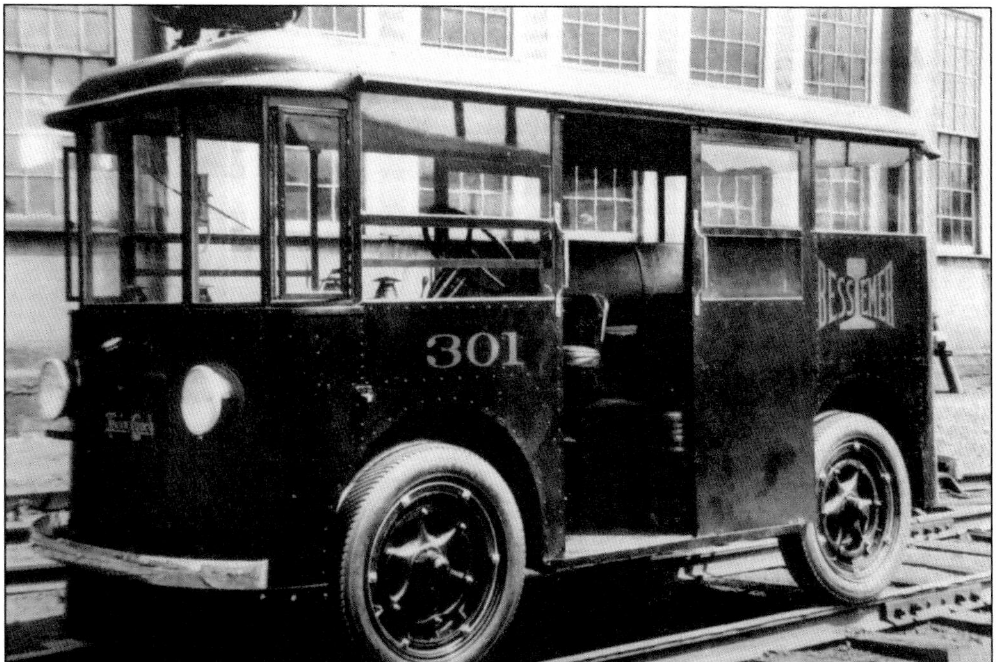

The Bellevue and Cascade narrow-gauge line was not the only railroad to try a vehicle like the Canary. The Bessemer and Lake Erie Railroad had a similar venture in its No. 301, which carried passengers. (Wood.)

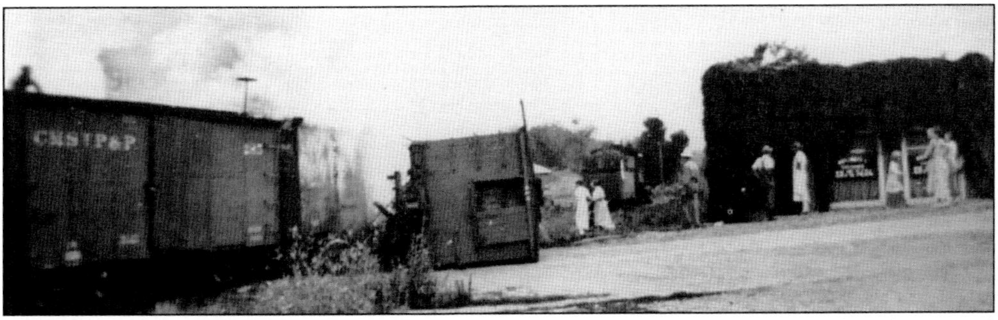

In 1934, people stand near Zwingle's ivy-covered bank building watching the gasoline fire started by a semitruck striking the early-morning train. On the other side of the track, the truck's gas tank erupted from the force of the crash. No. 2 waits beyond the bank. (Leffert.)

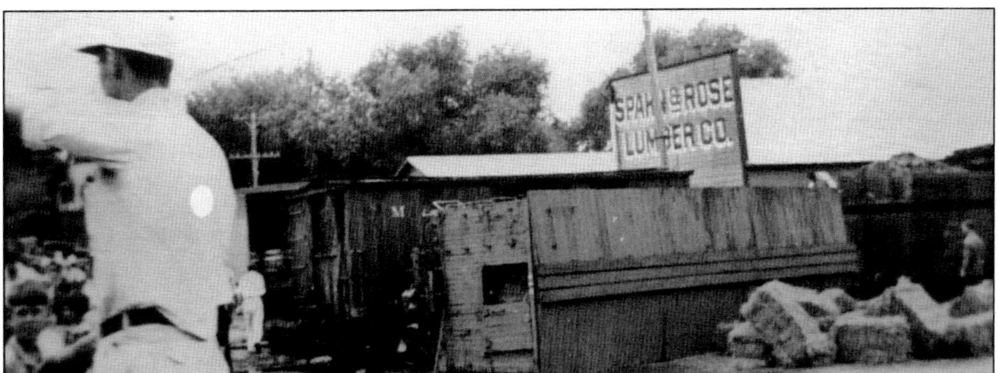

The truck driver lost control of his vehicle and struck the second boxcar, knocking it off the rails. The truck's tractor was crushed. Here No. 2 has backed up to its train. (Leffert.)

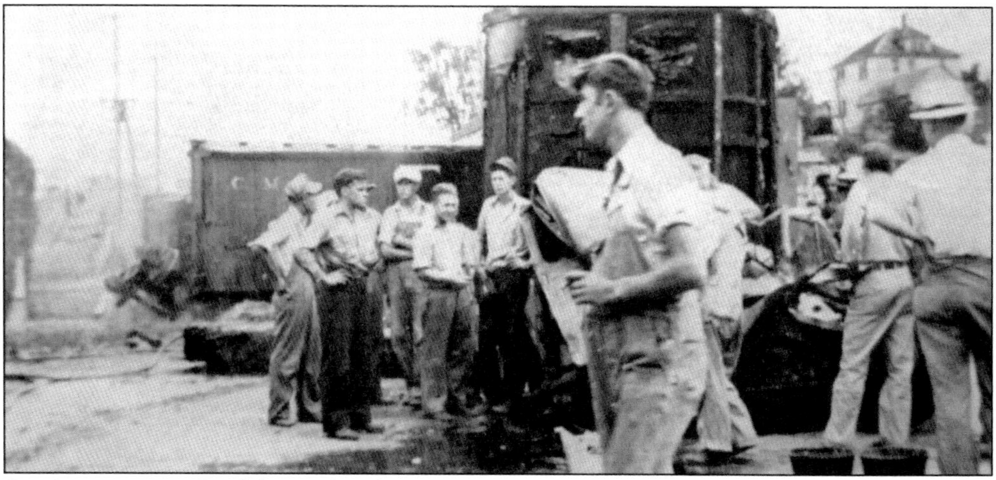

On the opposite side of the tracks, the trailer stands next to the demolished tractor. (Leffert.)

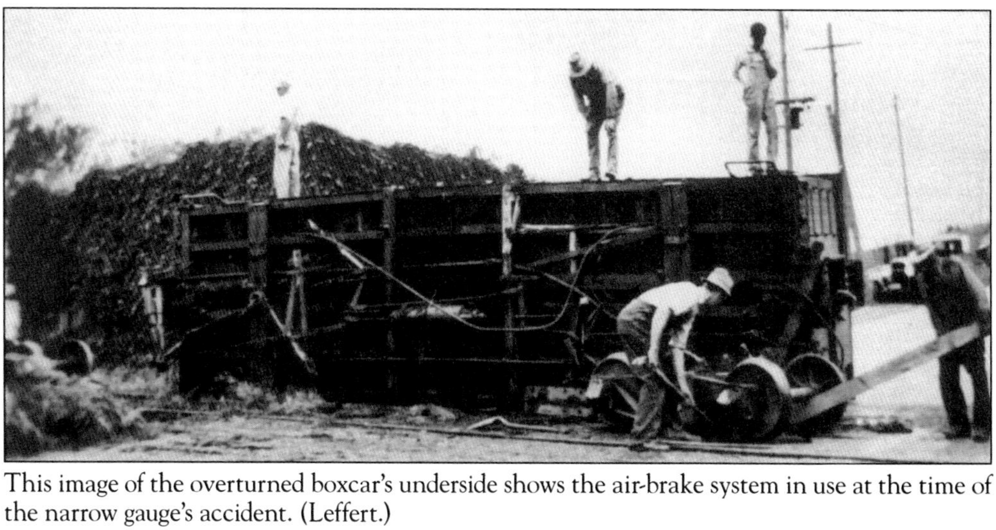

This image of the overturned boxcar's underside shows the air-brake system in use at the time of the narrow gauge's accident. (Leffert.)

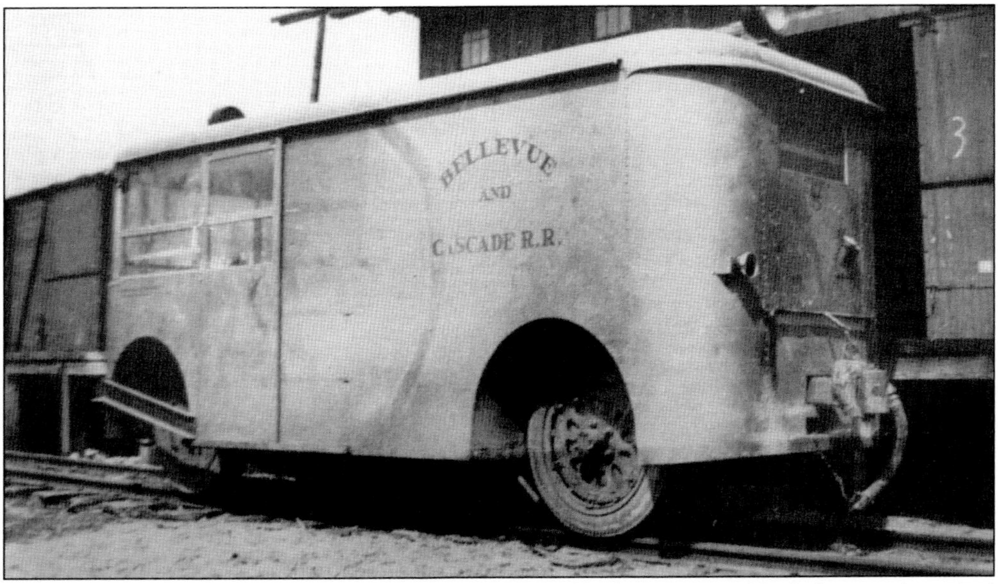

The 1934–1935 winter was cold but without snow. Still, the Canary's block froze and cracked when the water was not drained one November night.

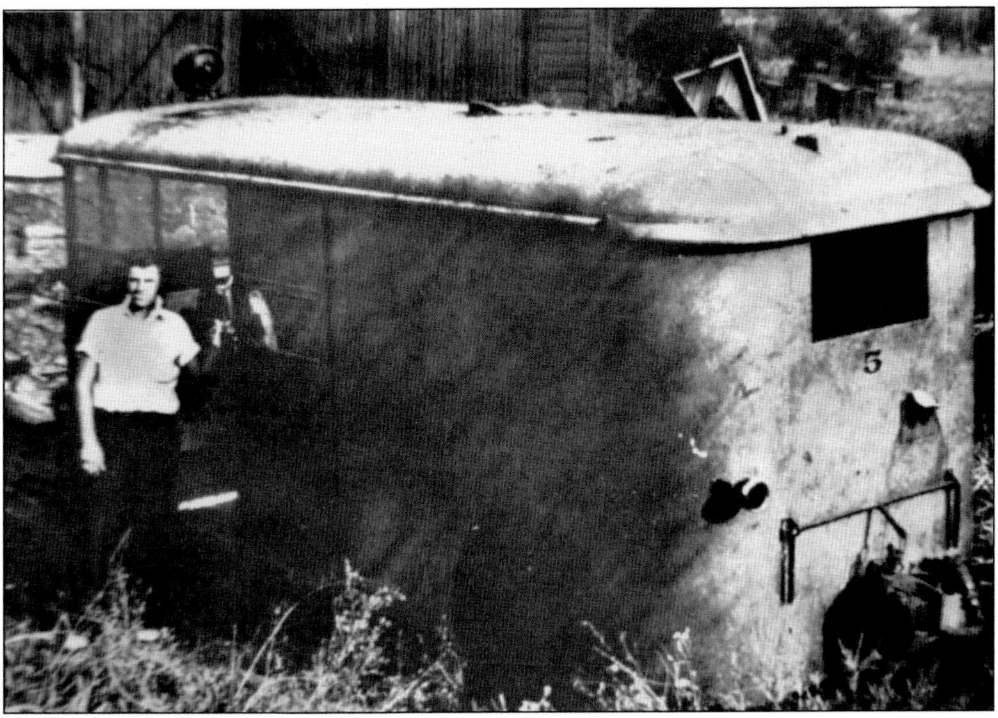
The Canary spent its last days on the Bellevue and Cascade sitting on a weedy siding in Bellevue. In the late 1930s, it would become a regular street vehicle.

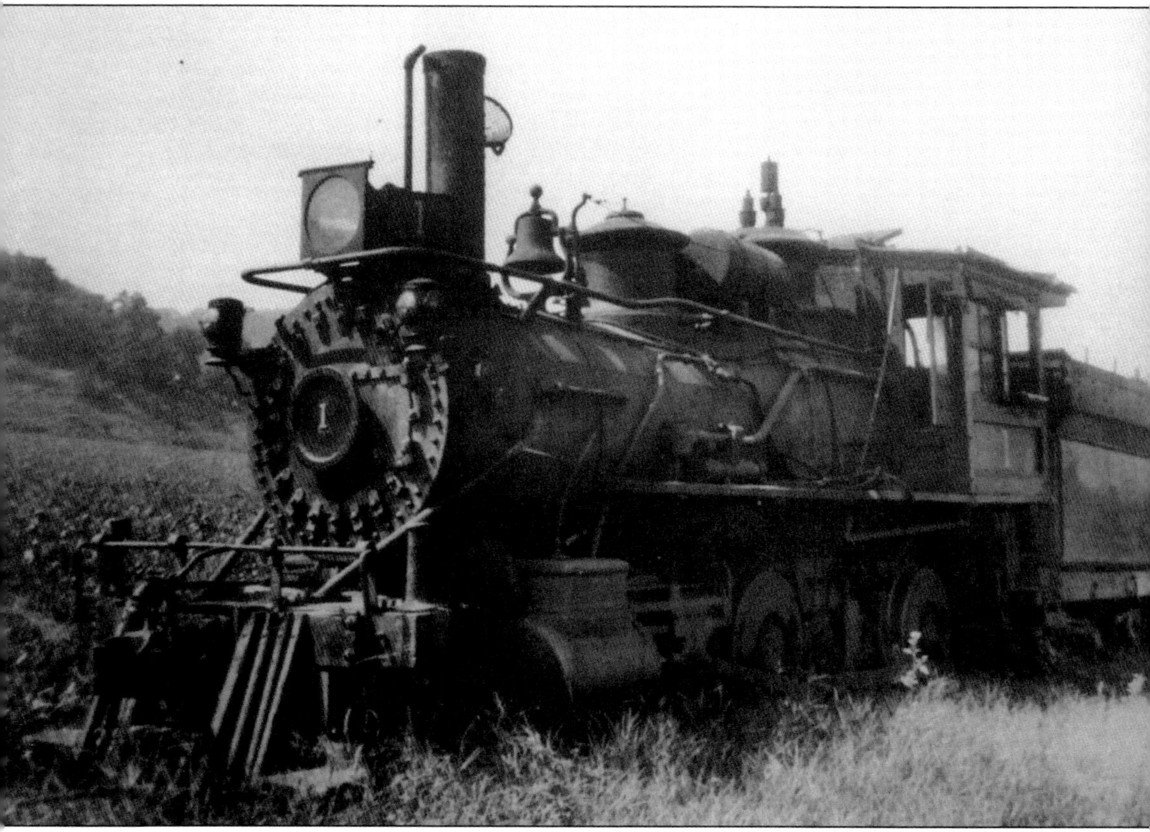

When No. 1 broke an axle in LaMotte, it was eventually pulled to Bellevue and left to rust with No. 4, the Cooke consolidation. No. 2, a Baldwin, continued operating as the only remaining engine, although it suffered from leaky flues and stay bolts like No. 3. (Adney.)

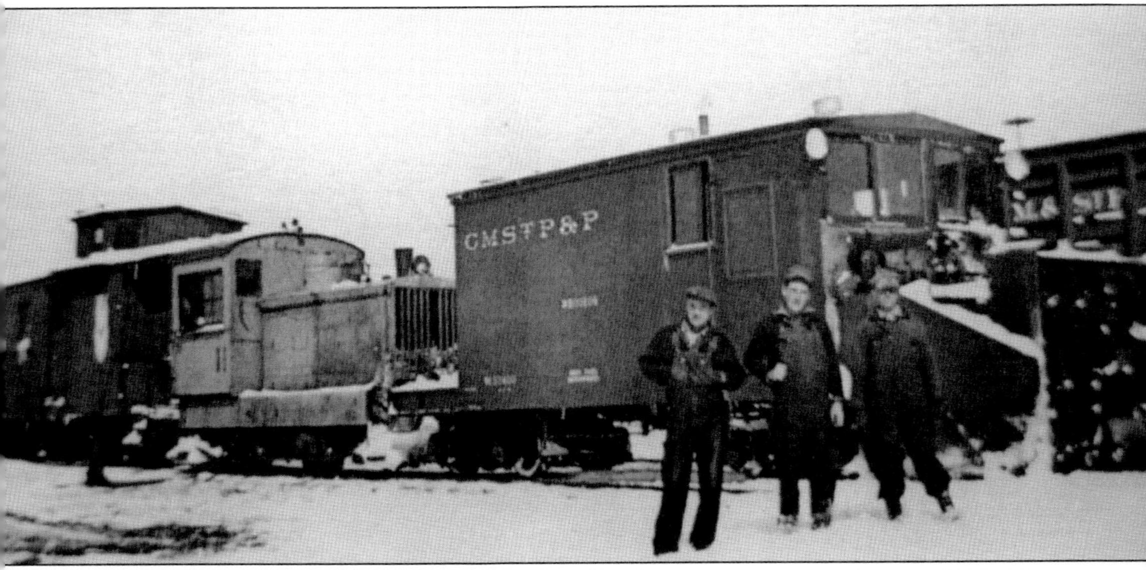

Steam locomotives had problems pushing the Sno-Go plow at a consistent, slow speed. The Ox, however, was capable of pushing the plow at two to three miles per hour. Benjamin Roehl (left) and Richard Bogue (right) are pictured here with an unidentified man. (Bradley.)

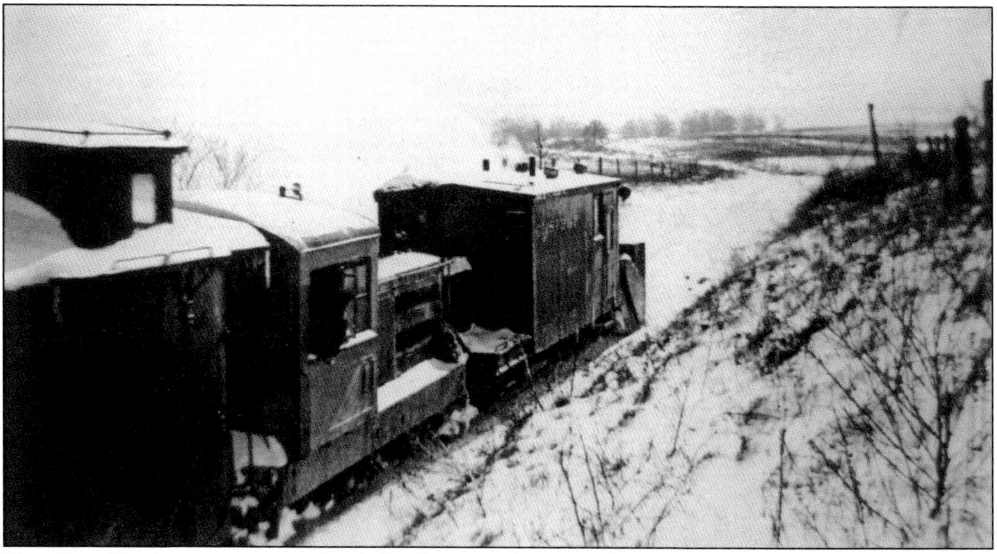

The Sno-Go throws snow to the left, clearing the main line between Fillmore and Cascade. Communications between the plow and the Ox were maintained by using a battery-powered bell system devised by plow operator Sylvester Otting. The Ox's engineer, Sylvester's brother Joseph was usually at the throttle. A third brother, Ralph, also worked on the narrow gauge while only a teenager. (Bradley.)

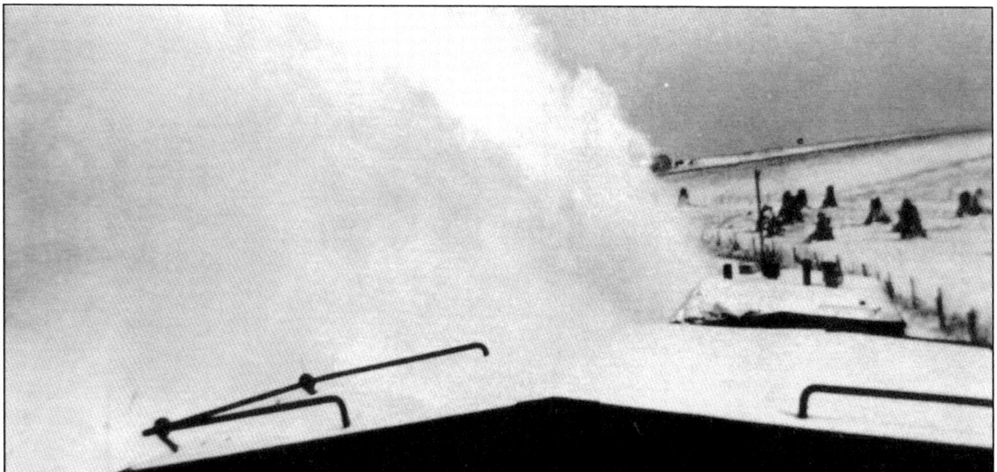

This image depicts the Klauer Sno-Go at work. Even 8- or 10-foot-high drifts were no problem with the Ox furnishing the motive power. Snow could be directed to either side. (Bradley.)

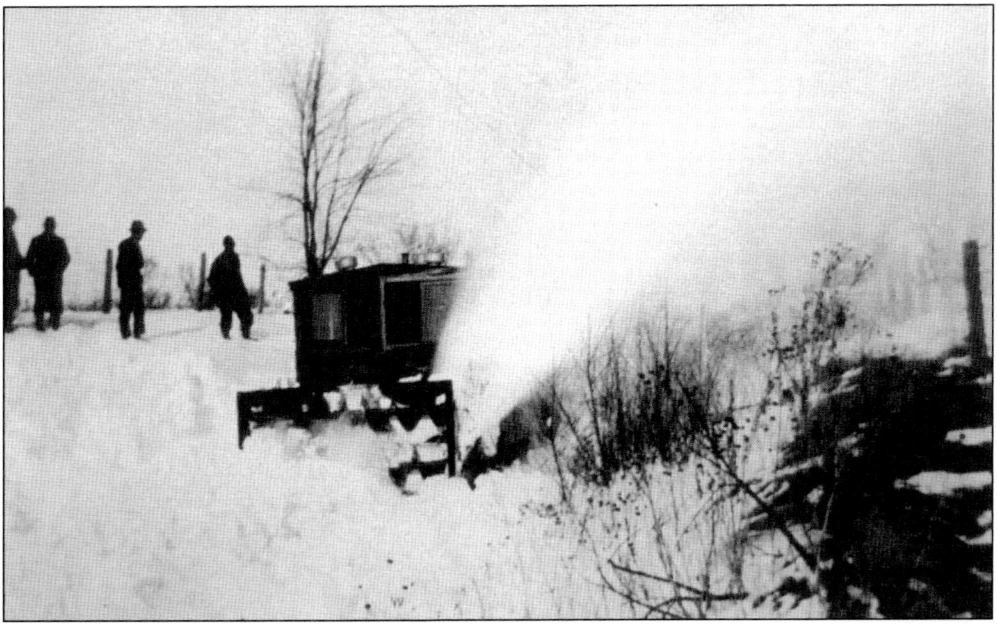

The unidentified shovelers on the left seem amazed at how easily the Sno-Go opens the line. (Kemerer.)

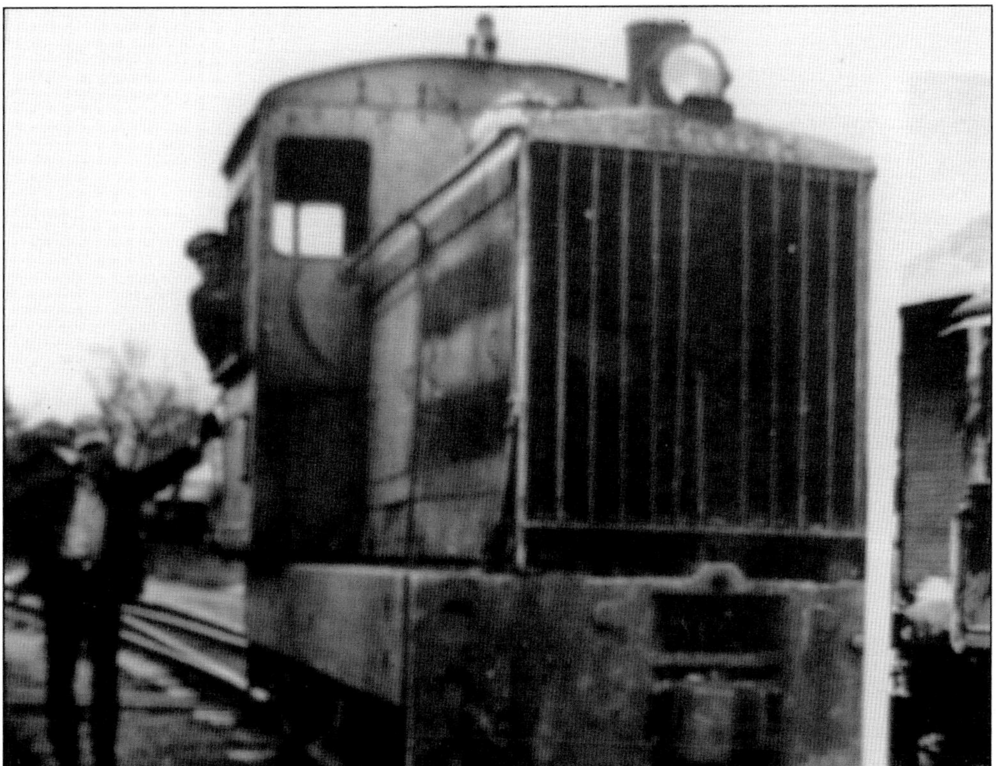

For whatever reason, the Ox threw a rod in early 1935. To keep the railroad running, the Sno-Go's six-cylinder engine was installed in the Plymouth switch engine. These men are unidentified.

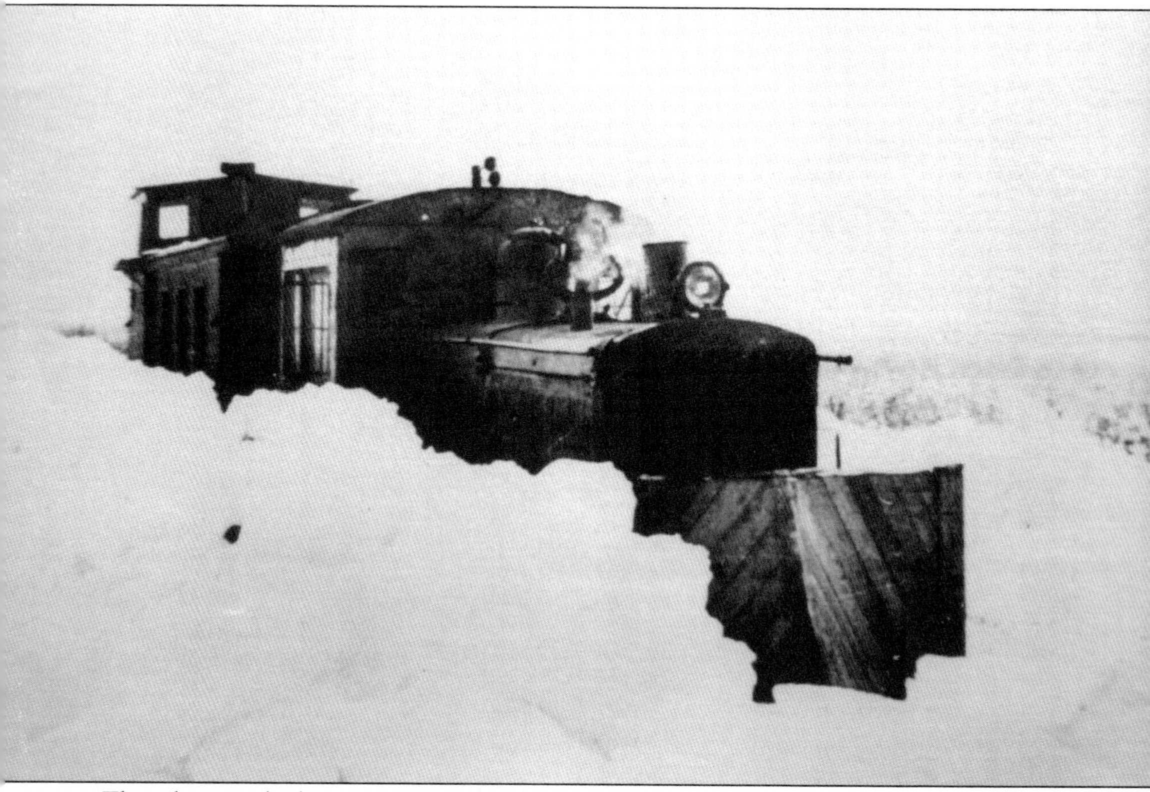

This photograph shows an accumulated Iowa winter's snow at its worst. In December 1935, an additional 9.9 inches of snow fell, and the Ox readily cleared the main line with its wedge plow. (Deppe.)

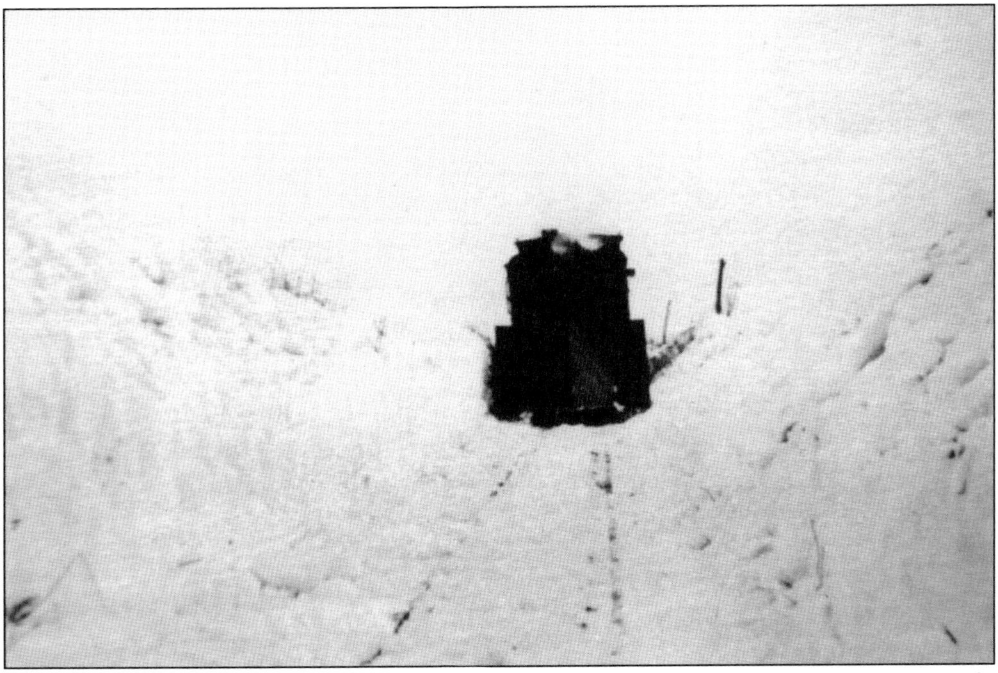

After the main line was opened, an even tighter clearance closed in on the little trains. (Deppe.)

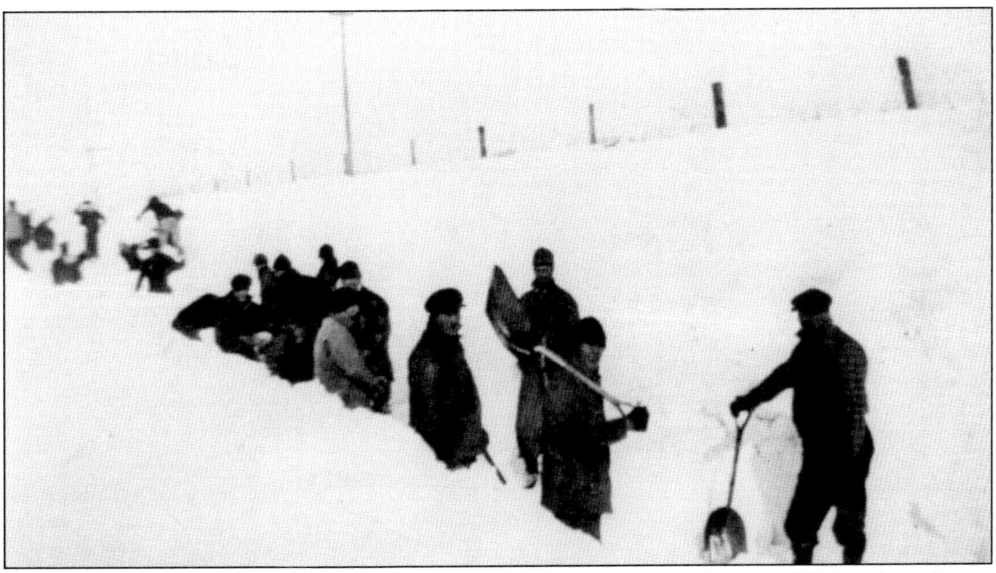

Old Man Winter struck with a vengeance in a six-week span of time. A total of 33.4 inches of snow fell and thick ice formed on the surface. Area residents were hired to clear the tracks. (Otting.)

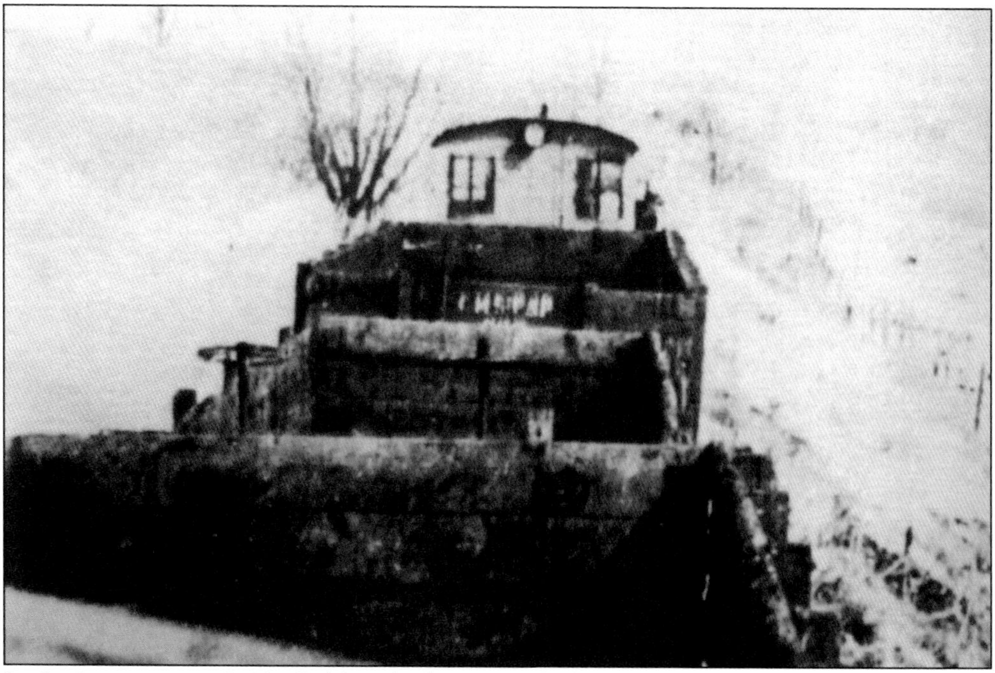

In the late summer of 1934, Baldwin-built No. 2, which had been sidetracked with leaks in its boiler system, was put on the disabled list because no funds were available for the locomotive's five-year overhaul. The Canary had a cracked block; only the under-powered Ox was still operating. (Bogue.)

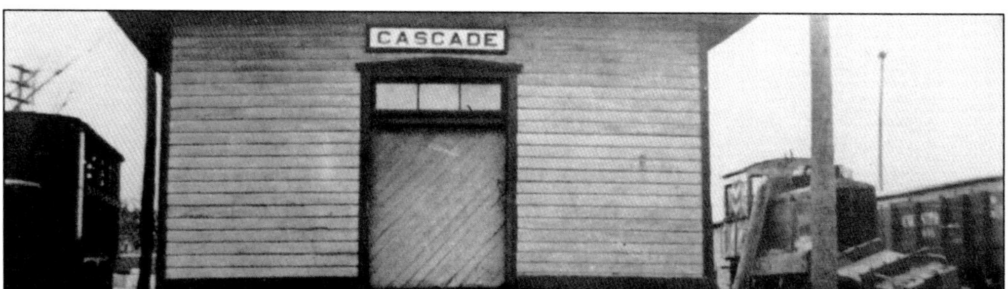

The Ox appears to be hiding from the stock truck on the south side of the Cascade depot in the spring of 1935.

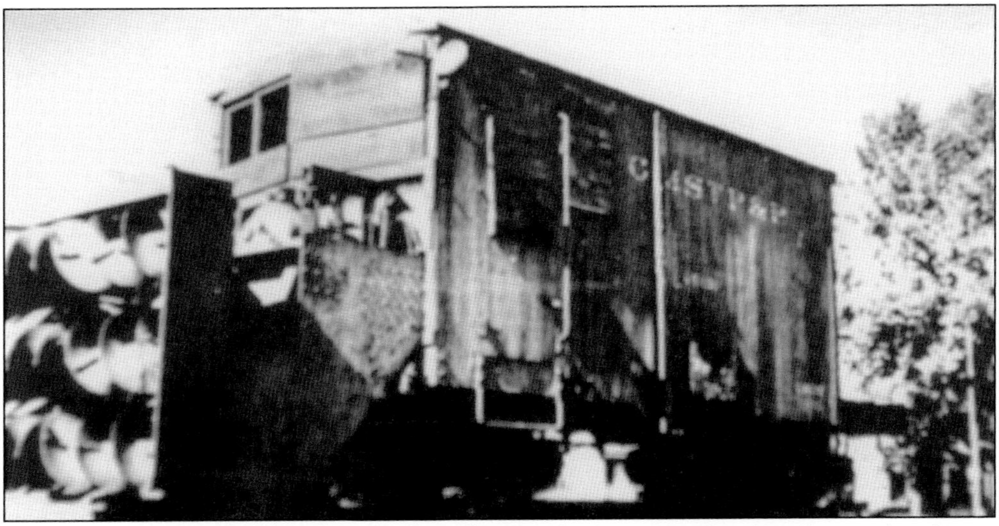

The Klauer Manufacturing Company agreed to buy back its Sno-Go plow. It was placed on a pedestal of 12-inch planks. In time, the blower, augers, and scoop were sold for scrap. (Pregler.)

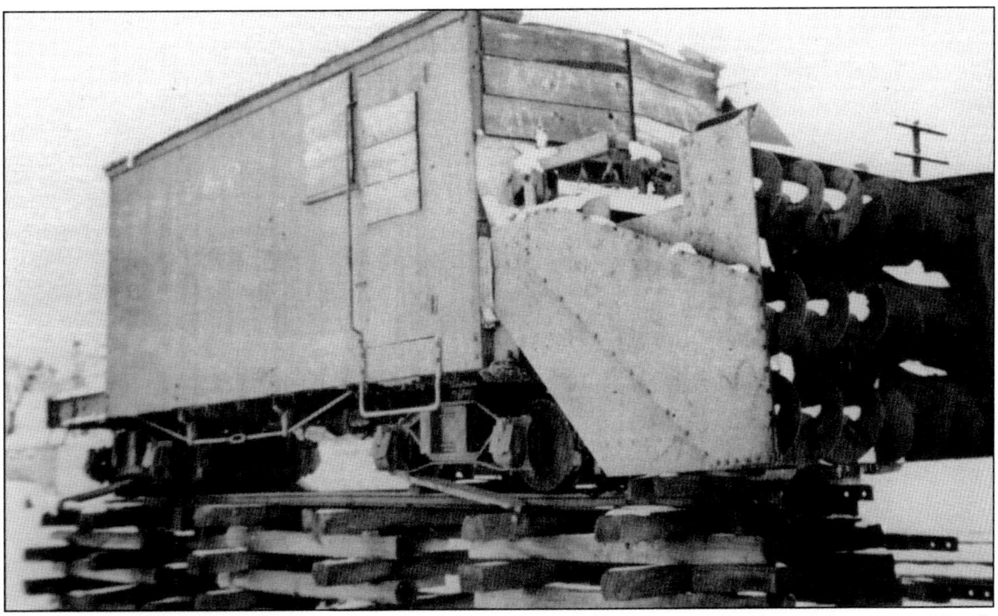

The Sno-Go's truck and coupler were donated to the Mid-Continent Railway Museum at North Freedom, Wisconsin. (Kreuzberger.)

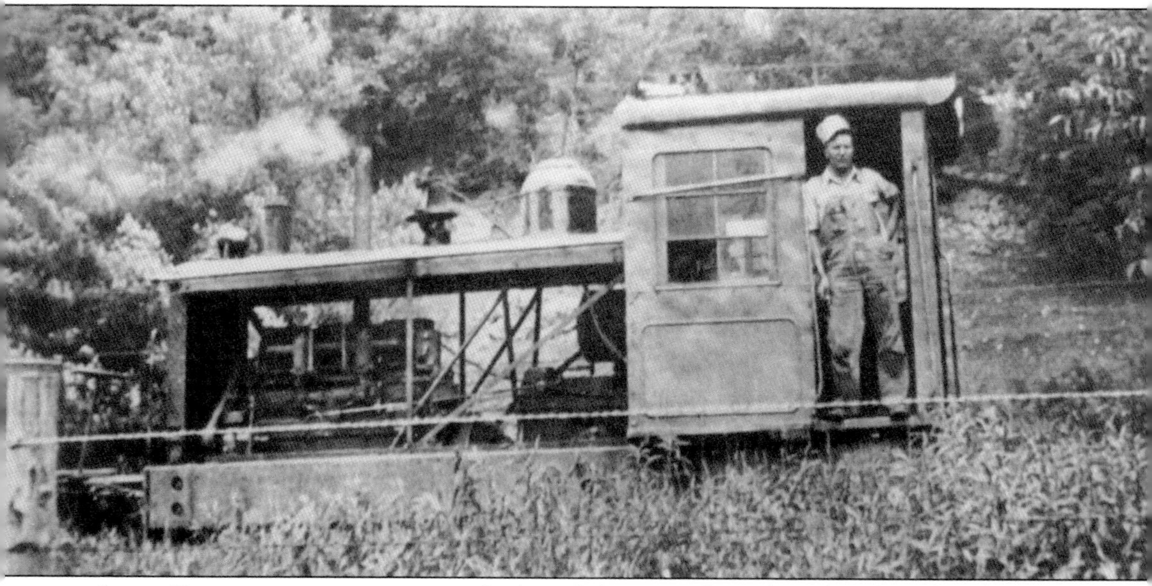

Lester Deppe, a young engineer on the branch line, stands in the cab to have his photograph taken. The exhaust of the Climax six-cylinder Sno-Go engine would eventually be cut shorter.

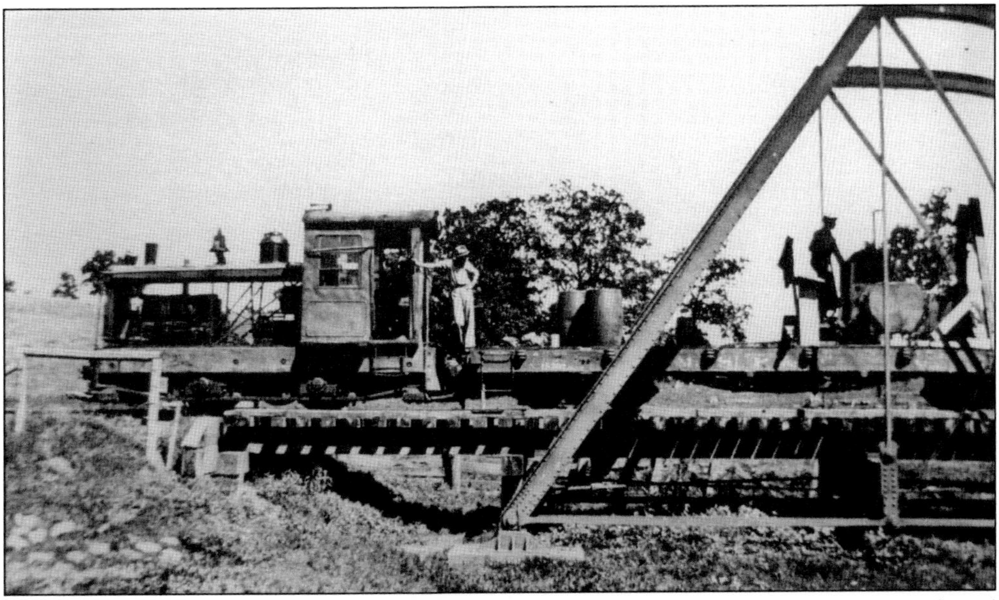

Pulling a work train, the Ox pauses on the bridge east of Zwingle. The engineer seems bored waiting for work on the bridge to be completed. (Leffert.)

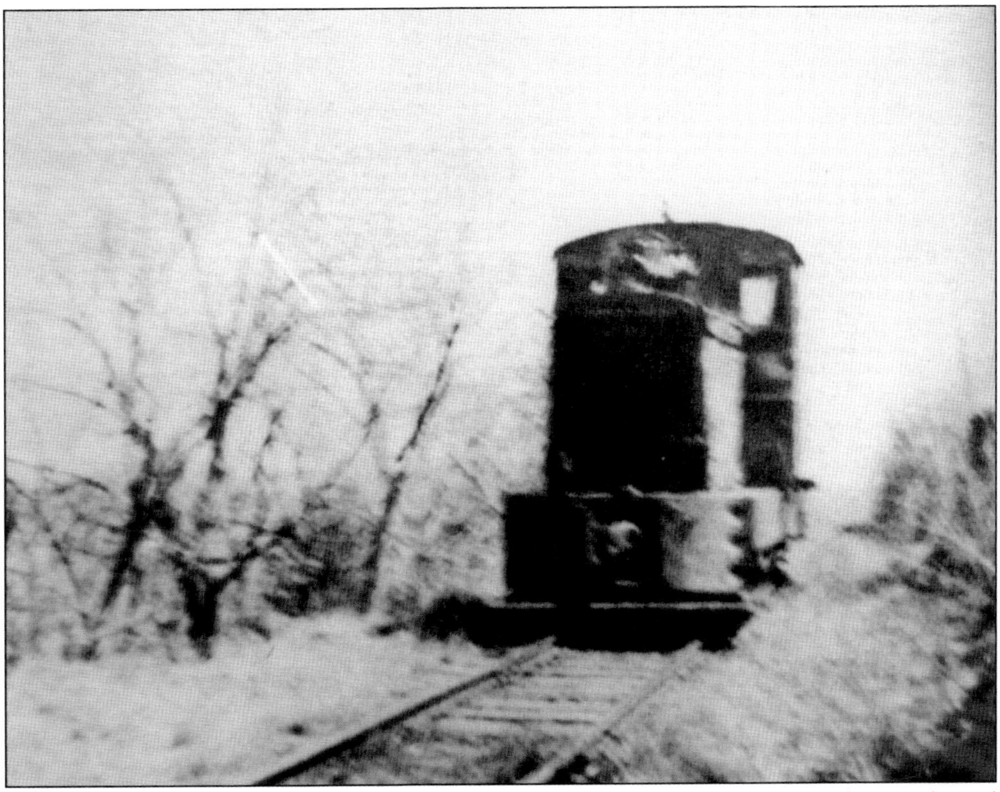

The Ox hurries along the line without a train. The weather has not yet warmed, as evidenced by the side panels on the hood. After 1934, when No. 2 was parked with leaks, only the Ox was working. (Bogue.)

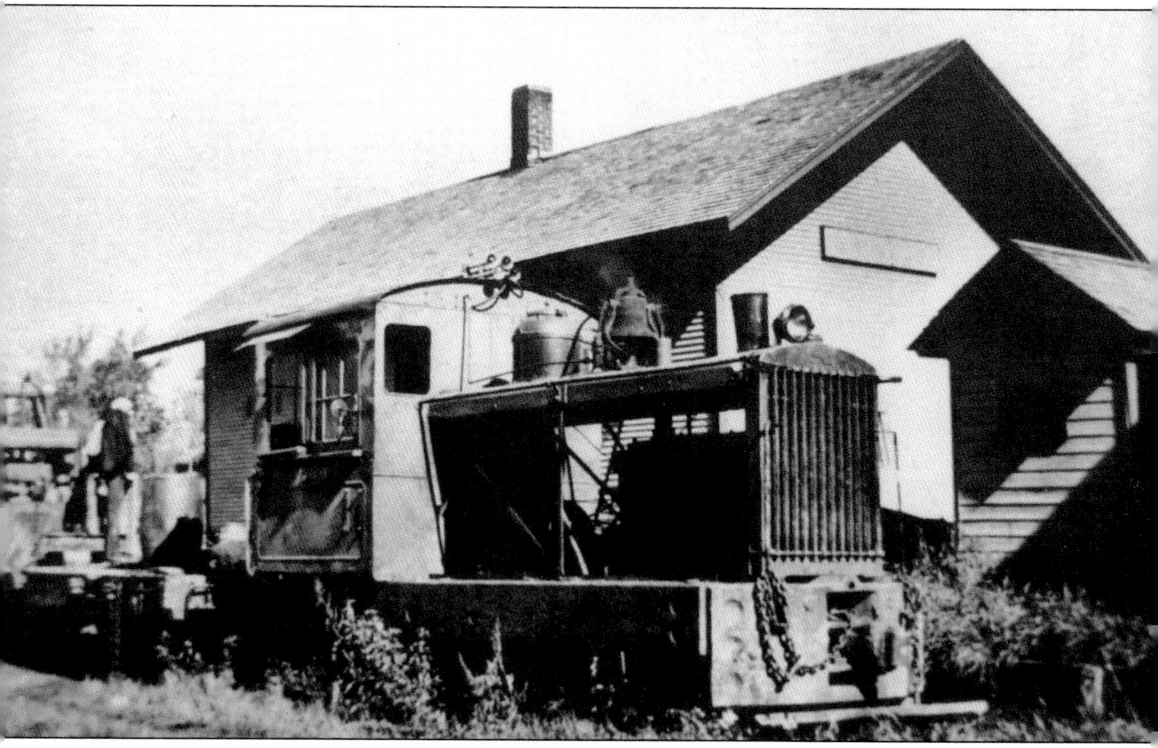

The Ox stops in Zwingle with its work train. About this time, Earl Bradley had not acquired his loan and contacted William G. Bell, who specialized in operating short railroads. (Leffert.)

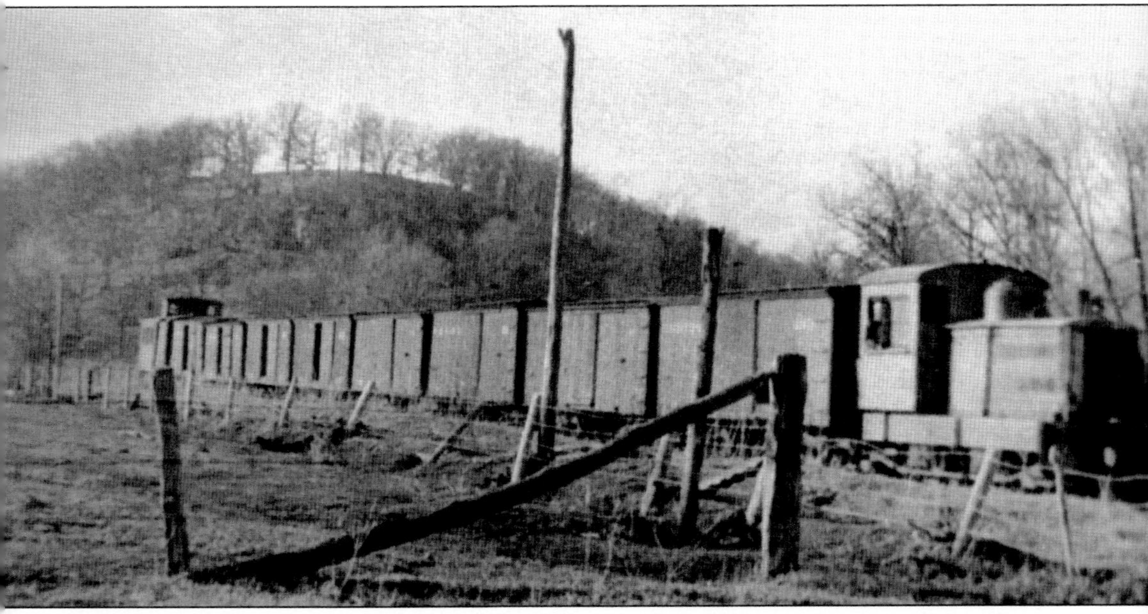

The date of this photograph is March 14, 1936. William G. Bell, who had acquired the little railroad in November 1935, came to the conclusion that the Bellevue and Cascade narrow-gauge railroad could not be saved. The last scheduled train came down the 2.8-percent grade west of Bellevue and stopped. The engineer stepped down and, camera in hand, took this photograph. (Deppe.)

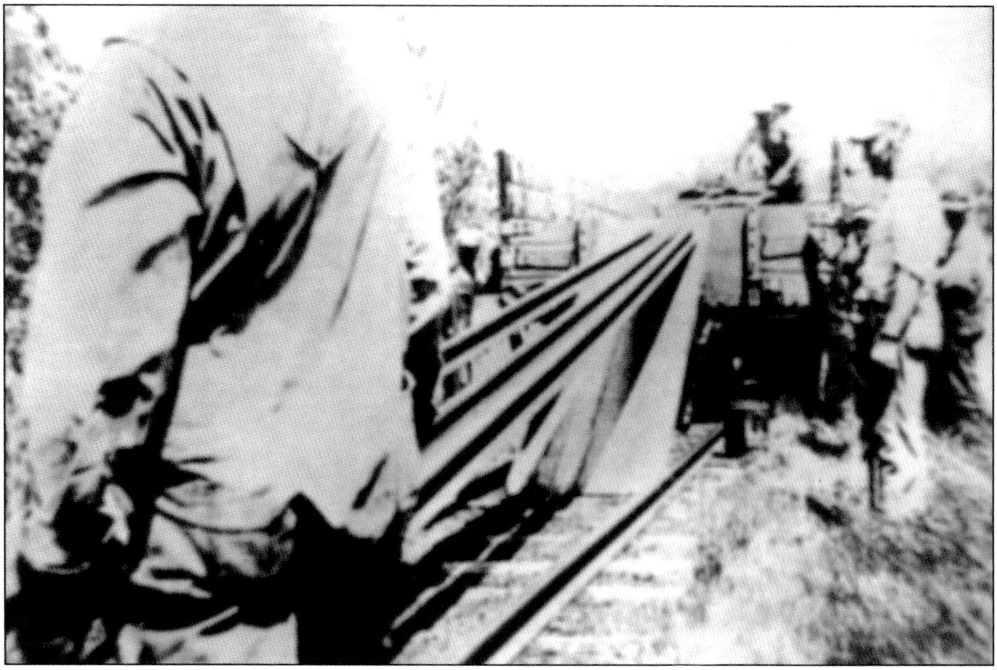
Once the spikes were pulled up, the rail was winched into a gondola. Jobs were scarce for men in 1936—even if the job was ripping out their own railroad. (Bogue.)

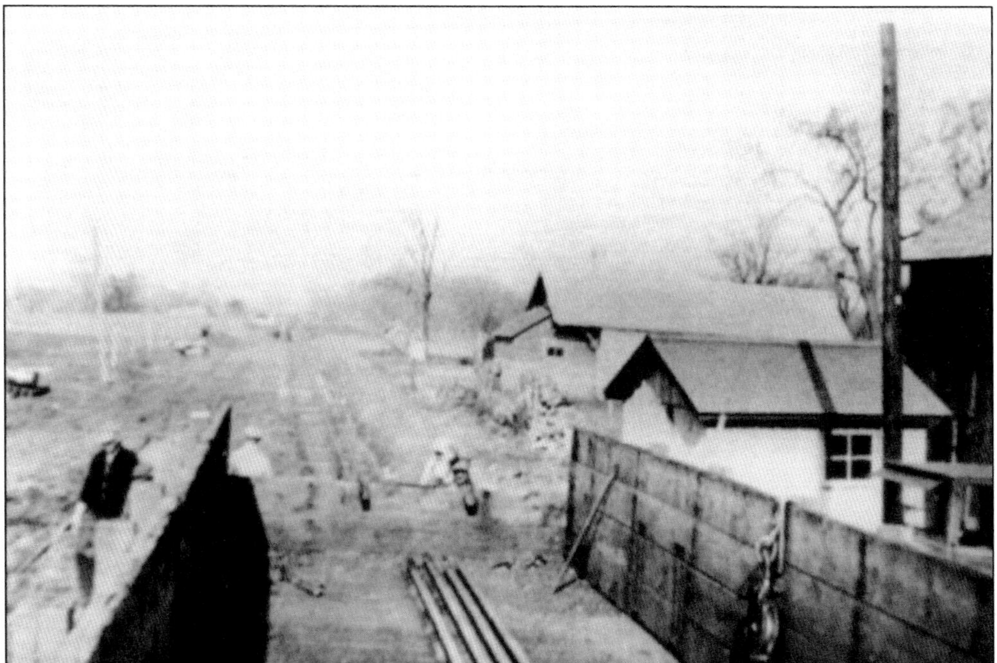
The small white building on the right served as the station in Fillmore. Here the rails are being pulled up to end the life of the Bellevue and Cascade. (Deppe.)

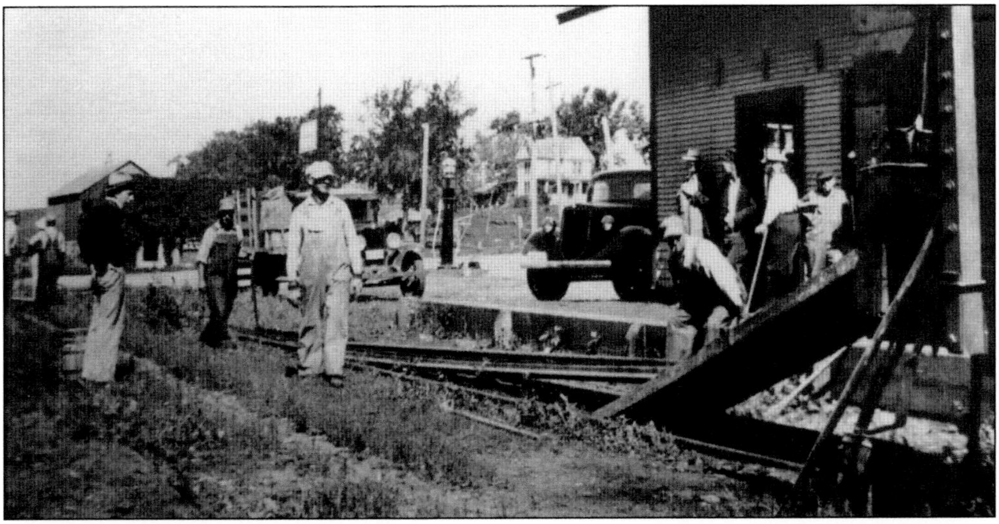

The Zwingle station building has been converted to a private home. Seen in the left distance is the ivy-covered bank. (Deppe.)

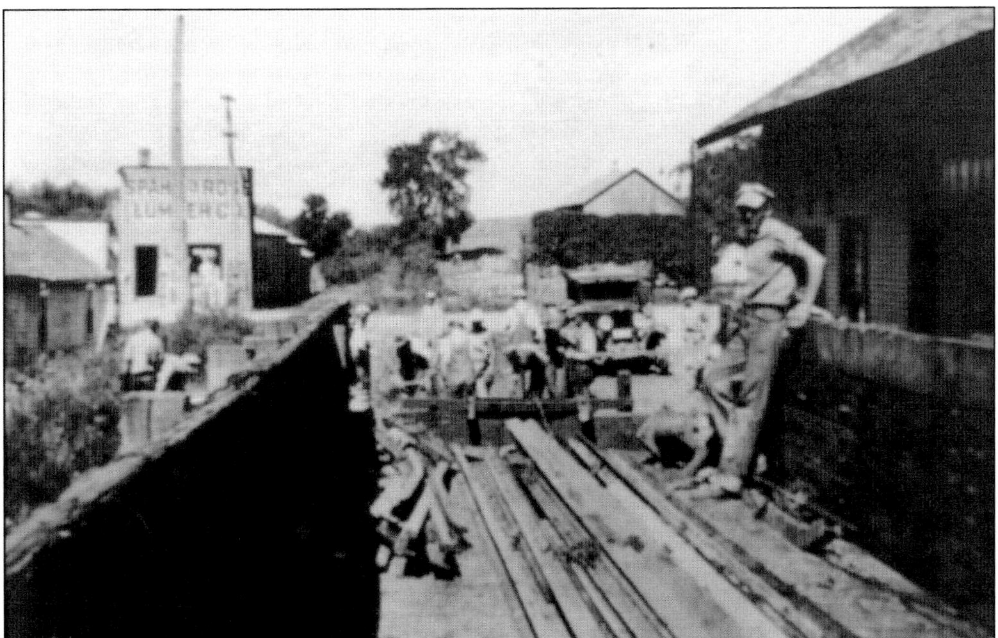

The rails will soon be only a memory in Zwingle. The grade is still visible in places from a small airplane. (Deppe.)

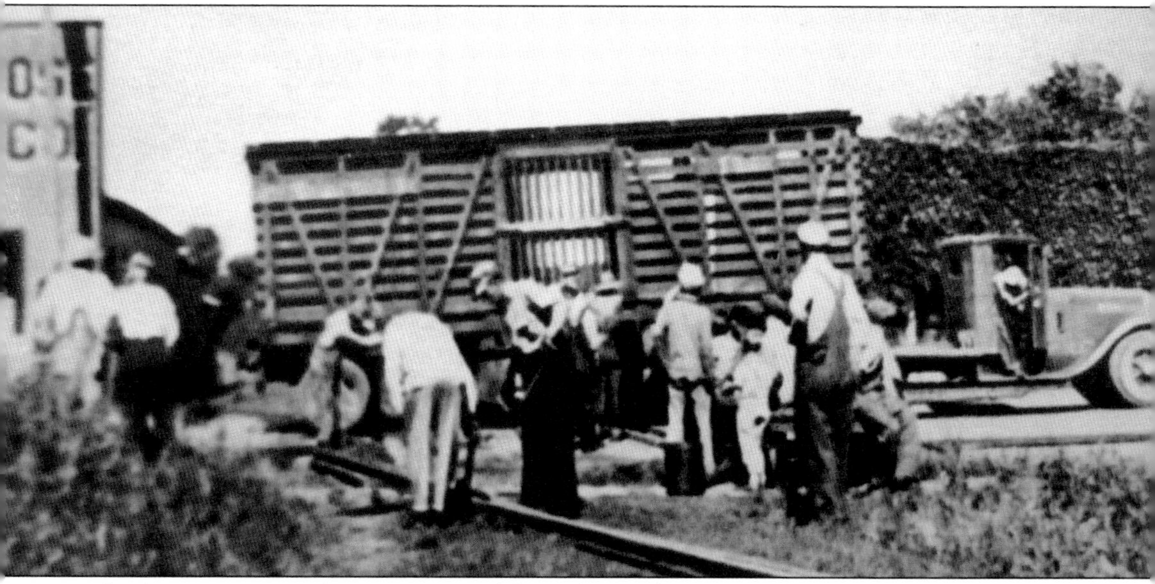

In this image, a stock car is removed from the tracks in Zwingle to be hauled to a farmer's property. During the early part of April 1936, Laverne Ferneau of Dubuque purchased the boxcars and stock cars and sold them at an auction sale. The rolling stock was put to many uses by the buyers. (Leffert.)

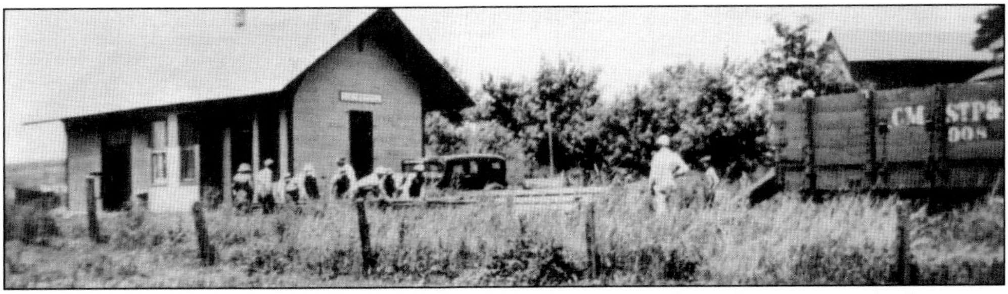

The salvage crew continued eastward, removing rails passing through LaMotte, the last town before reaching Bellevue. Today the station still stands and houses a museum that features artifacts of the narrow-gauge railroad. (Deppe.)

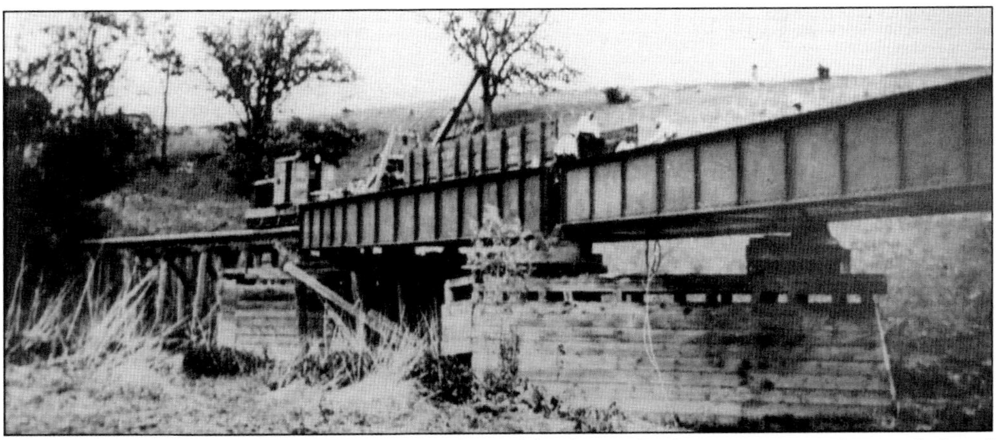

Many of the trestles had been replaced with steel bridges, which in turn were dismantled and sold for scrap. (Deppe.)

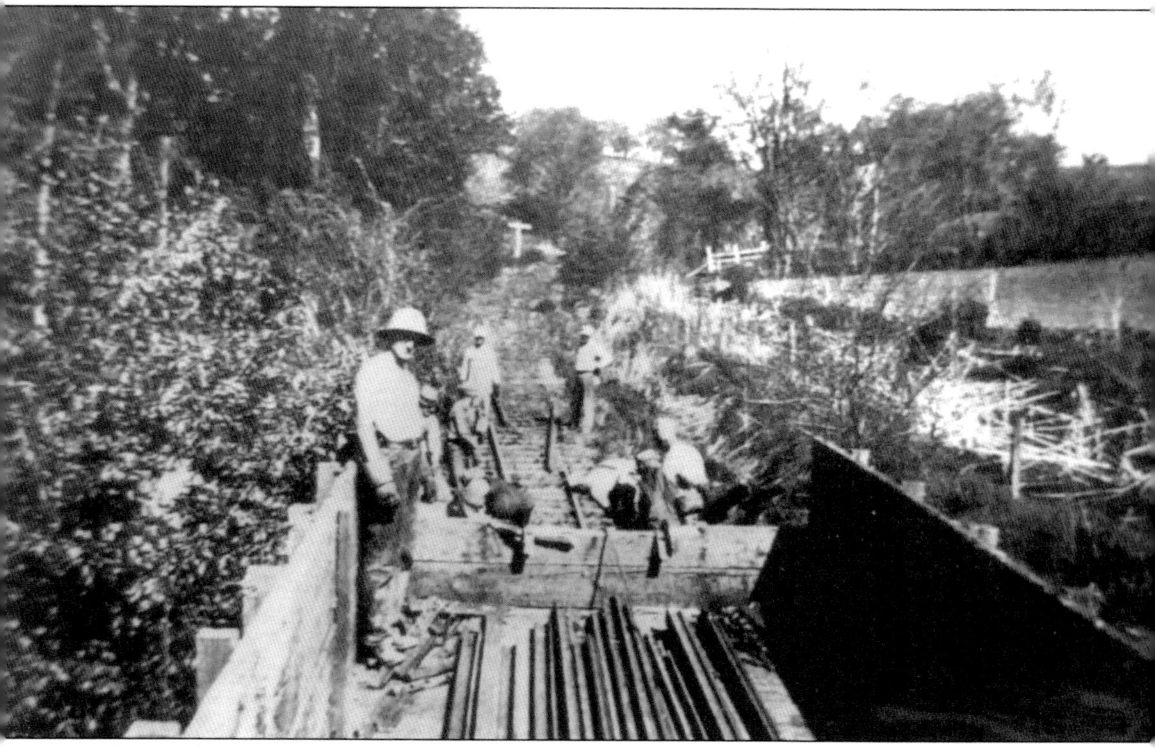

Here a salvage crew works in what was known as Paradise Valley. Stories circulated that the rails, locomotives, and steel from bridges were shipped as far away as Japan. (Deppe.)

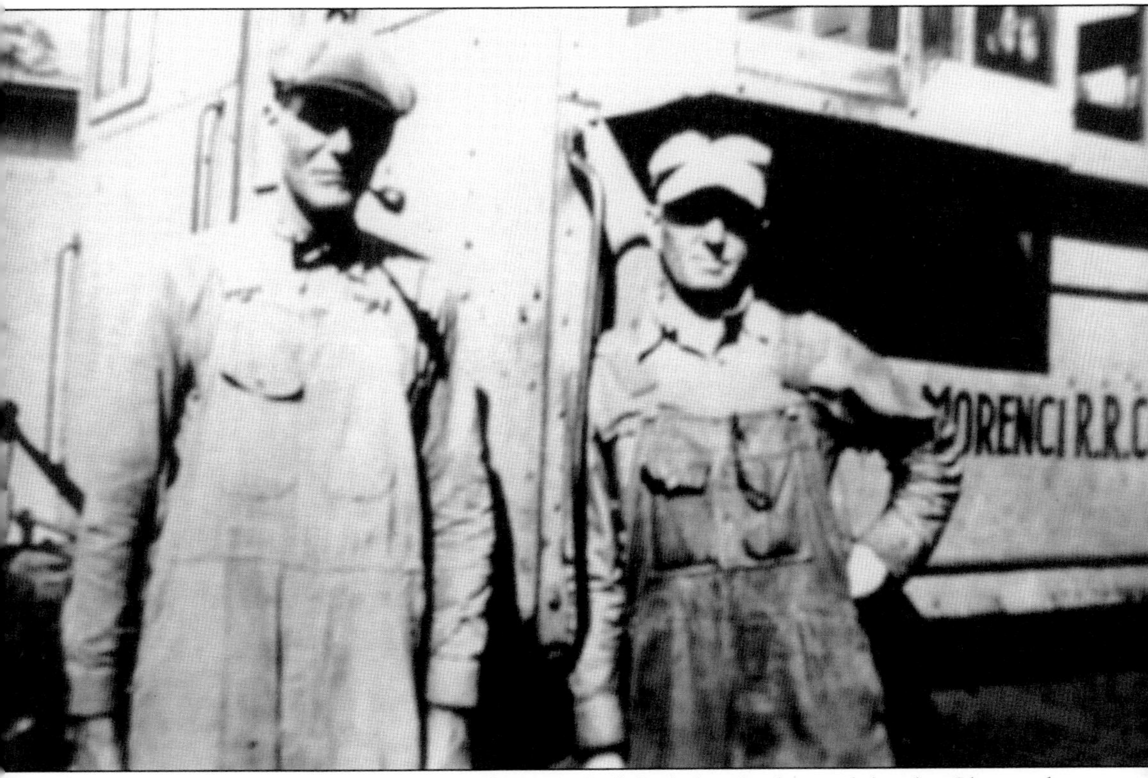

When the rails had been removed, William G. Bell had the Ox lettered for the Ohio and Morenci Railroad Company, one of his successful undertakings. It was shipped east shortly after this photograph was taken.

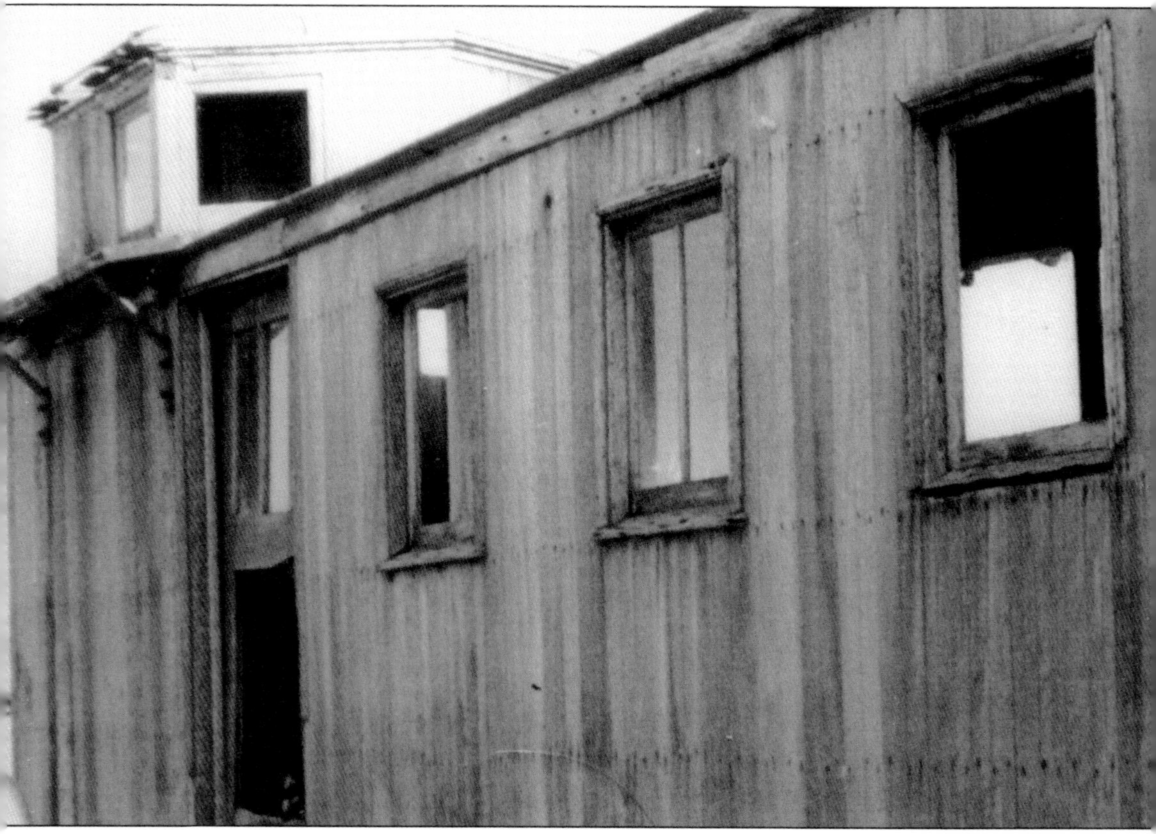

This caboose was purchased and used as a storage building on a farm some years later. The photograph was taken by Albin Lee, one of the earlier historiographers of the 36-mile-long railroad. (Lee.)

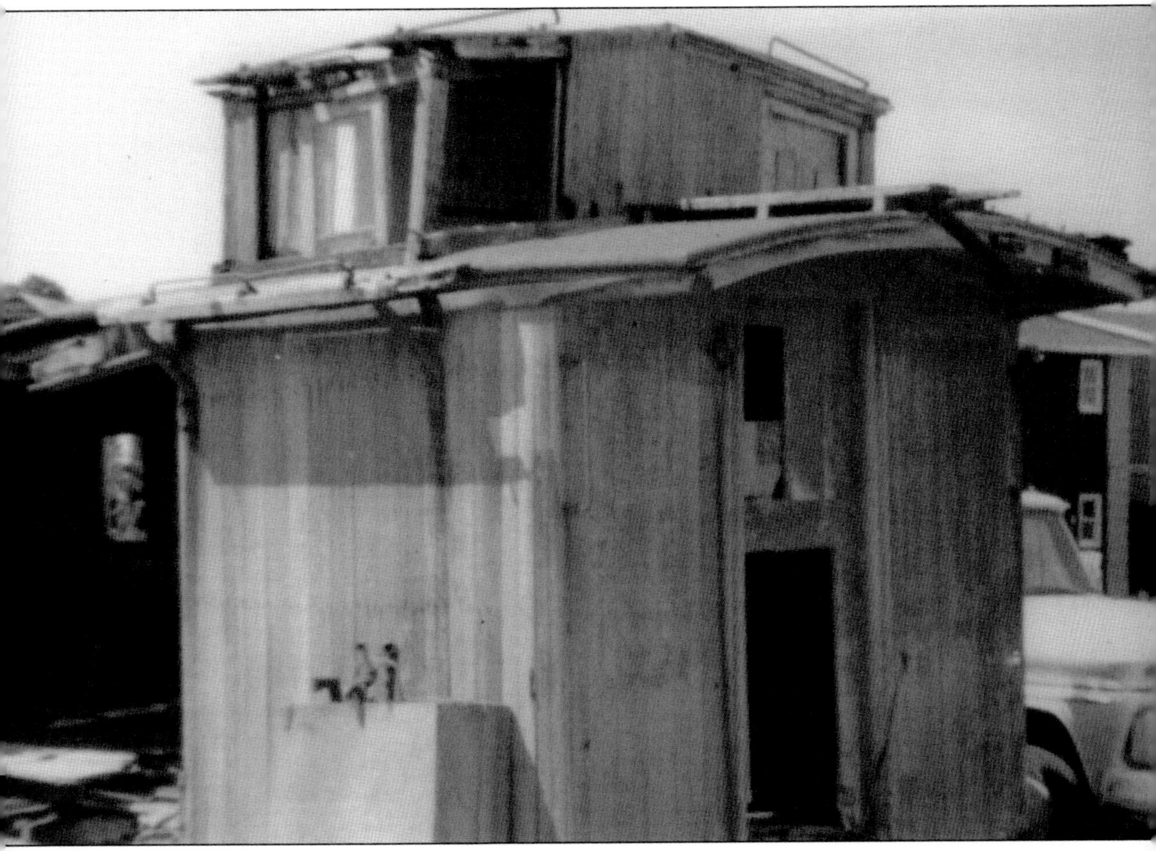

The caboose's opposite side is pictured here. (Lee.)

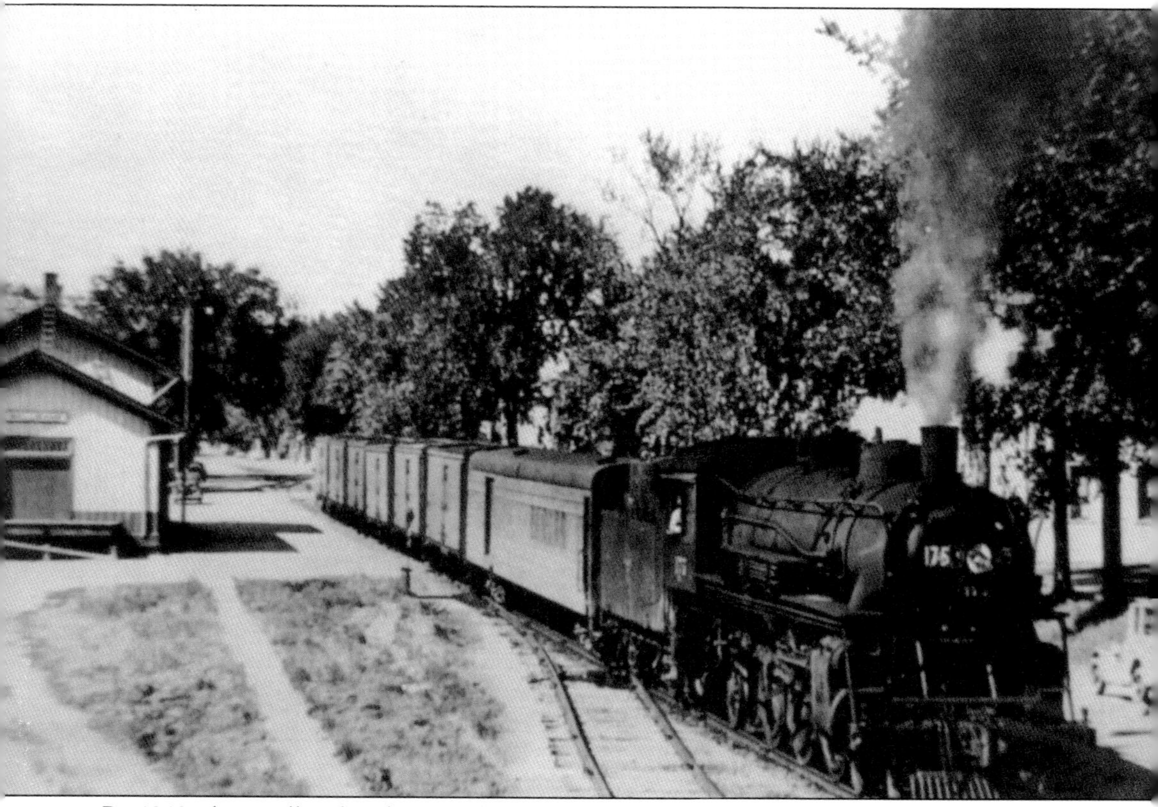

By 1940, the small railroad was only a memory. No. 175, a Milwaukee Road standard-gauge Pacific-type 4-6-2, pulls a streamlined combine and six refrigerator cars southbound through Bellevue to Savanna, Illinois, in late afternoon. (Courtney.)

Six

A Final Look

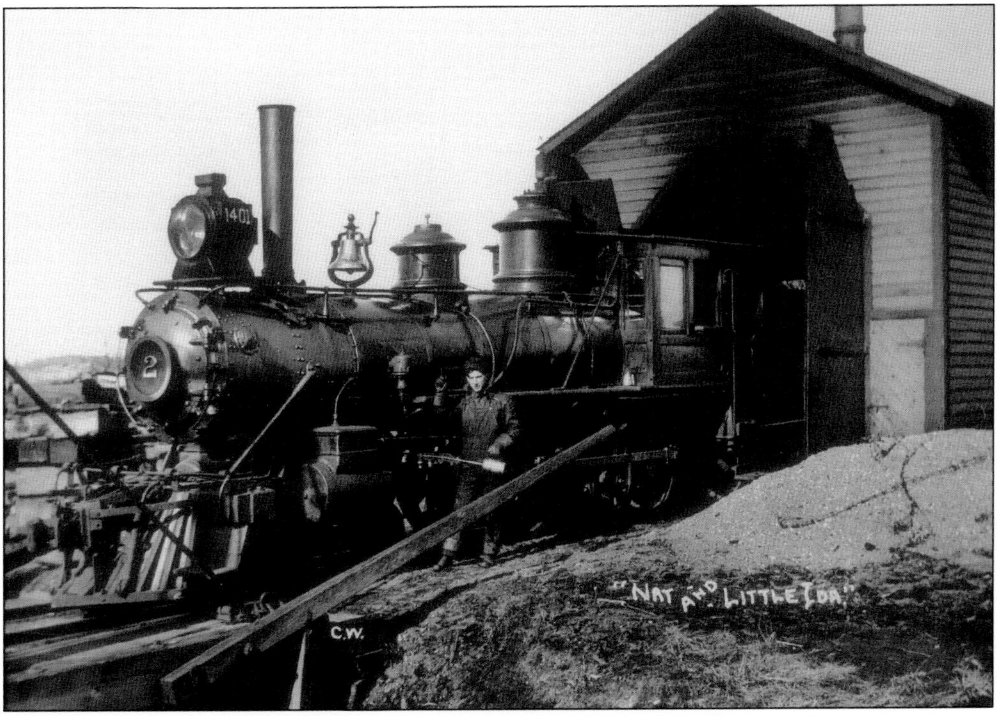

Although posed for Claude Wyrick, this photograph clearly shows how Nathan Hunter went about his job of caring for No. 2, or as he called her, "Little Ida." (Wyrick.)

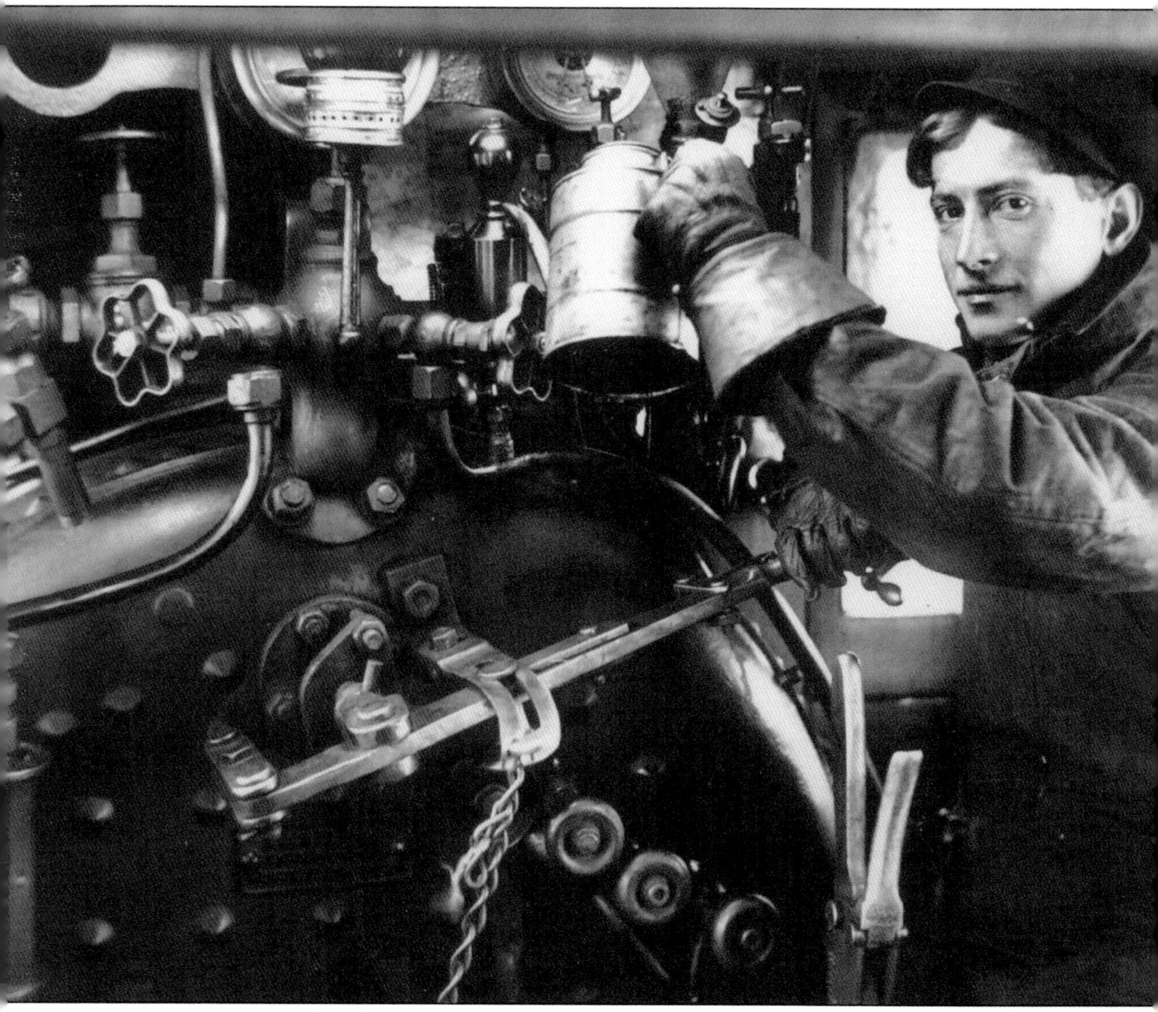

The interior of No. 2's cab is seen in clear detail. Although the setup was considered simple and basic, the components to operate a steam locomotive are all present. (Wyrick.)

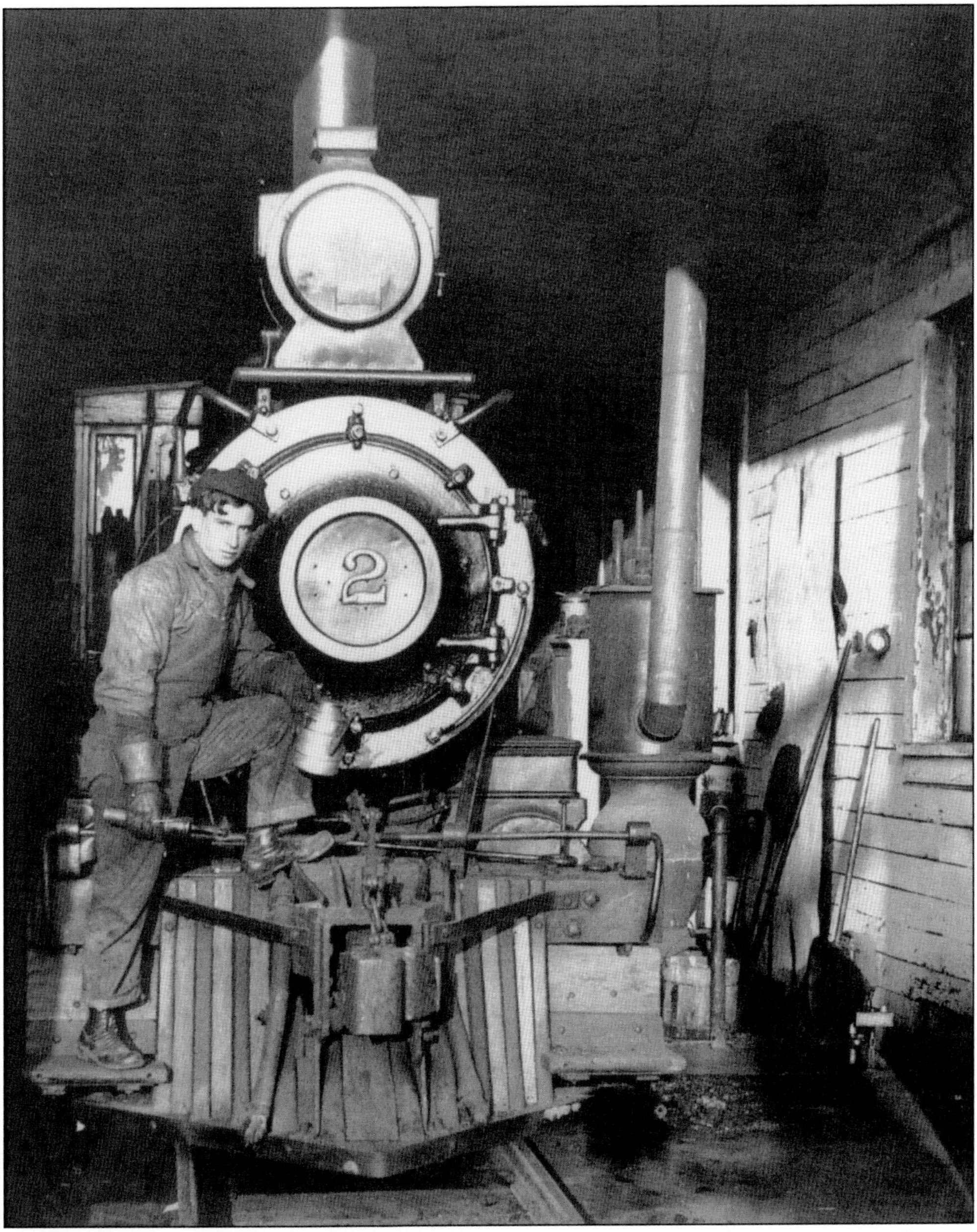

Nathan Hunter strikes a pose. While he apparently liked his job on the narrow gauge, he was lured away by a trucking firm and died in a truck accident in the late 1930s. (Wyrick.)

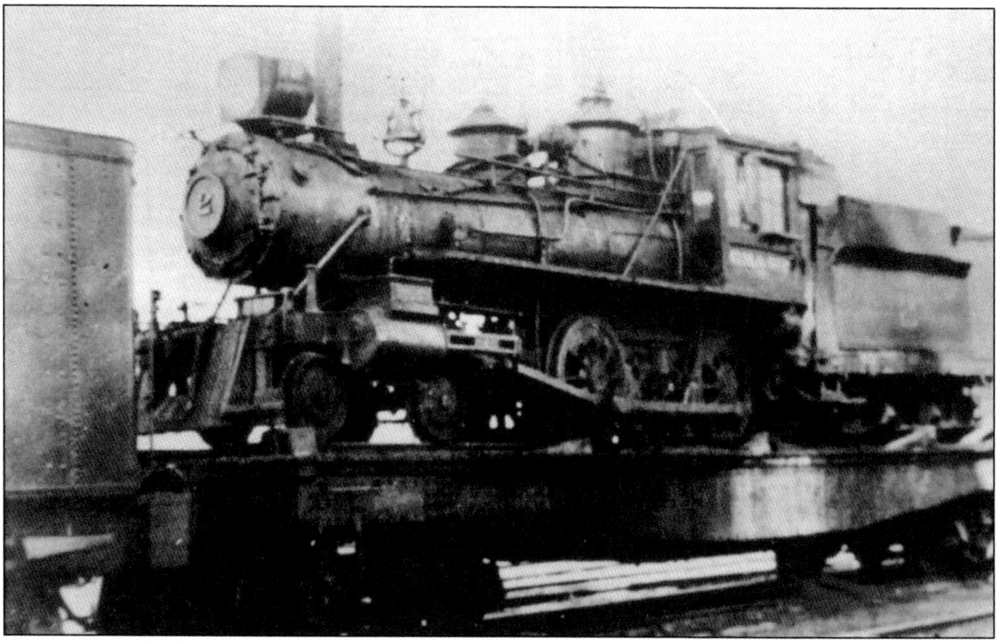

No. 2's 42-inch drivers aid in understanding the overall size of the Pittsburgh locomotive. The total wheelbase of the engine was 18 feet 4 inches. The fact that the tender is also on the flatcar could only mean that No. 2 is on its way to the cutting torch. If so, the date it was scrapped was August 16, 1928.

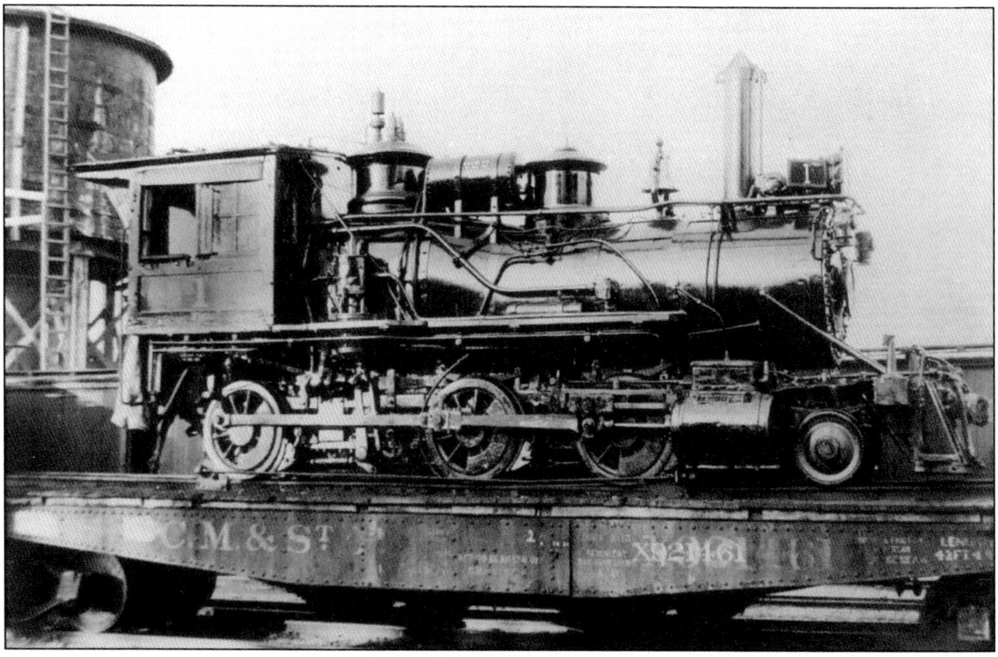

Seen here is the engineer's side of No. 1. The Brooks Mogul was built for the J. E. Potts Salt and Lumber Company in 1889. When it went to the Ausable and Northwestern Railroad, it had no number and so became 1400 when it arrived on the Milwaukee property. It was changed to No. 1 in 1912. (Adney.)

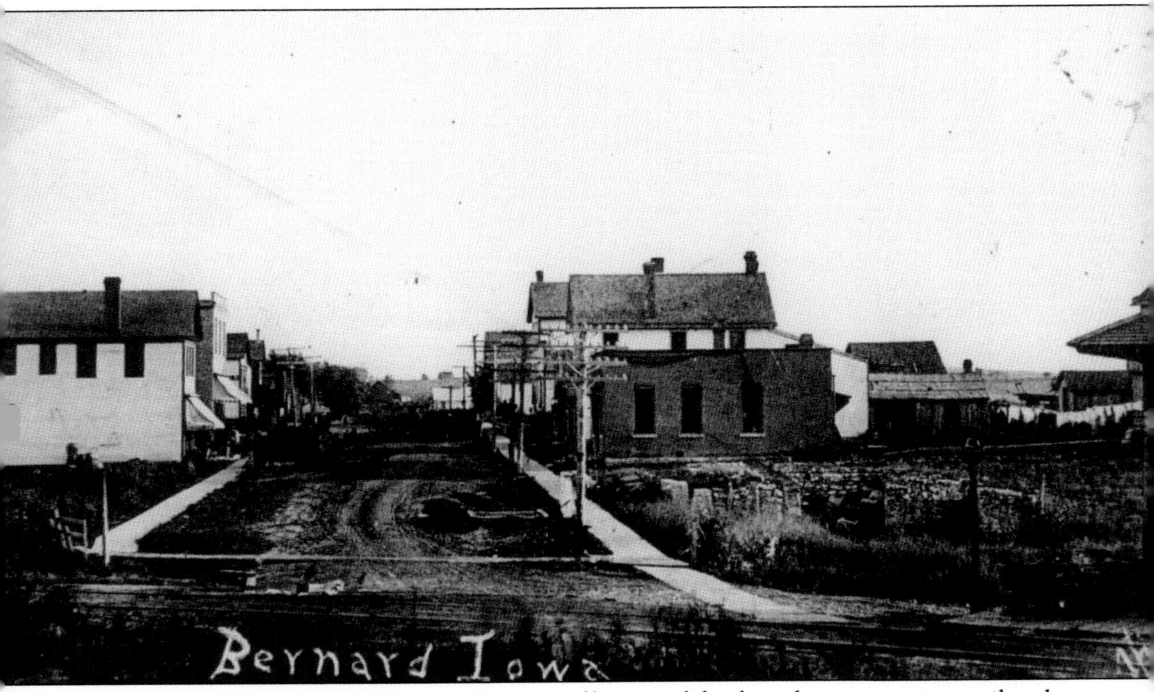

Small communities like Bernard enjoyed a surge of business life when the narrow-gauge railroad came to town. With new roads and commerce well established, they hardly missed a tick when the rails were pulled up. (Higbe.)

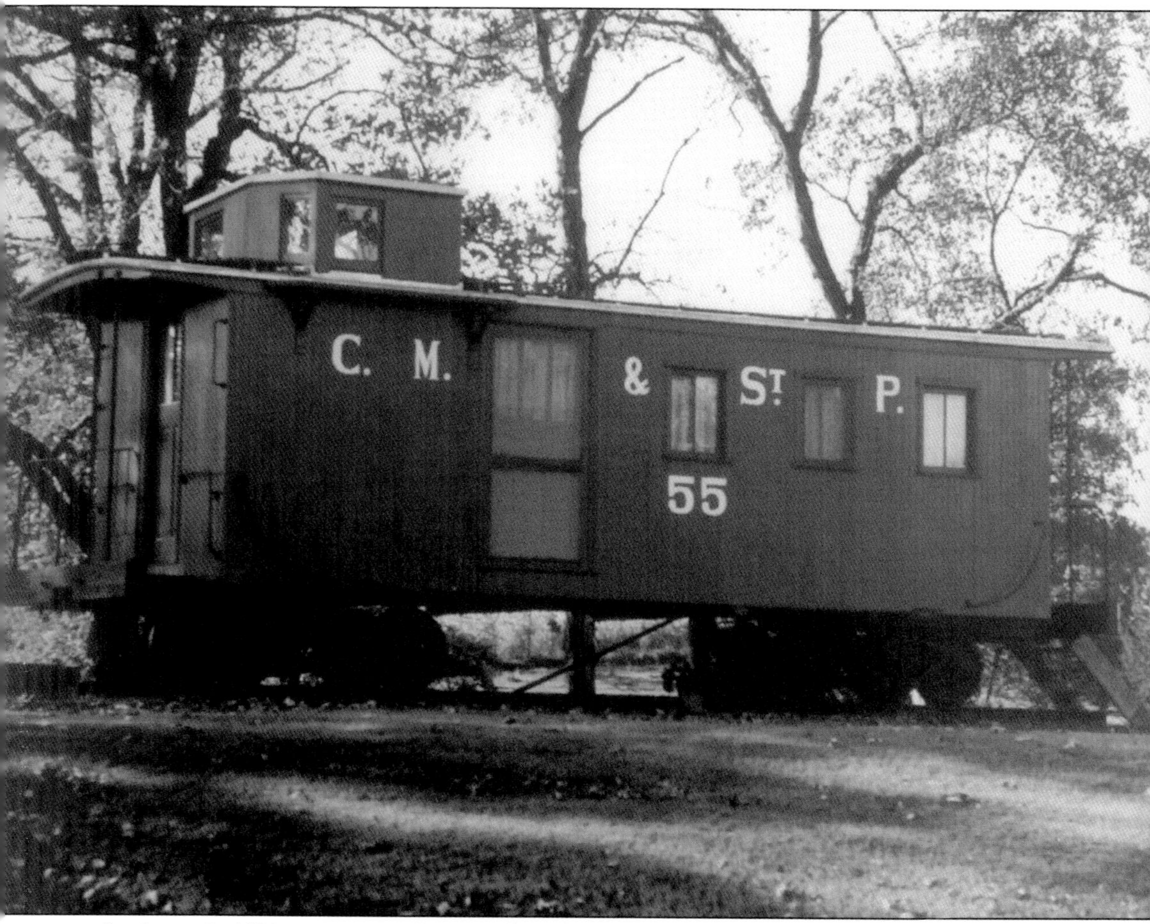

In the early 1980s, contractor James Schroeder of Bellevue acquired the remains of the narrow gauge's only caboose. Because it was beyond repair, Schroeder used the car's dimensions to completely duplicate the red caboose. It stood in his front yard. When he passed away, his wife, Margaret, donated it to the Midwest Central Railroad at Mount Pleasant. (Margaret Schroeder.)

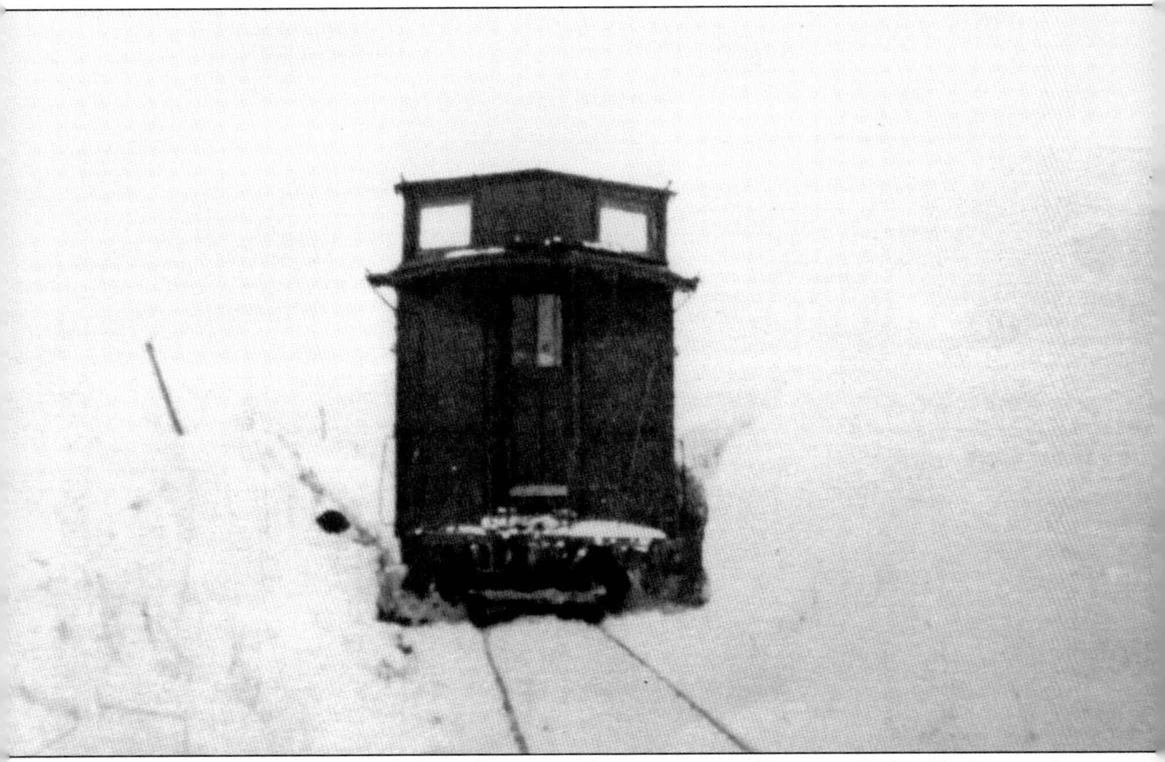

Today the Bellevue and Cascade branch is more than a memory. Young and old alike know of its history and, thus, keep it alive. Even though it may seem to have left, it still exists in books and images depicting that long-gone era. (Deppe.)